SPSS/PC+ Made Simple

OTHER TITLES OF RELATED INTEREST IN SOCIOLOGY

Research Methods and Statistics

Earl Babbie, THE PRACTICE OF SOCIAL RESEARCH, FIFTH EDITION
Earl Babbie, OBSERVING OURSELVES: ESSAYS IN SOCIAL RESEARCH
Earl Babbie, SURVEY RESEARCH METHODS, SECOND EDITION
William Sims Bainbridge, SURVEY RESEARCH: A COMPUTER-ASSISTED INTRODUCTION
James Grimm/Paul Wozniak, BASIC SOCIAL STATISTICS AND QUANTITATIVE RESEARCH METHODS: A COMPUTER-ASSISTED INTRODUCTION
Margaret Jendrek, THROUGH THE MAZE: STATISTICS WITH COMPUTER APPLICATIONS
John Lofland/Lyn Lofland, ANALYZING SOCIAL SETTINGS: A GUIDE TO QUALITATIVE OBSERVATION AND ANALYSIS, SECOND EDITION
Joseph Healey, STATISTICS: A TOOL FOR THE SOCIAL SCIENCES, SECOND EDITION
June True, FINDING OUT: CONDUCTING AND EVALUATING SOCIAL RESEARCH, SECOND EDITION

Computer Software for the Social Sciences

John Hedderson, SPSS^X MADE SIMPLE
Rodney Stark/Cognitive Development, Inc., STUDENT SHOWCASE: INTRODUCING SOCIOLOGY THROUGH THE COMPUTER, REVISED EDITION

SPSS/PC+ Made Simple

Simple

JOHN HEDDERSON
Urban Research Division
Internal Services Department
County of Los Angeles

Wadsworth Publishing Company
Belmont, California
A Division of Wadsworth, Inc.

To the students at the University of Texas at El Paso
who made me a better teacher.

Sociology Editor: Serina Beauparlant
Editorial Assistant: Marla Nowick
Production Editor: Richard Lynch, Bookman Productions
Print Buyer: Martha Branch
Designer: MaryEllen Podgorski
Copy Editor: Janet M. Hunter
Indexer: Katherine Stimson
Technical Illustrator: John V. Serna
Compositor: G&S Typesetters, Inc.
Cover: Al Burkhardt

SPSS, SPSS^x, and SPSS/PC+ are trademarks of SPSS Inc. for proprietary software.

Printed in the United States of America

2 3 4 5 6 7 8 9 10—95 94 93 92 91

ISBN 0-534-14376-8

Library of Congress Cataloging-in-Publication Data

Hedderson, John.
  SPSS/PC+ made simple / John Hedderson.
     p. cm.
  Includes index.
  ISBN 0-534-14376-8
    1. SPSS/PC Plus (Computer system) 2. Social sciences—Data
processing. I. Title. II. Title: SPSS/PC Plus made simple.
HA32.H42   1990
300'.285'5369—dc20   90-12381
                                                         CIP

CONTENTS

Chapter 10   Multivariate Comparison of Means: Analysis of Variance and Multiple Analysis of Variance 125

Chapter 11   Discriminant Function Analysis 139

PREFACE

After twelve years of teaching SPSS, SPSSx, and SPSS/PC+, I am convinced that SPSS/PC+ is not easy for the average college student to learn. I am also convinced that it is not easy to teach from the program manuals. Students who are experienced with statistics and programming or students with a high aptitude for this type of work will learn SPSS/PC+ easily. The rest suffer. Typically, my students have scant training in statistics or programming. Often they are not comfortable with mathematics, computers, and "that sort of thing." I wrote *SPSS/PC+ Made Simple* to help these students and their instructors.

Organization

As the title implies, this book does not attempt to present all the intricacies and capacities of SPSS/PC+. In Part 1, I have tried to discuss only what is essential for a student with little background in statistics and no background in programming to perform successful analyses with SPSS/PC+. Being able to produce interesting output quickly is a tremendous morale booster. In Part 1 of the text, my objectives are

- to minimize the errors the student is likely to make;
- to teach the student to think in terms of coding data into cases, variables, and formatted records;
- to introduce the student to basic data file cleaning through the LIST command;

- to introduce the student to univariate analysis through the use of the FRE-QUENCIES command;
- to teach the student how to focus on subsets of data files through the SELECT IF command;
- to teach the student how to transform variables and create new variables with the RECODE, COMPUTE, and IF commands; and
- to introduce the student to bivariate analysis with the CROSSTABS, MEANS, CORRELATION, and PLOT commands.

Part 2 covers multivariate statistical techniques that in themselves are not simple. Although I present simple approaches to using SPSS/PC+ for producing the analyses, the discussion of the meaning of the statistics is unavoidably more challenging than the discussion in Part 1. Part 2 also includes a chapter on using data files from the Bureau of the Census and a chapter on using Microsoft Chart with SPSS/PC+.

Acknowledgments

This book would never have been completed without the confidence and support of the staff at Wadsworth Publishing Company. Sheryl Fullerton and Cynthia Haus provided encouragement in the early stages of 1988 and that work passed over to Serina Beauparlant and Marla Nowick. Able production editing was done by Richard Lynch of Bookman Productions. Janet Hunter was that all-important player: a good copyeditor. I envision copyeditors as sitting at their desks or kitchen tables going through sentence after sentence discovering inconsistencies, omissions, and atrocities of language usage as they rush to meet a deadline after receiving the manuscript late from the author. They improve the text dramatically, and I hope I never meet one of mine in a dark alley. Since computer books are often read from the index forward, I must not forget to thank the indexer, Katherine Stimson, who added immeasurably to this text's usefulness.

The Department of Sociology and Anthropology at the University of Texas at El Paso, where I taught while writing this text, provided computer hardware, software, and students. More importantly, however, my colleagues and students there were always genuinely enthusiastic about the project.

I don't think anyone honestly looks forward to reading critical comments of early drafts, but often they are on the mark. The reviewers of this text improved it, and the fact that not all of their suggestions were incorporated reflects practical constraints and is not an implication that those omitted were meritless. I appreciate the numerous constructive comments of the following reviewers: Ron Anderson, University of Minnesota; John P. Broida, University of Southern Maine; Edward J. Duffy, Marshall University; Susan G. Janssen, University of Minnesota; Barbara Keating, Mankato State University; Lauren H.

Seiler, CUNY Queens College; William Skinner, University of Kentucky; and Anthony Walsh, Boise State University.

Most of all, I would like to thank my children, Shanti and Monique, and my wife, Sarah Ray. Without their incredible patience and their willingness to forgo other activities while I worked on the manuscript, it could never have become the text you hold in your hands.

Advantageous Features

Throughout this book I have tried to proceed step by step without making implicit leaps in logic or sneaking in new terms without definitions.

A single topic, the correlates of happiness, is used for examples to illustrate the various procedures as they are introduced. This extended example elaborates chapter by chapter how happiness corresponds with gender, age, education, income, health, marital status, and parenthood.

An easily conducted research project is incorporated into the text. Part of the work is done in the chapters and gives the student the experience of being involved in an analysis from data collection to final product.

Data from the 1984 General Social Survey conducted by the National Opinion Research Center is available from Wadsworth Publishing Company to instructors who adopt the book, so that analyses paralleling those in the text can be readily given as exercises.

The first fourteen chapters have Review Questions with answers (given in the back of the text) that enable the students to check their understanding of the chapter. These chapters also have Assignment Questions with answers provided only to the instructor.

The portion of code being introduced is highlighted by boldface type for emphasis within code segments. Outputs discussed in the presentation of new material are simplified to facilitate the learning of key statistics. Complete replications of SPSS/PC+ outputs are also provided to enable the student to see the context in which the statistics appear and to provide the instructor the option of discussing additional statistics.

Commands in text are written in CAPITAL LETTERS. A glossary enables the student to quickly look up command keywords and specifications and see examples of their use.

Finally, this text condenses into one book the most essential material covered in several SPSS manuals.

Note to the Student

SPSS/PC+ is a computer program for analyzing and displaying information. (The SPSS/PC+ acronym stands for the Statistical Package for the Social Sciences/

Personal Computer enhanced edition.) This book will show you how to use SPSS/PC+ versions V2.0 or V3.0.

If you are unfamiliar with statistics or computers, you may be a little nervous—perhaps very nervous. Relax. You do not have to be a genius to perform statistical analysis or to use a computer. Step by step, this book explains how to perform statistical analyses with SPSS/PC+. You will not become an expert on statistics or computers simply by studying this book. You will, however, be able to do the procedures used most often in academic, government, and business work. Be patient, be persistent, and don't be afraid to ask people who know more than you do for help. You'll survive and, I hope, develop an enthusiasm for what you can learn through quantitative analyses.

The SPSS/PC+ material is most easily learned by studying examples. To give continuity and realism to our examples, we conduct an analysis of happiness that proceeds from chapter to chapter. The analysis examines how happiness is affected by gender, age, education, income, marital status, parenthood, and health. Can you hazard a guess right now as to which of these variables will be most strongly associated with happiness?

PART 1

LEARNING THE BASICS

Part 1 opens with an introduction for beginners in Chapter 1. If you have no experience with computers, this is the place to start. Chapter 2 explains how data are coded for computer analysis. Chapter 3 presents three elementary analytical commands and Chapter 4 introduces the basics of using the SPSS/PC+ program. Chapter 5 examines how to transform variables into new categories, how to compute new variables, and how to label your output clearly. Chapter 6 shows the use of CROSSTABS to examine the association between two variables. Chapter 7 demonstrates the use of MEANS to compare group means. Finally, Chapter 8 guides you through the use of commands for correlations and scatterplots, two more ways of examining the association between two variables.

Part 1 provides practice in using an SPSS/PC+ system file. As an example, we use the National Opinion Research Center's 1984 General Social Survey, discussed in Appendix B. The text examples focus on those characteristics of respondents that are associated with happiness. The file, however, contains many other variables and covers a broad range of attitudes and background information.

Part 1 also has class assignments that involve the gathering and coding of data, using the Happiness Questionnaire in Appendix C. If your instructor uses this project you will collect information about people including their level of happiness. You will be then be instructed chapter by chapter on how to treat the information you collect, so it can be analyzed with SPSS.

1

WHAT HAVE YOU GOTTEN YOURSELF INTO?

Many people hate working with computers or statistics, and you are now in the position of having to do both. Often this hatred is grounded in an unspoken fear that "I won't be able to do it right." To become an expert at programming or statistics *is* a long and difficult learning process, but you need not be an expert to do useful statistical analysis with computers. *Learning to do basic statistics with SPSS/PC+ is no more difficult, than learning to read. You learned to read, and you can learn to use SPSS/PC+ correctly.*

The best way to learn to use SPSS/PC+ is by example. As a learning example, we will analyze how various types of people differ in their likelihood of being happy. Are men happier than women? Are college graduates happier than people who stop their education after high school? Are the affluent or the poor happier than the middle class? Are single people happier than married people? Are people with children happier than people without children? Are people less than forty years old happier than people forty and older. In the coming chapters, you will learn how SPSS/PC+ can help you answer these and a wide range of other questions.

This book's primary goal is to teach you to use SPSS/PC+. (In case you're still wondering, the SPSS/PC+ acronym stands for the Statistical Package for the Social Services/Personal Computer enhanced edition.) Although most statistical concepts are explained when they occur for the first time in the text, we presume that you have a little knowledge of statistics. You should take the Background Quiz at the end of this chapter to refresh your memory and see whether or not your statistical knowledge is at the expected level. If your grasp of these terms is shaky, you may wish to have handy an introductory statistics text for reference. An easy introduction is *Statistics without Tears* by Derek Roundtree (New York: Charles Scribner's Sons, 1981). A more advanced introduction is Hubert Blalock's *Social Statistics,* revised second edition (New York: McGraw-Hill, 1979). A statistics text that also discusses SPSS commands is *Through the Maze: Statistics with Computer Applications* by Margaret Jendrek (Belmont, Calif.: Wadsworth, 1985).

1.1 About SPSS/PC+: Friend or Foe?

This section provides some basic background about SPSS/PC+, programs, and data. These beginning terms are like your car tires. They are not the most exciting part of the vehicle, but you are not going anywhere without them.

What Is SPSS/PC+?

SPSS/PC+ is a set of programs for computers that enables researchers to do many types of statistical analyses. Sometimes researchers analyze data they have collected, sometimes they analyze data sets acquired from other researchers. With SPSS/PC+ you can

- learn the number of cases in each category of a variable;
- compute simple averages for your data;
- perform crosstabulations to examine associations among variables;
- compute correlations between variables;
- do multiple regressions, discriminant function analyses, log-linear analyses, factor analyses, and other sophisticated multivariate analyses; and
- display your data in a variety of table, graph, and map formats.

SPSS/PC+ has a number of features that make it easier to use than other statistical analysis programs, and it is the most widely used program dedicated especially to statistical analyses. There is also a version of SPSS (called, simply, SPSS^x) for use on large mainframe computers. The commandsare generally the same, so learning SPSS/PC+ will give you a foundation for using the mainframe version.

What Are Data and What Data Will We Use?

Broadly defined, **data** are any kind of information; however, the term often is used to refer particularly to information organized for computer processing. The word *data* is the plural form of the word *datum*. We use *data* with the plural form of verbs, as in "the data are accurate." This may sound peculiar at first.

SPSS/PC+ is a tool that can analyze all sorts of data about a countless variety of topics. What you use it for depends upon your interests. SPSS/PC+ has been used by people studying such diverse subjects as

- business payrolls
- school registrations
- earthquakes
- income distributions
- death rates
- population growth
- unemployment trends
- attitudes about nuclear weapons
- which kinds of people are most likely to be happy or unhappy

The subject of happiness is the focus for examples throughout this book. For these examples, we employ data gathered by the National Opinion Research Center (NORC), a nonprofit research branch of the University of Chicago. Founded in 1941, NORC is one of the oldest national survey research facilities in the country and works for a wide range of clients. Academic researchers, marketing managers, city planners, and political campaigners are some of the variety of people involved in survey research who have utilized the services or data of NORC.

Among its many research projects, NORC has conducted a General Social Survey almost every year since 1964. (The exceptions were 1979 and 1981, when government funding for the project was insufficient.) This survey measures people's social, psychological and political attitudes. The NORC General Social Survey also gathers information about age, sex, income level, level of education, ethnicity, race, marital status, and other social characteristics.

Our examples use data from the NORC 1984 General Social Survey (often referred to as NORC84). We also give assignments involving this data file as you progress chapter by chapter. Appendix B lists the questions used by NORC in their data collection. (Doing Assignment Question 1.1 at the end of this chapter will begin preparing you to use this file.)

You can also collect data of your own using the Happiness Questionnaire in Appendix C. These data can be used for comparisons with the data in the

NORC84 file. Look at Appendix C now to get an idea of what is entailed in the course research project. (The Research Project Work at the end of this chapter begins the research project.)

Perhaps you already have a data set concerning questions of interest to you. If so, this book will take you step by step through what you need to know to analyze it.

What Is a Program?

A **program** is a set of instructions to a computer to make it perform tasks that the user wants done. A **job** or **run** is the submission of a program to a computer for execution.

One mistake beginning students sometimes make is to think that a computer program already has the data and they need only ask their questions. This is not true. For example, if you want to know the mean length of employment at Wadsworth, Inc., a statistics program can calculate the mean only if you supply the employment data about the individuals working for Wadsworth. Unless someone has stored the necessary data set in a memory device of your computer system and your program makes reference to where it is, you must provide the data along with your commands.

The following is an example of an SPSS/PC+ program that includes data (the lines of numbers between BEGIN DATA and END DATA).

two   *separate files*   *file 1*   *file 2*

```
data list /
      idl          1–2
      educ|        3–4
      sex|         5
      happy|       6.
begin data.
   010912
   021223
   031521
   041222
   050611
   061612
   071522
   081612
   091821
   101412
   111321
   121611
   130922
```

data list /
id2   1–2
edu2   3–4
sex2   5
happy2   6.
begin data.
02 0913

save   outfile = "data2".

```
141212
151221
161821
170821
181222
191613
20142
end data.
frequencies educ sex happy.
```

(handwritten left margin: ave of file = "data")

(handwritten right margin:
juk3.
compute id3 = id1 – id2.
if (id3 ne 0) list id3.
compute educ3 = educ1 – educ2
if (educ3 neg list id1 educ3
↓
all variable.)

There is nothing magical about a program. When the user gives commands like DATA LIST or FREQUENCIES, certain procedures are carried out according to the instructions that are stored as part of the SPSS/PC+ program. (For now, do not worry about what this code does. The work done by DATA LIST is explained in Chapter 2, and the work done by FREQUENCIES is explained in Chapter 3.) The commands are a shorthand method to activate the more complete instructions contained in the SPSS/PC+ program stored in the computer.

Each space on a line represents a column. SPSS/PC+ commands do not have to begin in column 1, although most users begin them there. If the command will not fit on one line, it is continued on the following line. You cannot split any words or variable names between lines. The end of a command is indicated by a period. If by mistake you do not end with a period, SPSS/PC+ will try to read the following line as a continuation of the command, and an **error** will result.

Most SPSS/PC+ commands have two parts: (1) a command keyword, and (2) a specification field that provides details of the command. In our example, FREQUENCIES is a command keyword calling for a frequencies analysis. (Frequency analyses are explained in Chapter 3.) Following the command keyword FREQUENCIES is the specification field EDUC SEX HAPPY which names the specific variables for which the frequencies are to be produced. In a few commands, there is a command phrase containing two keywords: for example, DATA LIST. There are also a few command keywords that do not require specifications: for example, BEGIN DATA. (DATA LIST and BEGIN DATA are explained in Chapter 2.)

How Do You Learn to Use SPSS/PC+?

You learn SPSS/PC+ step by step, just as you learned to read. This book takes you through the process of learning to use SPSS/PC+ to analyze social science data. For further reference, see the *SPSS/PC+ V2.0 Base Manual* (Chicago: SPSS Inc., 1988). This large, intimidating volume is an encyclopedic reference tool; it should be available for reference at your computer installation. It is also sold at many college bookstores. A section at the end of each chapter, entitled Additional Resources, indicates where in the *SPSS/PC+ V2.0 Base Manual* you will find more discussion of the material covered in the chapter. Part 2 discusses more advanced statistical techniques; there a different reference manual, *SPSS/PC+ Advanced Statistics V2.0* (Chicago: SPSS Inc., 1988), is often cited. In addition, the Additional Resources section often references other articles and texts that you may find useful.

1.2 About Using Computers

If you have no experience with computers, learning to use a computer may be the hardest part about learning to use SPSS/PC+. Just remember that you cannot break a computer by using it—even if you make mistakes. A deliberate attack, perhaps with an ax or a sledgehammer, can damage a computer. (Sometimes you will feel like doing this. . . . Don't!) Dropping a computer down a flight of stairs can damage it. Pouring coffee into a computer can damage it. Making errors while using a computer will not damage it. So don't be nervous about hurting it.

What Is a Computer?

What is usually called a **computer** is actually a system of machines that can receive information, process information, store information, and send out information. Realize that you are dealing with a mindless system of machines that does only what it is instructed to do and remembers only what it is told to remember. (Human and mechanical malfunctions can mess up this ideal state of operation.) We use computers because, once programmed correctly, they perform tasks very quickly and accurately. What we hate about computers are the difficulties encountered in programming them correctly. User-friendly programs (those that are considered easy to use) such as SPSS/PC+ reduce the difficulties.

What Are the Basic Parts of a Computer System?

The basic parts of a computer system are the input devices, the central processing unit (CPU), the storage devices, and the output devices. The discussion in this book is confined to personal computers (PCs), the self-contained units that sit "conveniently" on your desk taking up all your comfortable writing and note file space. (The avid computer enthusiasts will tell you that all these tasks can now be accomplished with the computer so you don't need the space. Personally, I miss the elbow room, but my PC is indispensable.)

The part of the computer system that you usually will work with first is an input device. This consists of a keyboard and a video display screen to indicate what characters you are entering.

The CPU is the part of the computer that does the calculations and data transformations that you command.

There are programs and data that need to be stored in a way that allows the computer to access them when so instructed without requiring users to enter them each time the users want to use them. The most common storage devices are tapes, disks, or the memory core of the CPU itself. Tapes, disks, and memory core utilize magnetic charges to store information. Of course, to retrieve or store information on any of these media requires a machine designed for that purpose that is linked with the computer's CPU.

Often the output from the computer will be on the same video display screen that displays your input. For example, if you make an error entering a command, you may receive an error message on the screen. You may use the screen to display the information in a file stored on a disk.

Another option is to have your output printed on paper as a hard copy. This requires a printer and instructions telling the computer to print the output at that particular printer. A common practice is to examine an output file on the video screen to ensure that it is correct, and then, if it is correct, print it. (Think of the millions of trees that have been temporarily saved from the paper mills!)

A typical work session at your PC will entail turning it on, entering a command to call into memory the program you want to use, entering program commands, entering a command to exit the program you were using, and turning off your PC.

1.3 Summary

In this chapter you've learned some very basic information about SPSS/PC+ and computers. Let's briefly recap that information before plunging in and using SPSS/PC+ (a program that enables researchers to organize data sets, transform variables, and perform many types of statistical analysis).

Computers are machines that can receive, store, process, and transmit information. This information, particularly when organized for computer processing, is called data. The user must give programs (sets of instructions) to a computer to command desired operations. This is done via runs or jobs: the submission of a program to a computer for execution.

Terminals are machines for transmitting information to and receiving information from computers. Printers are machines that produce on paper the output from computers. Visual images of what is being input to or output from computers are produced on video display screens.

RESEARCH PROJECT WORK

Administer the Research Project Questionnaire in Appendix C to a sample of 20 people.

REVIEW QUESTIONS

1.1   What are the words behind the acronym "SPSS/PC+"?

1.2   What are the basic parts of a computer system?

1.3   Give an example of an input device.

1.4   What does the central processing unit do?

1.5   Give an example of a storage device.

1.6   Give an example of an output device.

1.7   What is a computer program?

1.8   What are the parts of an SPSS/PC+ command?

1.9   Can a word or variable name be split between two lines of an SPSS/PC+ command?

1.10 How is the end of an SPSS/PC+ command indicated?

1.11 What is a computer run or job?

ASSIGNMENT QUESTIONS

1.1   Look through the questions in Appendix B.

1.2   Make a list of the variable names that relate to
      a. family background
      b. satisfaction with aspects of one's life
      c. attitudes toward freedom of speech

BACKGROUND QUIZ

In this book, we assume that you are familiar with basic statistical terms and concepts. To check your knowledge and refresh your memory, fill in the blanks in the following statements using the terms provided. (The answers are provided after the last question.)

    a. case
    b. central tendency
    c. correlation
    d. interval measure
    e. *N*
    f. nominal measure
    g. mean
    h. median
    i. mode
    j. ordinal measure
    k. population
    l. range
    m. sample
    n. score
    o. standard deviation
    p. statistical significance
    q. *t*-test
    r. unit of analysis
    s. variable
    t. *Z* score

1.   One specific example of what is being studied is called a _____.

2.   The number of cases in your study is called the _____.

3.   The type of entity that is being studied is termed the _____.

4.   The total set of what you are studying is called the _____.

5.   A smaller number of the total set of what you are studying is termed a _____.

6.   This is a set of mutual exclusive attributes that can be used to classify all cases according to a characteristic. For example, income is a _____.

7.   The measure of a particular case on a variable is its _____ for that variable.

8.   The point in a distribution around which other scores tend to cluster is the _____.

9. A measure of central tendency that is the point above which and below which half the cases fall is termed the _____.

10. A measure of central tendency that is the average calculated by summing the scores and dividing by the number of cases is called the _____.

11. The score that occurs most frequently is called the _____.

12. A measure that has categories that can be ranked but are not of equal size is termed _____.

13. A measure that has categories of equal size that can be ranked is called _____.

14. A measure that has distinct categories that cannot be ranked is called _____.

15. The difference between the highest score and the lowest score is called the _____.

16. The _____ is a measure of the typical distance from the mean of cases in a distribution. It is the square root of the sum of the deviations from the mean squared, divided by the number of cases. $\sqrt{\dfrac{\Sigma (X - \bar{X})^2}{N}}$

17. A score minus the mean divided by the standard deviation—for example, $(X - \bar{X})/s$—is a _____.

18. The probability that a given result could be caused by sampling error is called the _____.

19. One test of the statistical significance of the distance between the means of two sets of scores is the _____.

20. A measure of the strength of association between two interval variables is the _____.

ANSWERS TO BACKGROUND QUIZ

1. a
2. e
3. r
4. k
5. m
6. s
7. n
8. b
9. h
10. g
11. i
12. j
13. d
14. f
15. l
16. o
17. t
18. p
19. q
20. c

create systems files —

merge systemfiles
get file = "data1"
jain match = "*".

compute —

(not subj)

yrbirth — subbirth2

yrbirth (etc)

subj1 - subj
yrbirth1 - yrbirth
mobirth1 - mobirth
dabirth1 - dabirth
yrtest1 - yrtest
motest1 - motest
datest1 - datest
gender1 - gender
iq1 - IQ
bac1 - back
orien1 - orient
color1 - color
form1 - form
nam1 - name

Change
files

2

GETTING STARTED

New SPSS/PC+ Commands:

```
DATA LIST
BEGIN DATA
END DATA
MISSING VALUES
SAVE
GET
INCLUDE
```

After the NORC researchers interviewed 1,473 people for the 1984 General Social Survey and recorded their answers, they needed to feed the data into the computer in a form it could use. If you've collected responses to the questionnaire in Appendix C, you're in the same boat. What you need to know now is how to code data and how to tell that code to the computer.

2.1 Coding Your Data to Be Computer Readable

In this section we discuss how to prepare information so that it can be analyzed with a computer. Suppose that you did the assignment in Chapter 1 that involved administering the research project questionnaire to 20 people. Now you have data from 20 people marked on questionnaires. What is the next step?

Computers store information in columns. Therefore, converting verbal responses to numbers that will require fewer columns is a good idea. For example, in our research project questionnaire in Appendix C, one question was "Would you say that you are very happy, pretty happy, or not too happy?" The person is asked to choose from three answers:

1	2	3
very happy	pretty happy	not too happy

To store the verbal responses on columns, we would need to reserve as many columns as there are letters and spaces in the longest response: that would be 13 columns for "not too happy." Instead of this approach, we can have each response correspond to the number above it. Fantastic! Now we only need one column reserved for whichever number corresponds to the response for that case.

At first converting the responses to numbers may seem odd; however, this convention saves a tremendous amount of column space. An equally important reason to use numbers is that we often are working with variables for which we want to calculate the mean (average of all scores) and other statistics. In our example, we might like to know what the mean was of the responses. If it was 1.6, we would know that in our sample the average response was between "pretty happy" and "very happy."

There may be times when you want to work with words instead of numbers. For example, you may be conducting a study for which you want to be able to make a directory of respondents with names and addresses. To work with words you need to use string variables, which are discussed in Appendix A. Once we have coded the data, we must store them in a way that enables the computer to find them. Think of the data for each case as being stored on a line. These lines are called **records**. Every column on a line of data is numbered sequentially starting with 1. Each **column** can hold one character—a number, letter, or other symbol. If columns 1–2 are the case identification numbers for case 1, columns 1–2 will be the case identification numbers for all other cases as well. This organization of data is called a **fixed format**, and it is the formatting we use in this book. Other types of formats are available, but the fixed format is the most commonly used for statistical data. (See Appendix A for a discussion of free format.)

The number of columns in each line is the **record length.** The record length for SPSS/PC+ is 80 columns. What if you need to enter more data for this case? You go to the next record—the next line—and use two or more records for each case.

TABLE 2.1 Example Data Set

Name	Years of Education	Sex	Happiness Level
Acuna	09	male	pretty happy
Adams	12	female	not too happy
Bates	15	female	very happy
Beall	12	female	pretty happy
Cunningham	06	male	very happy
Dunham	16	male	pretty happy
Estrada	15	female	pretty happy
Franklin	16	male	pretty happy
Graham	18	female	very happy
Hadi	14	male	pretty happy
Hedgepeth	13	female	very happy
Jordan	16	male	very happy
Kim	09	female	pretty happy
Lawrence	12	male	pretty happy
MacKenzie	12	female	very happy
Morrison	18	female	very happy
Palafox	08	female	very happy
Practor	12	female	pretty happy
Razkowski	16	male	not too happy
Zirl	14	female	no answer

The concepts of cases, columns, and records will be clearer if we go through an example of coding data for a set of cases. Table 2.1 contains a small data file before it is coded. The data in this file, except the names, are real cases taken from the NORC 1984 General Social Survey, described in Appendix B. This data set is used throughout Part 1 to provide examples of SPSS/PC+ procedures. We refer to it as our "example data set." There are many ways to code a data set, so the researcher has to make some decisions. We could code this data file as follows:

- *Case number.* The first two columns will be for the case number code; each individual will be given a unique code number to identify his or her data.

- *Education.* The third and fourth columns will be education, coded in years.
- *Sex.* The fifth column will be the respondent's sex (1 = male, 2 = female).
- *Happiness.* The sixth column will be happiness level (1 = very happy, 2 = pretty happy, 3 = not too happy).

We also need codes to indicate missing information. The simplest approach is to leave columns blank to indicate missing data. For example, the last person in our example data set, Zirl, did not answer the question about happiness, so the column for that variable will be left blank on the line for Zirl. If you want to distinguish between different types of missing data, you need to use the MISSING VALUES command discussed later in this chapter.

The coding system just described would result in the following data file:

```
010912
021223
031521
041222
050611
061612
071522
081612
091821
101412
111321
121611
130922
141212
151221
161821
170821
181222
191613
20142
```

Each line is one record and represents the variable codings for one person. Thus the first line of numbers, 010912, represents the responses of Acuna, the first case in our data file. The first two digits 01 are the case number that identifies Acuna. The second two digits (09) indicate that Acuna has 9 years of formal education. The 1 following the 9 shows that Acuna is a male. The 2 following the 1 shows that Acuna responded that he was pretty happy.

The second line, 021223, is the coded information for Adams, our second case. The digits 02 beginning the line are Adams's identification number. The 12 following the 02 indicates that Adams has 12 years of education. The 2 following the 12 indicates that Adams is a female. The 3 following the 2 indicates that Adams is not so happy.

Likewise each following line is for a subsequent case. The data on the third line are for Bates and the data on the fourth line are for Beall.

Note that the last column for Zirl, the last case, is blank because the information was missing for that variable, and we are using blanks to indicate missing data.

Having carefully coded and entered your data, you need to explain these codes and data locations to the SPSS/PC+ program. This communication with the SPSS/PC+ program is done via the DATA LIST command, which is discussed in the next section.

2.2 Telling the Computer How Your Data Are Organized: DATA LIST

The **DATA LIST** command tells the SPSS/PC+ program the name of each variable that you intend to use and the location of the columns being used for each of these variables. (You do not need to use all of your variables on every run.) Variable names must not be over eight characters long and must begin with a letter. Using variable names that are too long or that do not begin with a letter are common errors made by beginners. Blanks, commas, and periods are not permitted in a variable name, but numbers and other symbols are okay. A good practice is to give your variables names that will remind you of the nature of the variable. For instance, we gave the name HAPPY to the variable containing the responses to the question about happiness.

There are words that SPSS/PC+ reserves in its programming that the user cannot employ as a variable name. The **reserved words** are: ALL, AND, BY, EQ, GE, GT, LE, LT, NE, NOT, OR, THRU, TO, and WITH.

The DATA LIST command is the first command in a program unless you are working with an SPSS file which already has the DATA LIST information saved with the data. (See Section 2.5.) By itself, the DATA LIST command does not produce any output. It simply provides the SPSS/PC+ program with information needed to perform other commands.

Let's consider an example of a DATA LIST command:

```
data list /
    id 1-2.
```

The words DATA LIST alert the SPSS/PC+ program that the rest of the command will describe the names and locations of the variables for this run. The words DATA LIST must begin the command and there must be one space and only one space between DATA and LIST. There must be a slash after LIST.

The expression ID 1–2 indicates that the first variable name is ID and that the ID information is located in columns 1 and 2.

There must be at least one space between the variable name and the column numbers—in this example, between ID and 1–2. If the data span two or more columns, enter the number of the first column, a hyphen and then the number of the second column—in this example, 1–2.

Usually you will be concerned with more than one variable. The following DATA LIST command contains information for the four variables described in the coding example at the beginning of this chapter:

```
data list /
      id        1–2
      educ      3–4
      sex       5
      happy     6.
```

In this longer DATA LIST command the EDUC 3–4 indicates the name of the second variable and the location of the education responses in columns 3 and 4.

In the DATA LIST command, each variable name must be separated from the column numbers of the preceding variable by one or more commas or blanks. The same convention for separating a list of variable names is followed in other SPSS/PC+ commands. In this text, we sometimes, for the sake of clarity, use two spaces where one would suffice or use a comma instead of a space. For the same reason, sometimes each variable name is placed on a separate line. Writing commands that can be read quickly and correctly is as important as writing commands as compactly as possible.

The third variable is SEX; its data are located in column 5. The fourth variable is named HAPPY; its data are located in column 6.

The DATA LIST command is one of two places where you can indicate if your data contain decimal points. Indicate the number of digits that are to the right of the decimal point in parentheses following the column location information. For example, if you had a variable named WAGE (hourly wages) in columns 11–15 and you wanted a decimal point to the left of the last two columns, your code would be:

```
data list /
      wages 11–15 (2).
```

You could also simply enter the wage data with a decimal point before the last two digits; then the (2) would be unnecessary. For example, if an hourly wage of $7.50 were entered as 7.50, the decimal would not have to be indicated on the DATA LIST command. However, the practice of including decimal points in the data uses up more columns than indicating the decimal place in the DATA LIST command.

More examples of coding are provided by the NORC84 codebook in Appendix B and the research project questionnaire in Appendix C. (If you are still unclear about coding, take time to look at these appendixes now.) Throughout Part 1 we refer to the example data set in this chapter, the NORC84 Codebook in Appendix B, and the Happiness Questionnaire in Appendix C. They are used in the Research Project Work, the Review Questions, and the Assignment Questions because they are realistic examples of the types of data sets researchers collect and analyze.

2.3 Indicating Where Your Data Records Begin and End: BEGIN DATA and END DATA

Before doing a statistical procedure in SPSS/PC+, you need to instruct the computer to begin reading data. This is done with the BEGIN DATA command:

```
begin data.
```

This command is followed by the data records—the lines of data. After all the data are entered, you instruct the computer to stop reading data with the command:

```
end data.
```

The DATA LIST, BEGIN DATA, and END DATA commands, as well as the data themselves, are all omitted from your commands when you use an SPSS system file. (We discuss SPSS System files in Section 2.5.)

2.4 Indicating Where Data Are Missing: MISSING VALUES

As we explained earlier, the easiest way to handle missing data is to leave the columns for that variable blank when entering data. This signals the SPSS/PC+ program that the data are missing.

At times, however, the researcher will want to distinguish among different types of missing data. The **MISSING VALUES** command enables us to do this. As an example, information on education might be missing because the interviewer forgot to ask that question or because the respondent refused to answer. Since the person who refuses to answer is showing some reluctance about the interview, this is information we might want to know in evaluating other answers of that respondent. We could code the education variable as blank spaces when the interviewer forgot to ask the question and −9 when the respondent refused to answer. The choice of values is arbitrary. We could have used 98 or 99 or any number that would not be confused with an actual response to the education question. We could not use 9 as a missing value because there might be some respondents who had nine years of formal education.

The following example shows the SPSS/PC+ command necessary to give the variable named EDUC the missing value −9:

```
missing values
    educ (-9).
```

This code segment indicates that if the number in the EDUC columns is −9, then EDUC is missing for that case. We are limited to designating one missing value per variable, in addition to the blank which is a general system missing value. This is an unfortunate limitation. The RECODE command discussed in Chapter 5, however, allows us to change other values for a variable to the missing value. So we could have several missing value categories that are changed to the designated missing value when we want to drop cases with these values from the analysis.

If no numbers appear within parentheses immediately after a variable name, the missing values will be the same as those for the first variable following the MISSING VALUES command which does have missing value information. In the following example, HAPPY is not followed by a number in parentheses; SEX, the variable after HAPPY, is followed by a missing value of 0. This means that the missing value for HAPPY is also 0.

```
missing values
    happy sex (0).
```

Not all the variables in the DATA LIST command need to be listed in the MISSING VALUES command, nor does the order of variable names on the MISSING VALUES command have to be the same as the order on the DATA LIST command.

A nice convention is to give all the variables the same missing values, but sometimes this practice is awkward. For income or years of education, one would not use the number 0 to designate missing, because that could be a legitimate response. Often a negative number is used for variables that have 0 as a response category. A negative number takes up two columns, however, and you would not want to use it universally if your data set has many variables that can be fit on one column. The use of blanks as missing values is not only convenient, because it does not require a MISSING VALUES command; it also is efficient in the use of columns.

There are procedures available in some of the SPSS/PC+ analyses for assigning missing values another value, such as the mean for the variable, so that those cases will be included in the analysis. (See the *SPSS/PC+ V2.0 Base Manual* where it discusses the OPTIONS available for the technique you want to use.) This is often done when one is doing an analysis including so many variables that the number of cases with missing data on one or more variables is quite high. It is possible, especially in an analysis with many variables, for every case to be missing data on one or more of the variables. Under these circumstances, the analysis is impossible unless values are assigned to the cases missing data or unless some of the variables are dropped from the analysis.

Where in the program you place the MISSING VALUES command is important. It must be placed somewhere after the DATA LIST command and before the first statistical procedure command for which the specified values are to be treated as missing. The missing values will stay in effect for the entire run after the MISSING VALUES command unless it is superceded by a second MISSING VALUES command. In the following code segment, we have added a MISSING VALUES command to our example.

```
data list /
      id          1-2
      educ        3-4
      sex         5
      happy       6.
begin data.
010912
021223
031521
```

```
041222
050611
061612
071522
081612
091821
101412
111321
121611
130922
141212
151221
161821
170821
181222
191613
20142
end data.
missing values
      educ      (−9)
      happy
      sex       (0).
frequencies educ sex happy.
```

As you can see, when the data and commands are in one file, the file can soon become very bulky. SPSS system files, which we discuss in the next section, provide a solution to this problem.

2.5 Using SPSS System Files

Think of an SPSS system file as a data file that is saved along with the DATA LIST and MISSING VALUES commands. This type of file is a great convenience because you need not enter all this information every time you want to perform an analysis of the file. If you use an SPSS system file, DATA LIST, MISSING VALUES, BEGIN DATA, the data, and END DATA are omitted from your commands.

SPSS system files can be combined easily. This is useful when you have a set of related data files that you use in different combinations. For example, you may have a file' for each census tract in a city, but want to do a series of analyses using different groupings of tracts.

Creating an SPSS System File

To create an SPSS system file, the only SPSS/PC+ command that you need is **SAVE**. This command needs to be accompanied by the specification **FILE** followed by the name under which to store the file. To create a system file with the name PROJECT, you would use the command

```
save file 'project'.
```

Normally this command is placed at the end of your program so that any transformations and variables created during the program will be saved as well. The commands and data needed to create an SPSS file from our example data set are

```
data list /
      id        1-2
      educ      3-4
      sex       5
      happy     6.
begin data.
010912
021223
031521
041222
050611
061612
071522
081612
091821
101412
111321
121611
130922
141212
151221
161821
170821
```

```
181222
191613
20142
end data.
missing values
        educ        (-9)
        happy
        sex         (0).
save file 'project'.
```

Note that you need DATA LIST, BEGIN DATA, END DATA, and the data themselves among your commands when you create an SPSS file. Once the file is created, however, you need not include these commands or the data when you use the file. In the run creating the file PROJECT, statistical procedure commands like FREQUENCIES could have followed after the END DATA.

Accessing a System File

You would use the **GET** command to access the system file named PROJECT as saved in our previous example. A **FILE** specification field is also necessary, so the entire GET command would be

```
get file 'project'.
```

To produce the frequency distributions (see Section 3.2) for all the variables in the SPSS file PROJECT, the entire set of commands would be

```
get file 'project'.
frequencies educ sex happy.
```

The GET command, however, cannot be used to access data not in an SPSS file. GET also cannot be used to bring a file of commands into a program. To perform these tasks, you need to use the INCLUDE command discussed in the next section.

2.6 Submitting Commands and Data from a File: INCLUDE

A file containing commands, data, or both can be submitted as a batch to be executed all together with the command **INCLUDE**. Follow the command with the name of the file you want submitted enclosed in single quotation marks.

Thus to submit a file named PROGRAM, the complete INCLUDE command would be

```
include 'program'.
```

If, for the first example in this chapter, the data were stored in a file named data, our total set of commands for a frequencies procedure would be

```
data list /
      id          1-2
      educ        3-4
      sex         5
      happy       6.
missing values
      educ        (-9)
      happy
      sex         (0).
begin data.
include 'data'.
end data.
frequencies educ sex happy.
```

You cannot, however, use the INCLUDE command to access SPSS system files; these must be accessed with the GET command discussed in Section 2.5.

2.7 Additional Resources

The information on coding that is presented in this chapter is also addressed in the *SPSS/PC+ V2.0 Base Manual.* DATA LIST is discussed on pages C37–49; BEGIN DATA–END DATA, on page C22; MISSING VALUES, on pages C91–92; SAVE, on pages C175–176; GET, on pages C70–71; and INCLUDE; on pages C78–79. SPSS system files are discussed on pages B22–23.

2.8 Summary

In this chapter we explained how to code information into numbers.

We explained how to use a DATA LIST command to tell the computer what our variables are and what columns contain each variable's information.

We showed how to set off data with the BEGIN DATA and END DATA commands and explained how to indicate missing data with blanks or with the MISSING VALUES command. We also explained how to create and access SPSS system files using the SAVE and GET commands and how to use the INCLUDE command.

RESEARCH PROJECT WORK

2.1   Code the data you gathered doing the Chapter 1's Research Project. For all but the last question, you can use the codes provided by each response on the Research Project Questionnaire. The last question is not precoded, however, so you will have to decide how to categorize the answers and what code value to give each category.

2.2   Write a DATA LIST and MISSING VALUES statement to go with the data you collected.

REVIEW QUESTIONS

HINT: There is more than one way of coding the variables in the following questions.

2.1   Using the variables and the coding system from our example data set, what would be the data record for the following case? Hedderson, whose identification number is 25, whose sex is male, who has 21 years of formal education, and who states that he is very happy?

2.2   How would you code the variable age?

2.3   How would you code the variable political affiliation?

2.4   How would you code the variable annual salary?

Review Using DATA LIST

2.5   Write a DATA LIST command that would allow you to use the education variable from the example data set presented in this chapter.

2.6   Do you need to use a DATA LIST command if the file you are using is on an SPSS system file?

2.7   For the file that would be created from the Happiness Questionnaire discussed in Appendix C, write a DATA LIST command that would allow you to use the variables named INCOME and SEX.

Review Using MISSING VALUES

2.8 Write a MISSING VALUES command that would assign a missing value of −9 to EDUC.

2.9 Write a MISSING VALUES command that would assign missing values of −9 and −8 to the variable INCOME.

2.10 Write a MISSING VALUES command that would assign a missing value of 0 to variables SEX, RELIGION, and PARTY.

2.11 What would have to be done in order for a blank to be treated as a missing value?

ASSIGNMENT QUESTIONS

2.1 Using the variables and the coding system from our example data set, what would be the data record for the following case? Foster, whose identification number is 33, whose sex is female, who has 18 years of formal education, and who states that she is very happy?

2.2 How would you code the variable number of months working for Wadsworth?

2.3 How would you code the variable number of dependents?

2.4 How would you code the variable religious affiliation?

2.5 Write a DATA LIST command that would allow you to use the happiness variable from our learning example data set.

2.6 Would a DATA LIST command be needed to use the variables named AGE and INCOME on the SPSS file named NORC84 discussed in Appendix B?

2.7 Write a DATA LIST command for the variables in the Happiness Questionnaire given in Appendix C.

2.8 Write a MISSING VALUES command that would assign a missing value of −9 to INCOME.

2.9 Write a MISSING VALUES command that would assign a missing value of −8 to the variable INCOME and a missing value of −9 to the variable EDUCATION.

2.10 Write a MISSING VALUES command that would assign a missing value of 0 to variables MARITAL, STATE, and RELIGION.

3

TAKING A FIRST LOOK AT YOUR DATA

New SPSS/PC+ Commands:

```
LIST
FREQUENCIES
SELECT IF
```

In Chapter 4 you will learn how to enter data and commands with SPSS/PC+. Before setting you loose on the computers, however, we want to introduce you to a few SPSS/PC+ data processing commands. That way you'll be able to do something once you have entered SPSS/PC+. This chapter explains the use of the LIST, FREQUENCIES, and SELECT IF commands.

When you analyze your data for the first time, one of your obvious concerns will be the general distribution of cases for each variable. For instance, in considering the example data set presented in Chapter 2, you might ask what percentage of the cases were "very happy," "happy," and "not too happy," respectively. This is the frequency distribution of cases for the variable HAPPY, and in this chapter you will learn how to produce frequency distributions with SPSS/PC+.

Less obvious concerns that should take precedence over analyzing the distribution of cases for each variable are to ensure that the data were entered correctly into memory and that your program is reading them correctly.

It is very important to check your data for errors in coding and data entry.

If the data set is given to you on cards, tapes, or disks by someone who has already checked it extensively, it may be "clean"—that is, free of errors. However, if you or someone else enters the data from a coding sheet, questionnaires or scribbled class notes, errors in data entry are likely to occur.

The LIST command allows you to list by case the values entered for each variable. The FREQUENCIES command allows you to learn about the frequency distribution of the cases for each variable. Interesting in itself, the frequency distribution is also useful for revealing errors in data entry. The SELECT IF command allows you to limit an analysis to whatever types of cases you choose to specify.

Together the FREQUENCIES, LIST, and SELECT IF commands provide you with tools for tracking down errors in data entry and for taking a first look at the distribution of your cases by variable category.

3.1 Printing Out Data for Cases of Interest: LIST

Perhaps you have received a data set on a tape and want to see if it matches an accompanying codebook that explains the variable codings. Perhaps a data set has just been entered onto a storage device and you want to check each case's data to be sure they were entered correctly. Perhaps a statistical analysis has led you to suspect that the data are incorrect for a particular case and you want to list all the data entries for that case. You accomplish these types of tasks with the LIST command.

A listing is an output that gives the values that have been entered in your data file. You may want to LIST the scores for some or all of your cases. You may want to list some or all of your variables. If you want to see all the data entries for all your cases, the command is simply

```
list.
```

For example, to LIST all the data entries for our example data set from Chapter 2, the data and necessary commands would be as follows:

```
data list /
      id        1—2
      educ      3—4
      sex       5
      happy     6.
```

```
begin data.
010912
021223
031521
041222
050611
061612
071522
081612
091821
101412
111321
121611
130922
141212
151221
161821
170821
181222
191613
20142
end data.
list.
```

The output produced by this set of commands is given in Table 3.1. Note that a period is printed for the final case, which has missing data in the column for HAPPY. The SPSS/PC+ commands that you submitted will also be printed. If the job did not run properly, you may see an error message. An **error message** is a statement produced by the SPSS/PC+ program when it encounters something amiss in trying to read or execute your commands. The message will be a statement that tries to explain what went wrong. It will normally be printed in the output immediately after the command with the error. If your data file has a large number of variables and you do not want to print them all, you can specify which ones to print.

```
list id happy.
```

If you do not want to list all the cases of a data file, you can specify the number of cases you want listed with the **CASES =** subcommand. This is very useful when you do not want to see all of a large data set. For example, CASES = 10 will limit the list to the first ten cases. CASES = ALL lists all the cases, and this

TABLE 3.1 Output from the LIST Command

ID	EDUC	SEX	HAPPY
1	9	1	2
2	12	2	3
3	15	2	1
4	12	2	2
5	6	1	1
6	16	1	2
7	15	2	2
8	16	1	2
9	18	2	1
10	14	1	2
11	13	2	1
12	16	1	1
13	9	2	2
14	12	1	2
15	12	2	1
16	18	2	1
17	8	2	1
18	12	2	2
19	16	1	1
20	14	2	

is also the default if CASES = is omitted. With a CASES = subcommand added, our example becomes

```
list id happy/
cases = 10.
```

3.2 Learning the Distribution of Cases: FREQUENCIES

The **FREQUENCIES** command instructs the computer to print out all the code numbers that occur for each variable and the number of cases in each of the code-number categories. For example, the variable SEX in our learning example data set has the code numbers 1 for males, 2 for females, and a blank if the information was missing. The FREQUENCIES command would print out that there was a category coded 1 and the number of cases in this category; it would also print out that there was a category coded 2 and the number of cases in this category. Similarly, it would print out the number of cases for which the data are missing.

In addition to giving the distribution of cases by variable, the FREQUEN-CIES command is an excellent way to check the validity of your data file. If a value that is impossible appears to have cases, you can be sure that the data were entered incorrectly for those cases or that the DATA LIST command contains an error. Thus, if cases appear in category 3 for SEX, when only code values 1, 2, and blanks for missing are being used, you know to check the DATA LIST command. If that command is correct, errors occurred in data entry.

The FREQUENCIES output will not catch misentries that are realistic in appearance. For example, if for the variable SEX, a 1 was entered instead of a 2, nothing will look wrong. You would assume that the case was a male and not realize that it was a female whose gender data had been entered incorrectly. (The LIST command covered in the previous section must be used to detect less obvious errors by checking the printout against the original data.)

To do a FREQUENCIES procedure for the variable named HAPPY in our example data set, you would use the following command:

```
frequencies happy.
```

Variable names must be separated by at least one comma or space.

Placed in the context of our example, the following FREQUENCIES command instructs SPSS/PC+ to produce the frequencies for the variable HAPPY:

```
data list /
        id        1-2
        educ      3-4
        sex       5
        happy     6.
begin data.
010912
021223
031521
041222
050611
061612
071522
081612
091821
101412
111321
121611
130922
141212
```

```
151221
161821
170821
181222
191613
20142
end data.
missing values
       educ        (-9)
       happy
       sex         (0).
frequencies happy.
```

These commands and data will produce the output in Table 3.2. The column headed VALUE indicates the code categories for the variable HAPPY. The column headed FREQUENCY indicates the number of cases in each category. The column headed PERCENT indicates the percent of all the cases that are in each category.

Recall from the coding we did in Chapter 2 that in our example data set, value 1 stands for "very happy," value 2 stands for "pretty happy," and value 3 stands for "not too happy." In our sample of 20 people, there is one whose response is missing. Of the 19 people who did respond, 42.1 percent responded that they were very happy, 47.4 percent responded that they were pretty happy, and 10.5 percent responded that they were not so happy.

To produce a table that presents the number of cases in each category for all variables, you would substitute the following FREQUENCIES command in the preceding example:

```
frequencies all.
```

TABLE 3.2 Simplified Output from a FREQUENCIES Command

HAPPY

VALUE	FREQUENCY	PERCENT
1	8	42.1
2	9	47.4
3	2	10.5
.	1	MISSING
TOTAL	20	100.0

The **ALL** in this command is a specification keyword that has the same meaning in SPSS/PC+ that it does in everyday usage. (**Keywords** are words used in commands and subcommands to facilitate the expression of what you want done. Their meaning is generally apparent, and we will cover them as we introduce the SPSS/PC+ commands and subcommands.) In this example, ALL calls for FREQUENCIES to be done for all the variables on the DATA LIST command.

Before doing a FREQUENCIES run, review your variables to be certain that none of them contains more categories than you want printed out. Otherwise your output may be far bulkier than you want. For example, family income to the nearest dollar would have nearly as many categories as the number of cases, and for a large data set the frequencies for INCOME would be an enormous table. The best way to solve this problem is to combine many values into fewer large categories. This combining of values is done with the RECODE command discussed in Chapter 5.

You might not want to produce a frequency table for the ID variable in a large data set. Fortunately, portions of a variable list can be specified using the **TO** keyword.

```
frequencies education to happy.
```

This command would print the frequencies for EDUC, SEX and HAPPY, but not ID.

3.3 Using FREQUENCIES with an SPSS System File

The use of FREQUENCIES with an SPSS system file differs from the example in the previous section. The GET command accesses a file that already has the information from DATA LIST, MISSING VALUES, BEGIN DATA and END DATA commands stored with the data. To do a FREQUENCIES run of all the variables in the SPSS system file NORC84, you would use the following commands:

```
get file 'NORC84.'
frequencies all.
```

Part of the output produced by the preceding commands is replicated in Table 3.3. In this table for the 1,473 case NORC84 file, you can see a few differences in format from Table 3.2. First there are VALUE LABELS for the VALUES because NORC84 was saved with VALUE LABELS. (Creation of VALUE LABELS is discussed in Chapter 5.) Second there are two categories of missing data. A

TABLE 3.3 Partial Output of FREQUENCIES for HAPPY Using the NORC84 SPSS System File

HAPPY

VALUE LABEL	VALUE	FREQUENCY	PERCENT
VERY HAPPY	1	502	34.7
PRETTY HAPPY	2	756	52.3
NOT TOO HAPPY	3	187	12.9
DK	8	1	MISSING
NA	9	27	MISSING
	TOTAL	1473	100.0

check of the codebook for NORC84 in Appendix B will show that NA stands for "no answer" and DK stands for "don't know."

There are also very noticeable differences in the frequency distribution of HAPPY for this sample compared to our earlier example. The percent very happy is 34.7 percent instead of 42.1 percent, the percent pretty happy is 52.3 percent instead of 47.4 percent, and the percent not too happy is 12.9 percent instead of 10.5 percent. The NORC84 sample is much larger than our 20-case example, so we presume that it more accurately reflects what the percentages would be if we surveyed the entire population of the United States.

From this table we learn that about half the respondents in the NORC84 sample reported being pretty happy, a third reported being very happy, and the remaining sixth were not so happy. In Chapter 5 we will begin to investigate how various types of people differ in their likelihood of being in each of these categories.

3.4 Producing More with FREQUENCIES: Subcommand STATISTICS

Using the subcommand STATISTICS on a FREQUENCIES command will produce the high score, low score, mean, and standard deviation for each variable.

```
frequencies all/
          statistics.
```

Note how the subcommand STATISTICS is separated by a slash. For greater visual separation we have placed the STATISTICS subcommand indented on the next line. A good practice is to make it as easy as possible to pick out the various parts of your SPSS/PC+ commands.

The complete output from the preceding commands for the variable HAPPY in the NORC84 SPSS system file is given in Table 3.4. It includes the mean, standard deviation, minimum score, and maximum score. Also in Table 3.4 are two percent columns: the PERCENT column contains percents calculated including the missing data; the VALID PERCENT column contains percents calculated omitting the missing data.

For a simple description of the characteristics of a set of cases, the information provided by FREQUENCIES will often be sufficient. But what if you want to focus on a subset of your cases? For example, your employer's personnel department may have assigned you the task of doing a description of the salaries, positions, and length of employment of all female personnel. Or you may want to select those cases with invalid data and list their ID numbers. This would give you the identification number of these cases which need to have corrections made in their data. The SELECT IF command presented in the next section will allow you to focus on such subsets of your data file.

TABLE 3.4 Partial Output of FREQUENCIES with STATISTICS

HAPPY   GENERAL HAPPINESS

VALUE LABEL	VALUE	FREQUENCY	PERCENT	VALID PERCENT
VERY HAPPY	1	502	34.1	34.7
PRETTY HAPPY	2	756	51.3	52.3
NOT TOO HAPPY	3	187	12.7	12.9
DK	8	1	.1	MISSING
NA	9	27	1.8	MISSING
	TOTAL	1473	100.0	100.0

MEAN	1.782	STD DEV	.655	MINIMUM	1.000
MAXIMUM	3.000				

VALID CASES   1445   MISSING CASES   28

3.5 Focusing on Cases of Interest: SELECT IF

Often in an analysis you will not want to include all the cases in your data file. Perhaps you want to obtain a description of just the women in your sample. The SELECT IF command allows you to do this. Study the following command (remembering that female is coded 2 for the SEX variable):

```
select if (sex eq 2).
```

There must be one space and only one space between the SELECT and the IF. After that the spacing on this command is flexible. The EQ symbolizes equal, hence this command selects out only the women in the data file. The specification of the set of cases being selected must be in parentheses.

The file placement of the SELECT IF command must be after the DATA LIST command and before any commands for which you want it to apply. The following example illustrates the normal placement of the SELECT IF command:

```
data list /
      id        1-2
      educ      3-4
      sex       5
      happy     6.
begin data.
010912
021223
031521
041222
050611
061612
071522
081612
091821
101412
111321
121611
130922
141212
151221
161821
170821
```

```
181222
191613
20142
end data.
missing values
     educ        (-9)
     happy
     sex         (0).
select if (sex eq 2).
frequencies educ sex happy/
          statistics.
```

To do the same procedures for the SPSS system file NORC84, the SPSS/PC+ commands would be

```
get file 'NORC84'.
select if (sex eq 2).
frequencies all/
          statistics.
```

If we did two runs, one selecting for females and another selecting for males, we would obtain on separate outputs one frequencies distribution for females and one for males. Pooling the information from these outputs, we could put together Table 3.5. (In Chapter 5 we will learn how the PROCESS IF

TABLE 3.5 Table Constructed for HAPPY from FREQUENCIES Outputs

MALES		
VALUE LABEL	FREQUENCY	PERCENT
VERY HAPPY	196	30.7
PRETTY HAPPY	355	55.6
NOT TOO HAPPY	88	13.8
TOTAL	639	100.0
FEMALES		
VALUE LABEL	FREQUENCY	PERCENT
VERY HAPPY	303	35.0
PRETTY HAPPY	455	52.5
NOT TOO HAPPY	108	12.5
TOTAL	866	100.0

command would enable us to select for females and then later select for males in the same run.) The numbers in the table indicate that 30.7 percent of the males are very happy. (Recall that the response "very happy" was given the value 1.) The second part of the table concerns females, and indicates that 35.0 percent of the females report being very happy.

You can see then that females are slightly more likely than males to report that they are very happy. We will look at this relationship more closely in later chapters, as we examine how other variables are associated with the likelihood of being happy.

Perhaps you want to perform an analysis using only the people with over 15 years of education among your cases. The following command would select out that subset:

```
select if (educ gt 15).
```

The **GT** symbolizes "greater than," so GT 15 indicates that only those whose score on EDUC is greater than 15 will be used in this analysis. If LT was used in place of GT only those whose score on EDUC was less than 15 would be used. If EQ was used in place of GT, only those whose score on EDUC equaled 15 would be selected.

The following abbreviated expressions, called **relational operators,** may be used with SELECT IF:

EQ   symbolizes equal
NE   symbolizes not equal
LT   symbolizes less than
GT   symbolizes greater than
LE   symbolizes less than or equal to
GE   symbolizes greater than or equal to

What if you want to select people between two scores? For example, you only want to study adults with 13 to 16 years of education. No problem. Note the following example:

```
select if (educ gt 12 and educ lt 17).
```

The (EDUC GT 12 AND EDUC LT 17) part of the command means that only cases that have EDUC scores above 12 and below 17 will be selected.

You can select people from two or more of the categories on one variable. For example, the following command would select both those who had 13 years of education and those who had 14 years of education:

```
select if (educ eq 13 or educ eq 14).
```

If you want to use two or more variables in your selection process, you can use the following construction:

```
select if (educ gt 12 and sex eq 2).
```

This command would select only those respondents who were coded 12 or more on EDUC and 2 on SEX. In our data set, these would be women with more than 12 years of education.

You may want to select people who are in a particular category in either of two variables. That is no problem either. For example, to select people who have less than 16 years of education or who responded that they are "not too happy," you would use the following command:

```
select if (educ lt 16 or happy eq 3).
```

SELECT IF commands can become quite convoluted. Often you will want to place your conditions on several commands, rather than have one complex command. Be careful! A series of SELECT IF commands will be interpreted as if they are linked by AND. In other words, only those cases that meet all the specifications of all the commands will be selected for the analysis. For example the two commands

```
select if (educ gt 16).
select if (sex eq 1).
```

together would dictate that only those both over 16 on EDUC *and* with a value of 1 on SEX will be included in the analysis.

The SELECT IF command can also be used to examine cases for which the data seem incorrect. This cleaning operation (to correct data entry errors) is done together with the LIST command. For example, you might want to list the ID numbers of cases that obviously have false data entered. Suppose you have a variable named SEX coded 1 for males, 2 for females, and blank for missing. If another value had been entered in the data file in the column containing the SEX data, it would be an error that you would want to discover and correct. The following code segment would list the ID numbers of cases for which SEX had not been coded as either 1 or 2:

```
select if (sex ne 1 or sex ne 2).
list.
```

The first line of these commands selects cases that have not been coded as 1 (male) or 2 (female). The second command instructs SPSS/PC+ to print all the variable codings for these cases. This will give you the ID number of the cases so that you can go back to the file or questionnaire to see what error occurred when the datum for SEX was entered. Having the values of the other variables may also help you detect the error. Perhaps a variable was omitted so that all the other variables after it were offset by the number of columns in that variable.

To select missing value cases, such as those coded blank, the specification MISSING is used followed by the variable name in parentheses. For example,

```
select if missing(sex).
```

This command would select the cases coded blank for missing on the variable SEX.

3.6 Additional Resources

LIST is discussed on pages B21–22 and C86–87 of the *SPSS/PC+ V2.0 Base Manual*. FREQUENCIES is discussed on pages B71–79, B89, and C65–69. SELECT IF is discussed on pages B39–40 and C177–178.

3.7 Summary

In this chapter we explained the LIST command, which produces the data entered by case. It can be used for all the variables or a subset of them. It also can be used for all the cases or a subset of the cases.

The FREQUENCIES command produces the distribution of cases by categories of a variable. It can be used for all the variables or for subsets of the variables.

STATISTICS is a subcommand that causes particular statistics to be added or deleted from the output. Most SPSS/PC+ procedure commands allow tailoring of output by STATISTICS.

The SELECT IF command causes SPSS/PC+ to focus its analyses on subsets of the cases in the data file. The cases kept in the analyses following SE-LECT IF are those that meet the conditions specified on the SELECT IF command. If you use more than one SELECT IF command, then a case must meet the conditions specified on all the commands to be kept in the analysis.

RESEARCH PROJECT WORK

Write a program that would produce a listing and the frequencies for all the variables in the data set you created as a research project in Chapter 2.

REVIEW QUESTIONS

Review Using LIST

3.1   Write a set of commands that will output the data entries for all variables for all the cases of our example data set in Chapter 2.

3.2   Write a set of commands that will output the data entries for all the variables for the first 20 cases of the SPSS file NORC84 presented in Appendix B.

3.3   Write a set of commands that will list all the data entries for the variable INCOME from the SPSS file NORC84 presented in Appendix B.

Review Using FREQUENCIES

3.4   Write all the commands necessary to produce all the frequencies for the variables in our example data set given in Chapter 2.

3.5   Write all the commands necessary to produce the frequencies for the variables AGE, SEX, and MARITAL from the SPSS file NORC84 described in Appendix B.

3.6   What would you need to do before doing a FREQUENCIES command for a variable named INCOME which was the annual income of the respondent to the nearest dollar?

3.7   What would be the meaning of the following output?

NEIGHBOR

VALUE	FREQUENCY	PERCENT
1	3	30.0
2	5	50.0
3	2	20.0
MISSING CASES	1	

Review Using an SPSS System File

HINT: You need to be familiar with the SPSS file NORC84 explained in Appendix B to work the following questions.

3.8   Write the commands necessary to produce a FREQUENCIES procedure for all the variables in the NORC84 file.

3.9 Write the command necessary to print out the FREQUENCIES for variables in the NORC84 file that concern attitudes toward abortion.

3.10 Write the commands necessary to produce FREQUENCIES for the variables concerning the respondent's education, health, and happiness in the NORC84 file.

Review Using SELECT IF

3.11 Write a SELECT IF command that will select only those cases that are coded 1 on the variable named SEX.

3.12 Write a SELECT IF command that will choose only those cases that have a value of 65 or greater on a variable named AGE.

3.13 Write a SELECT IF command that will choose only those cases that are over 16 on EDUC or over 30,000 on INCOME.

3.14 Write a SELECT IF command that will choose only those cases that are greater than 15 and less than 66 on the variable AGE.

3.15 Write a SELECT IF command that will choose only those cases that are coded 2 on a variable named SEX and are also coded between 14 and 45 on a variable named AGE.

3.16 Write a set of commands that will list the data entries for all the variables, for the first 25 cases that are coded above 15 on EDUC and coded 2 on SEX from the SPSS file NORC84 presented in Appendix B.

ASSIGNMENT QUESTIONS

3.1 Write all the commands necessary to produce all the frequencies for the variable named EDUC in our example data set given in Chapter 2.

3.2 Write all the commands necessary to produce the frequencies for the variables AGE and INCOME from the SPSS file NORC84 described in Appendix B.

3.3 What would you need to do before doing a FREQUENCIES command for a variable named SQFEET, which was the area of housing units to the nearest square foot?

3.4 What would be the meaning of the following output?

POLPARTY

VALUE	FREQUENCY	PERCENT
1	7	35.0
2	9	45.0
3	4	20.0
MISSING CASES	1	

HINT: You need to be familiar with the SPSS file NORC84 explained in Appendix B to work the next questions.

3.5 Write the SPSS/PC+ commands necessary to produce a FREQUENCIES procedure for all the variables in the NORC84 file. We know you worked on this question before as a review question, but this is a task you will want to perform frequently and we want to be sure you remember. Besides, this is one of the easy questions.

3.6 Write the SPSS/PC+ commands necessary to print out the FREQUENCIES for variables in the NORC84 file that concern anomie.

3.7 For the NORC84 file write the commands necessary to produce FREQUENCIES for the variables concerning whether the respondent has ever been unemployed in the past ten years and his or her current employment.

3.8 Write a SELECT IF command that will select only those cases that are coded 1 on the variable named RACE.

3.9 Write a SELECT IF command that will choose only those cases that have a value of 40 or less on a variable named AGE.

3.10 Write a SELECT IF command that will choose only those cases that are below 12 on EDUC or under 10,000 on INCOME.

3.11 Write a SELECT IF command that will choose only those cases that are less than 16 or greater than 65 on the variable AGE.

3.12 Write a SELECT IF command that will choose only those cases that are coded 2 on a variable named RACE and are also coded any value from 21 to 65 inclusive on a variable named AGE.

3.13 Write a LIST command that will output the data entries for all the variables for the first 20 cases.

3.14 Write a LIST command that will output the data entries for the variable ID for all the cases.

3.15 Write a set of commands that will list the data entries for the variable ID for all the cases coded above 3 on the variable RACE.

3.16 For the SPSS file NORC84 write a set of commands that will, for the first 20 cases that are coded above 15 on EDUC and above 2 on SEX, list the data entries for all the variables.

4

BEGINNING TO USE
THE SPSS/PC + PROGRAM

Now that you know a little about SPSS/PC+, let's see the mechanics of using the program. This chapter describes how to create your personal directory, enter the SPSS/PC+ program, enter data, execute commands, save your output, and save your commands. There are two approaches for entering data and commands: one is the Review editor program and the other is the Menu mode. As you become proficient, you will use both of these approaches, switching from one to the other in the same session. This chapter assumes that SPSS/PC+ Version 2.0 or Version 3.0 has been installed on your machine.

4.1 Entering the SPSS/PC+ Program

The recommended method for using SPSS/PC+ is to create a separate directory for your work apart from the directory containing the SPSS/PC+ command files. (A **directory** is assigned work space in your disk memory.) We will name the directory YOURID to remind you that you should make a directory for your own work to keep it apart from that of other users.

For most PC systems, once you turn the machine on, it runs through about a minute of system checks. Then the DOS prompt C) appears with the cursor next to it. At that point, type the command

```
md yourid
```

Then press the Enter key (on some keyboards this will be labeled Return or ↵). These actions create a new directory named YOURID. The name we've used is arbitrary; choose one that is easy to remember and easy to type. Change to this new directory by executing the command

```
cd yourid
```

Normally, YOURID directory would be used to store your data files, command files, and output files. Your instructor, however, may have you store these files on your own diskette to save space on the systems hard disk. If this is the case, you would add a designator of where this diskette is when saving or retrieving files. Most likely it will be in a disk drive called A. To refer to a diskette on that drive, add A: as a prefix to the file name. In this case, to save the file project you would use the command

```
save file 'a:project'.
```

Once in the YOURID (or whatever you've named it) directory, you start the SPSS/PC+ program by entering the command

```
spsspc
```

In the SPSS/PC+ program there is more than one way to enter commands. Our next section describes using the Review editor in its Edit mode.

4.2 Using SPSS/PC+ through the Review Editor

When you first enter the SPSS/PC+ program, a box titled Main Menu (see Figure 4.1) appears at the top left of your screen. On the top right is a box titled Orientation. The bottom half of the screen is a blank space which is identified as "scratch.pad" by a title along the bottom.

At this time you are in Menu mode (we'll explain this mode later in this chapter) and even though the cursor is in scratch.pad, if you try to type characters there, unexpected menu commands can occur.

Shift into the Review program Edit mode by holding down the Alt key while you press the M key. Do that now.

In Edit mode, the Main Menu is gone from the top of your screen. The top part of the screen is now a display area for the listing or output of your com-

FIGURE 4.1 REVIEW Editor Program Main Menu

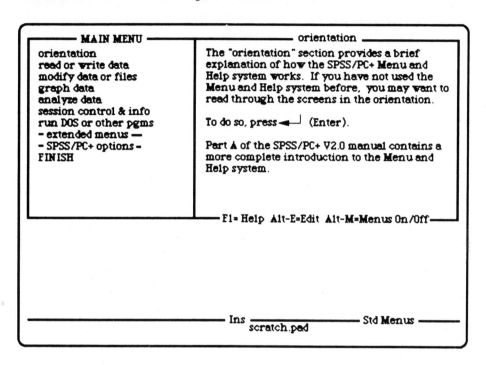

mands. "Edit mode—press Esc to resume menu mode" should appear at the bottom of your screen. This indicates that you are in the Edit mode. Although pressing the Escape key will resume the Menu mode, we recommend that you develop the habit of using the Alt-M key combination to move back and forth between the Menu mode and the Edit mode. The advantage of Alt-M is that it will shift you either way between the Review modes.

Now you can enter numbers and letters on the line where the cursor is positioned simply by typing what you want. This enables you to type into scratch.pad (we'll call this the scratch pad) the commands, variable names, and data you wish to use. Press the F10 key and then the Enter key to run the commands from the cursor line on.

What if you make a typing mistake? While in the Review editor, use the Backspace key to move the cursor back over the error—this will cause it to be erased.

The Review editor can be used in two modes: Insert and Replace. In the Insert mode, what you type will be inserted to the left of the cursor. In the Replace mode, what you type will replace or type over the character indicated by the cursor. When Review is in Insert mode, the word *Ins* appears at the bottom right of the screen. If you press the Insert key, the editor shifts from Insert mode to Replace mode and the word *Ins* disappears. Press the Insert key again, and the editor goes back into Insert mode.

4.3 Using the Review Editor to Perform a Run and Save the Output

Once into SPSS/PC+ you are ready to begin your own program. You can perform a run by typing data definition commands, BEGIN DATA, the data, END DATA, and the control commands into the scratch pad.

Use the Review editor to enter the following lines. (This example adds a SAVE command to the examples in Chapter 3.)

```
data list /
      id        1-2
      educ      3-4
      sex       5
      happy     6.
begin data.
010912
021223
031521
041222
050611
061612
071522
081612
091821
101412
111321
121611
130922
141212
151221
161821
170821
181222
191613
20142
end data.
```

```
missing values
      educ        (-9)
      happy
      sex         (0).
list.
save file 'project'.
```

To run this program, place the cursor on the line of the first command that you want entered (DATA LIST), and then press the F10 key. SPSS/PC+ will print a prompt asking whether you want to "Run from the cursor" or "Exit to prompt". "Run from the cursor" is highlighted, indicating that this action will be performed if you press the Enter key. This is what we want to happen continuing until the last line in the scratch pad. (If you had wanted the other option, you would need to move the highlight to "Exit to prompt" with the LeftArrow key.)

As the commands are executed, the output will appear on the screen; at the same time the output is stored in a file named SPSS.LIS. When the output from your commands is printed on the screen, the MORE is displayed in the upper-right corner to indicate that there is more output to follow. Press the Enter key to print further output on the screen. Until all the lines have printed once, you cannot scroll back to previous screens.

Once the commands have run, you will no longer be in Edit mode. You will be in Menu mode with the submitted commands in the scratch pad. By reentering Edit mode (hold down the Alt key and press the M key), you can view your program's output on the top half of the screen. Press the F2 key and SPSS/PC+ will give you a Switch window's prompt. Press the Enter key and you will enter the upper part of the screen where your output is. You can use the Arrow, PageUp, and PageDown keys to move through the output. You can insert, delete, and perform other word-processing functions in this screen just as you can in the scratch pad.

Your output should match that given in Table 3.1 of the previous chapter. It shows the variable names and entries for each case in your file. You can save it by pressing the F9 key and responding to prompts. Do this now, and name the listing OUT1. If your instructor wants you to save the output on your own diskette, call the file to be saved A:OUT1. The A: indicates that the file is to be saved on a diskette in your computer's A drive.

The reason for saving the output in the SPSS.LIS file to a different file is that SPSS.LIS will be erased the next time you enter the SPSS/PC+ program.

To print the output, press the F9 key and follow the prompts. If you are content with the output, you may also want to save the file that created it. Switch back to the scratch pad by pressing the F2 key. Then press the F9 key and follow the prompts to indicate that you want to save the file and name it

PROG1. That way you will know which program file produced the output, and you will be able to reuse it.

To retrieve files that you have saved back into the Review editor, press the F3 key. A prompt will ask you to enter the name of the file you want to retrieve. (If your file is on a diskette in the A drive you will have to add the A: prefix to the file name.) If you do not remember the file name, before pressing the F3 key, hold down the Alt key and press F.

If there is a command error in a run, SPSS/PC+ will give an error message and then return you to the menu concerning the command in which there was an error. Go to the Review editor mode (hold down the Alt key and press M). Then correct the errors and resubmit the commands by positioning the cursor on the line of the first command you want to run and press F10.

If it was a large output with more errors than you can easily note in the listing, enter the Review editor mode and submit the command REVIEW LOG. This will bring up on the screen the submitted commands and SPSS/PC+'s responses to the commands including error messages; it omits the procedure output. You can correct the errors in this file. Then resubmit the run by placing the cursor on the line of the first command you want run and pressing F10. The bracketed comments will be ignored, so you do not have to delete them.

The SPSS.LOG file is deleted when you reenter the SPSS/PC+ program. To save this file, press the F9 key, highlight that you wish to save the whole file, and press the Enter key. Then following the prompt, enter the name you want the saved file to have. (Remember to add the A: prefix if the file is to be saved on a diskette in the A drive.)

The Alt-E key combination will take you out of the SPSS.LOG and back to the Review editor.

4.4 Review Editor Line and Block Commands

Review also allows you to perform more complicated operations. If you press the F1 key while in the editor, it will change the bottom line of the screen and highlight the choice "Review Help". Since at the bottom of this screen the words *Review Help* are highlighted, pressing the enter key will summon up the Review Help screen. In this screen, shown in Figure 4.2, you can see the function keys to press to perform various operations. Reading down the left column, you see that you have choices ranging from "Information" to "Run". The fourth choice down from the top is "Lines". To the right appears *F4;* this indicates that the F4 function key allows you to perform line operations. To the right

FIGURE 4.2 REVIEW Editor Program Help Screen

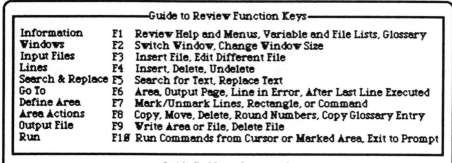

```
┌─────────────── Guide to Review Function Keys ───────────────┐
│                                                              │
│  Information        F1   Review Help and Menus, Variable and File Lists, Glossary │
│  Windows            F2   Switch Window, Change Window Size    │
│  Input Files        F3   Insert File, Edit Different File     │
│  Lines              F4   Insert, Delete, Undelete            │
│  Search & Replace   F5   Search for Text, Replace Text        │
│  Go To              F6   Area, Output Page, Line in Error, After Last Line Executed │
│  Define Area        F7   Mark/Unmark Lines, Rectangle, or Command │
│  Area Actions       F8   Copy, Move, Delete, Round Numbers, Copy Glossary Entry │
│  Output File        F9   Write Area or File, Delete File      │
│  Run                F10  Run Commands from Cursor or Marked Area, Exit to Prompt │
│                                                              │
│  ┌──────────────── Guide To Menu Commands ─────────────────┐ │
│  │  Enter  (←┘)        Paste Selection & Move Down One Level in Menu │ │
│  │  Tab or (→)         Temporarily Paste Selection & Move Down One Level │ │
│  │  ESC or (←)         Remove Last Temporary Paste & Move Up One Level │ │
│  │  Alt-ESC            Jump To Main Menu (Also Ctrl-ESC)     │ │
│  │  Alt-K              Kill All Temporary Pastes             │ │
│  │  Alt-T              Get Typing Window                     │ │
│  │  Alt-E              Switch to Edit Mode                   │ │
│  │  Alt-M              Remove Menus                          │ │
│  │  Alt-X              Switch between Standard and Extendend Menus │ │
│  │  Alt-Cursor Pad     Scroll Help Windows and Glossary (if NumLock Off) │ │
│  └──────────────────────────────────────────────────────────┘ │
│                                                              │
│      Enter Command or Press F1 for More Help or Escape to Continue │
└──────────────────────────────────────────────────────────────┘
```

FIGURE 4.3 REVIEW Editor Program Cursor Control Help Screen

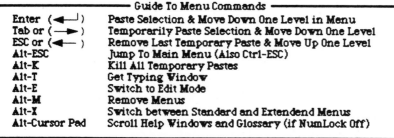
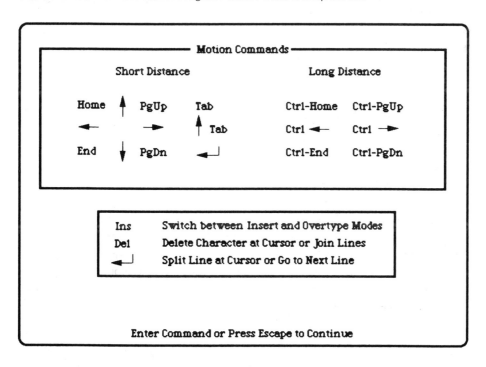

```
┌──────────────────── Motion Commands ────────────────────┐
│                                                          │
│         Short Distance              Long Distance        │
│                                                          │
│   Home  ↑  PgUp   Tab         Ctrl-Home   Ctrl-PgUp      │
│   ←      →      ↑ Tab          Ctrl ←      Ctrl →         │
│   End   ↓  PgDn   ←┘           Ctrl-End    Ctrl-PgDn      │
│                                                          │
└──────────────────────────────────────────────────────────┘

┌──────────────────────────────────────────────────────────┐
│   Ins      Switch between Insert and Overtype Modes       │
│   Del      Delete Character at Cursor or Join Lines        │
│   ←┘       Split Line at Cursor or Go to Next Line         │
└──────────────────────────────────────────────────────────┘

           Enter Command or Press Escape to Continue
```

of F4 are the words *Insert, Delete, Undelete;* these are the operations that can be performed on lines.

The F7 key marks blocks of lines for moving, copying, and deleting; the F8 key executes these operations. Blocks of lines from SPSS.LOG can also be run or saved. Use the F7 key and the prompts that follow to indicate the line beginning the block and the line ending the block.

At the bottom of the screen appears a message indicating that you can obtain more information about using the Review editor by pressing the F1 key. Press the F1 key. The screen reproduced in Figure 4.3 will appear. This information indicates how you can move the cursor around the scratch pad when you are in the Edit mode.

4.5 Review Editor Context Menu

When editing a command you can use a Review feature called the Context menu, which provides descriptions, examples, and options of the command. Holding down the ALT key while pressing M brings the Context menu to the screen. Be sure the cursor is on the command you want information about, before you press Alt-M. To return to the Review editor from the Menu mode, hold down the Alt key while pressing M.

4.6 Using Other Word-Processing Programs

Review has a number of limitations. Its files are contained in the random access memory (RAM) of your computer; this limits the size of files it can edit more than word-processing programs that edit files on a disk. It lacks some of the functions of more powerful word-processing programs such as WordStar or WordPerfect, which can find and replace words, or allow you to undo a command entered by mistake. These other programs can be used in their non-document or ASCII mode for compiling SPSS/PC+ files. In using other editors *note the following cautions:*

- Line length cannot exceed 80 characters.
- Line wrap-around features cannot be used. End each line with a carriage return keystroke.
- Special features such as boldface or underline cannot be used.

- See the *SPSS/PC+ V2.0 Base Manual* pages G3–G4 for a more detailed description of the use of other editors.

You can exit the SPSS/PC+ program by typing the line FINISH at the end of your scratch pad. Then press the F10 key. The "Run from cursor" option will appear as a highlighted prompt. Press Return and you will be taken out of the SPSS/PC+ program.

4.7 Using the NORC84 File

Let's look at a larger data set and practice using the GET command at the same time. Presuming your instructor has stored the NORC84 data set on the SPSS directory, you can call up this large data set with the GET FILE command and then use the FREQUENCIES command to discover the distribution by education, sex, and happiness. The necessary program would be

```
get file 'norc84'.
frequencies educ
            sex
            happy/
            statistics.
```

Enter those lines now and run them by placing the cursor on the GET FILE NORC84 line and pressing the F10 key. The output should match that displayed in Table 3.2. When the output has scrolled by and you are in the Menu mode, press Alt-M to return to the Edit menu. Press F2 and then press the Enter key to switch to the output screen. This output can be edited with the Review editor and then saved by pressing the F9 key followed by the Enter key. Do this now and save it as OUT2. (Remember to include the A: prefix if you are saving it to a diskette in the A drive.)

Return to the scratch pad by pressing the F2 key and then the Enter key. Save the program as PROG2 by pressing the F9 key and entering PROG2 as the file name and pressing the Enter key.

In this and previous sections we have shown you how to enter SPSS/PC+ and use the Review editor to enter commands and data, to save programs and save output. In the next section we explore how the same type of work can be done using the Menu mode.

4.8 Using the SPSS/PC+ Menus and the Review Editor

If you have not exited SPSS/PC+, do so now. Otherwise when you call up the PROJECT file with the SPSS/PC+ Menus mode, you'll receive an error message that the PROJECT file is already the active file.

The Menu mode allows you to "paste" commands into the scratch pad without typing. It's great for those of us with ten thumbs! But it requires some attention, practice, and patience to learn to use this mode.

When you go into SPSS/PC+, the program is in Menu mode. You know you are not in Edit mode because the line "Edit mode—press Escape to resume menu mode" is *not* on a line beneath the top boxes. Using direction arrows or typing the first letter of a command will shift the highlight up and down the column of menu choices. Pressing the Enter key (labeled Return or ↵ on some keyboards) or the RightArrow key will shift the screen to a submenu, and once again you move the highlight to the keyword or specification that you want. Pressing the Enter key when a command is highlighted will "paste" it into the scratch pad. When you enter SPSS/PC+, the box titled Main Menu is in the upper-left portion of the screen.

Do not press any keys until told to do so in this section. Throughout this section if you press keys before instructed to do so you may jump into submenus and become hopelessly lost. If this happens, you can press the Escape key a series of times. Each time you press the Escape key you will move further up the submenu hierarchy until eventually you will have returned to the Main Menu screen. (Holding down the Alt key and pressing the Escape key is a one-step method of returning to the Main Menu screen.) But then you will have to retrace your steps to catch up with the text discussion.

If you type a letter that corresponds to the first letter of one of the Main Menu lines, the highlight that is behind Orientation at the beginning will move to that line. Try typing an R (lowercase and uppercase letters will be treated the same by SPSS/PC+). The highlight moves down to the "Read or write data" line and the writing in the Orientation box changes to a description of what the commands in the "Read or write data" section will allow you to do.

The highlight can also be moved by using the Arrow keys. Press the DownArrow key and the highlight will move from the "Read or write data" line to the "Modify data or files" line.

As the highlight moves, the Orientation box contents change so that it contains a description of what is highlighted. Press the UpArrow so that the highlight returns to the "Read or write data" line. Note that there is a right arrow indicator at the end of the line. This means that there is more information available about this topic than is in the Orientation box. You can move further into the "Read or write data" menus in two ways, one in the Menu mode and one in the Edit mode.

First you can simply press the Enter key on your keyboard. Press the Enter key now and see what happens. You should now be looking at a screen that has a box labeled "Read or write data" on the top left. The highlight is behind DE and the box on the top right contains a description of what the DE command does. Type G to move the highlight to GET. Then press the Enter key and note how GET is placed into the scratch pad.

At the same time you are moved to the next GET submenu. The highlight covers !/FILE ' '. The ! indicates that this command is required. Press the Enter key and note that FILE ' ' is added to the GET command. You can see the file names in your directory by striking the Esc key and then holding the Alt key while pressing the Enter key. This brings up a screen which has a list of your directory files. Assuming you have already saved the file PROJECT on your directory, move the highlight with the Arrow keys to PROJECT and press Enter. That file name is placed on the GET FILE line between the single quotation marks. The line should now read

```
get file 'project'.
```

To add a FREQUENCIES command, move the highlight to the "Analyze data" line and press the Enter key. The menu presents a new set of choices. Highlight F and press the Enter key. You are shown examples of FREQUENCIES commands.

If there are errors in your command, shift to the Review editor by holding down the Alt key and pressing the E key. Once in the Review editor, make whatever corrections are necessary. Now pressing the F10 key and Return will run this command.

The alternative to pasting in commands with the Menu mode is to enter the commands using the Review Edit mode as described in Sections 4.1 to 4.6. The Edit mode of entering lines is easier to control and is the best approach for most new users of SPSS/PC+.

4.9 Additional Resources

The Review editor is discussed on pages A17-A22 of the *SPSS/PC+ V2.0 Base Manual.*

4.10 Summary

This chapter introduced the Review editor. The Review editor has many features of word-processing programs. Furthermore, it allows you to

1. run commands from within SPSS/PC+;

2. obtain help about a command the cursor is on by holding down the Alt key while pressing the M key;

3. see the list of variable names in an active file by holding down the Alt key while pressing the V key;

4. see the list of files in your directory by holding down the Alt key while pressing the F key.

Pressing the F1 key while in Review will bring up a Help menu that explains line and file management function keys. Pressing the F1 key when in the first Help menu will bring up a second Help menu that explains cursor movement function keys.

Commands are executed by moving the cursor to the first command in the run, pressing the F10 key, and then the Enter key.

Commands are stored after execution in the SPSS.LOG file. Output is stored after appearing on the screen in the SPSS.LIS file. To retain the information in these files for use in future sessions you must save them under a different name, because they are erased each time you enter SPSS/PC+.

RESEARCH PROJECT WORK

1. Use the Review editor to enter and store in a permanent file the data you gathered on the questionnaires doing the research project in Chapter 1.

2. Use the Review editor to create a permanent file with the commands you wrote for the research projects in Chapters 2 and 3.

3. Write a LIST ALL and a FREQUENCIES ALL program for your research project data.

REVIEW QUESTIONS

4.1 How would you create a directory named YOURID from which to work?

4.2 How would you enter a directory named YOURID?

4.3 How would you enter the SPSS/PC+ program once you were in the YOURID directory?

4.4 How would you enter the Edit mode once you were in the SPSS/PC+ Review editor?

4.5 What key will erase an error? What key will delete an error and move to the left the remaining text?

4.6 How do you find out what the Review editor function keys do?

4.7 How do you find out how to move the cursor more effectively while in the Review editor?

4.8 What key combination will move you to the top of a Review file?

4.9 What key combination will move you to the bottom of a Review file?

4.10 What key will move Review back and forth between the insert mode and the Replace mode?

4.11 How do you run a program that is in the Review editor?

4.12 What do you have to do when the word *MORE* appears in the upper-right corner of the screen?

4.13 When the commands in your Review program have executed will you be in the Edit mode or the Menu mode?

4.14 How do you move Review back and forth between the Edit mode and the Menu mode?

4.15 On what file is your output stored?

4.16 Will your output file be stored permanently?

4.17 How would you save your output to be used in another SPSS/PC+ session?

4.18 How would you print your output?

4.19 On what file are your commands stored?

4.20 How would you save your commands to be used in another SPSS/PC+ session?

4.21 How would you retrieve a stored file of commands back into Review?

4.22 How would you obtain help concerning a command you were entering or editing?

ASSIGNMENT QUESTIONS

4.1 Describe the commands necessary to create and move to a directory named JH.

4.2 Once your computer was turned on and you were at the C) prompt, how would you enter the SPSS/PC+ Review editor mode from an existing directory named JH?

4.3 Once in the Review editor mode, how would you retrieve a program named PROG1 from the MYID directory?

4.4   Having retrieved a file named PROG1 into Review, how would you run it?

4.5   If your program did not run correctly, how would you return to Review's Edit mode?

4.6   If there was an error in your FREQUENCIES command and you wanted to look at an example of a correct FREQUENCIES command in Review, what would you do?

4.7   If you could not remember the name of a file you wanted to retrieve, how could you see a list of the files on your directory?

4.8   If PROG1 ran, how would you scroll through the output.

4.9   If the output was correct, how would you print it?

4.10 How would you save a listing to a permanent file named OUT3?

5

TRANSFORMING VARIABLES AND LABELING OUTPUT

New SPSS/PC+ Commands:

RECODE
COMPUTE
IF
PROCESS IF
VARIABLE LABELS
VALUE LABELS

In Chapter 3 we used the FREQUENCIES and SELECT IF commands to find that in the NORC84 data file 35 percent of the respondents reported that they were very happy and that women were more likely than men to report being very happy. In this chapter we learn whether the likelihood of being very happy is affected by the variable AGE. Before we begin, we need to cover some of the data transformation commands available in SPSS/PC+. A problem frequently encountered is that you have data coded differently than you want them coded for a particular analysis. This annoyance can be remedied using the RECODE, COMPUTE, and IF commands described in this chapter. The PROCESS IF command, also covered in this chapter, allows you to confine the effects of the data transformation commands to the immediately following statistical procedure instead of being in effect for all the following procedures.

Finally we explain how to use the VARIABLE LABELS and VALUE LABELS commands to make the output easier to read.

5.1 Changing Variable Categories Where Necessary: RECODE

Suppose you coded information on education that ranged from 0 to 22 years of formal education, and now you need to do an analysis in which there will be only three education categories: respondents who did not complete high school, those who completed high school but not college, and those who completed college. The data you enter for a variable can be reclassified using the RECODE command. Carefully study the following example:

```
recode educ  (0 thru 11=1) (12 thru 15=2) (16 thru 30=3).
```

The RECODE command indicates that some changes follow in one or more variable codings. EDUC indicates that the first data to be recoded will be for the variable named EDUC. The segment (0 THRU 11 = 1) indicates that the numbers 0, 1, 2, 3, 4, 5, 6, 7, 8, 9, 10, and 11 will now all be treated as if they have the value 1. The segment (12 THRU 15 = 2) indicates that the numbers 12, 13, 14, and 15 will all be treated as if they had the value of 2. Finally, the segment (16 THRU 30 = 3) indicates that the numbers 16 through 30 will all be treated as if they had the value of 3. A statistical procedure done after the RECODE command will use the new values. Thus, a new FREQUENCIES of the EDUC variable would now reveal that the case scores have a range of from 1 to 3 instead of from 0 to 22.

For a variable that is being recoded, if some of the numbers fall outside the range of the RECODE command, these numbers will keep their original values. For example, if someone had 31 years of education, that value in the data columns for education would remain unchanged, because the commands only recode the values up to 30.

RECODE allows the use of two terms—HI and LO—to encompass extreme scores. Using these terms, our previous example would read

```
recode educ  (lo thru 11=1) (12 thru 15=2) (16 thru hi=3).
```

A hazard of using the LO and HI terms, however, is that you might accidentally encompass your missing values. In the previous example, if 99 were the missing value for EDUC, all the cases with missing values would be recoded from

99 to 3 and no longer treated as cases with missing data. Likewise, if −9 were the missing value for EDUC, it would be recoded to 1.

The RECODE command must follow the DATA LIST command and appear somewhere before any command for which you want to use the recoded information. The RECODE command, however, need not *immediately* precede commands for which you want to use the recoded information.

The following set of commands illustrates the file placement of the RECODE command using our example data set:

```
data list id 1-2 educ 3-4 sex 5 happy 6.
begin data.
010912
021223
031521
041222
050611
061612
071522
081612
091821
101412
111321
121611
130922
141212
151221
161821
170821
181222
191613
20142
end data.
missing values educ(-9,99) happy sex (0).
recode educ (lo thru 11=1) (12 thru 15=2) (16 thru hi=3).
frequencies id educ sex happy.
```

5.2 Making New Variables from Old Variables: COMPUTE

At times you will want to create new variables from variables already in your data file. For example, you may have a variable for family income named INCOME and a variable for family size named FAMSIZE. In addition to these two variables, you might want to have a variable for family income per capita—the family income divided by the number of people in the family.

An income per capita variable named INCOMPER can be created with a COMPUTE command as follows:

```
compute incomper=income/famsize.
```

Note that a slash (/) is used to indicate division. Anywhere in your program after this COMPUTE command, you can refer to the INCOMPER variable just as you can refer to all the variables on your DATA LIST command.

The SPSS/PC+ equivalents of the basic arithmetic symbols are as follows:

+	addition
−	subtraction
/	division
*	multiplication
**	exponentiation (raising to a power)
SQRT	taking the square root

These operations can be done with actual numeric values, with variables, or with a mixture of both. First we give examples of doing the arithmetic operations with numbers. Then we give examples of doing the arithmetic operations with variables. Finally, we show what to do when some values are missing.

COMPUTE Commands with Numbers

Addition
In this example, after the COMPUTE command, ANSWER1 would equal 650.

```
compute answer1=450+200.
```

Subtraction
In this example, after the COMPUTE command, ANSWER2 would equal 250.

```
compute answer2=450−200.
```

Division
In this example, after the COMPUTE command, ANSWER3 would equal 9.

```
compute answer3=450/50.
```

Multiplication

In this example, after the COMPUTE command, ANSWER4 would equal 900.

```
compute answer4=450*2.
```

Exponentiation

In this example, after the COMPUTE command, ANSWER5 would equal 125—that is, 5 to the third power.

```
compute answer5=5**3.
```

Square Root

In this example, after the COMPUTE command, ANSWER6 would equal 9.

```
compute answer6=sqrt(81).
```

COMPUTE Commands with Variables

The previous examples were done with numbers. The following examples illustrate each of the operations with variables.

Addition

To compute a new variable total income (TINC) equal to Wife's Income (WINC) plus husband's income (HINC) you could use the following:

```
compute tinc=winc+hinc.
```

Subtraction

To compute a new variable, years until retirement (RETIRE), equal to 65 minus age (AGE):

```
compute retire=65-age.
```

Division

To compute a new variable, average salary (AVESAL), equal to payroll (PAYROLL) divided by number of employees (NEMPLOYS):

```
compute avesal=payroll/nemploys.
```

Multiplication

To compute a new variable, total pay (TPAY), equal to daily salary (DSALARY) multiplied by number of days worked (DAYS):

```
compute tpay=dsalary*days.
```

Exponentiation

To compute a new variable, the deviation from the mean squared (DEVSQ), equal to income minus the mean of income (INC−MINC) squared:

```
compute devsq=(inc-minc)**2.
```

Square Root

To compute a new variable, absolute deviation (ABDEV), equal to the square root of the deviation from the mean squared (DEVSQ):

```
compute abdev=sqrt(devsq).
```

There are many other functions that can be used with the COMPUTE command—nearly 50 in all. (See pages C24–27 in the *SPSS/PC+ V2.0 Base Manual* for a more complete description of these functions.)

COMPUTE Commands and Missing Values

What happens if a variable that you use in a COMPUTE command has missing values? For example, you may want to COMPUTE the income per person for households, but the income variable is missing for some of the households. SPSS/PC+ will assign the **system missing value** (usually blanks) for the variable being computed to any case that has missing values for any of the variables used in the computation. The system missing value will be displayed as a period in the output. For example, if you do a FREQUENCIES command for a variable and the value for one of the categories is a period, the category of cases has missing data on that variable.

The system missing value will also be assigned to cases for which the computation is mathematically impossible. For example, you cannot divide by 0 or take the square root of a negative number. If you had the command COMPUTE INCCHILD = INCOME / CHILDS, the system missing value would be assigned for all cases for which the value for CHILDS was 0.

5.3 The IF Statement

At times you will want to COMPUTE new variables for some cases, but not for others. The IF command allows this type of operation. You can think of it as a combination of a SELECT IF command and a COMPUTE command. The first part of the command selects the cases for which the procedure is to be done. The second part of the command computes the new variable. For example, you may want to use an individual's income if that person does not live with his or her parents, but use the parents' income if the individual does live with his or her parents. To do so, the following SPSS/PC+ commands could be used. Assume we have a variable named LPARENT, for "living with parent(s)," coded 1 for yes. Assume also that we have a variable named PARENT$, for income of the parent(s). Then the following command would make a respondent's IN-COME equal to PARENT$ when the individual lives with his or her parent(s):

```
if (1parent eq 1) income=parent$.
```

Notice the similarity in syntax between each of the two parts of this command and the SELECT IF and COMPUTE commands.

(like SELECT IF syntax)   (like COMPUTE syntax)

```
if (1parent eq 1)      income=parent$
```

All the relational operators used in the SELECT IF command can be used in the IF command. As a reminder, the relational operators are:

EQ   equal
NE   not equal
LT   less than
GT   greater than
LE   less than or equal to
GE   greater than or equal to

All the functions used in the COMPUTE command can be used in the second part of the IF command. (These functions were explained in Section 5.2 this chapter.)

Parentheses must be used where necessary to set off the conditional part of the command. In this respect also the IF command is like the SELECT IF command.

Another example using IF would be to create a new variable AGEGROUP, which groups age into ten-year categories, from AGE, which records an individual's actual age. (Note that the IF command must be used instead of the RECODE command in this case, if you wanted to retain the original values for AGE.)

Grouping AGE into new categories for a new variable AGEGROUP could be accomplished with the following commands:

```
if (age le 9) agegroup=1.
if (age ge 9 and age le 19) agegroup=2.
if (age ge 19 and age le 29) agegroup=3.
if (age ge 29 and age le 39) agegroup=4.
if (age ge 39 and age le 49) agegroup=5.
if (age ge 49 and age le 59) agegroup=6.
if (age ge 59 and age le 69) agegroup=7.
if (age ge 69 and age le 79) agegroup=8.
if (age ge 79) agegroup=9.
```

The treatment of missing data and impossible computations for the IF command is the same as for the COMPUTE command (discussed in Section 5.2.)

5.4 Making a Selection for Only One Procedure: PROCESS IF

The PROCESS IF command signals SPSS/PC+ to do the data selection procedures that follow it only for the next statistical procedure. This useful command allows you, for example, to do separate FREQUENCIES for different subsets on the same run. To do two frequencies—one for males and one for females—on the same run, the following procedure could be used. After one PROCESS IF, select for males and then do a FREQUENCIES run. Following this FREQUENCIES, select for females and then do another FREQUENCIES. The result would be two frequencies outputs: one for males and one for females.

```
data list id 1-2, educ 3-4, sex 5, happy 6.
begin data.
010912
021223
031521
041222
```

```
050611
061612
071522
081612
091821
101412
111321
121611
130922
141212
151221
161821
170821
181222
191613
20142
end data.
process if (sex eq 1).
frequencies all/
            statistics.
process if (sex eq 2).
frequencies all.
```

The first PROCESS IF would select males for the first FREQUENCIES. This selection would only be for the first statistical procedure following the command, so afterwards we would have our entire sample back. Then the second PROCESS IF would select females, and they would be used for the second FREQUENCIES. Putting together the output from these two FREQUENCIES commands, we can compare men and women in our sample data.

To do the same procedures for our SPSS system file NORC84, the commands would be

```
get file norc84.
process if (sex eq 1).
frequencies all/
            statistics.
process if (sex eq 2).
frequencies all/
            statistics.
```

Pooling the information from the two frequency distributions these commands would produce, we could put together Table 5.1. We can see that—as

TABLE 5.1 Happy by Sex for the NORC84 Data File

MALES

VALUE LABEL	FREQUENCY	PERCENT
VERY HAPPY	196	30.7
PRETTY HAPPY	355	55.6
NOT TOO HAPPY	88	13.8
TOTAL	639	100.0

FEMALES

VALUE LABEL	FREQUENCY	PERCENT
VERY HAPPY	303	35.0
PRETTY HAPPY	455	52.5
NOT TOO HAPPY	108	12.5
TOTAL	866	100.0

we learned in Chapter 3—females are slightly more likely than males to report that they are very happy.

As another example, we could select first the respondents in the SPSS file NORC84 under 40 and then the respondents over 40. Then we will do a separate FREQUENCIES for each group and see whether being in the younger group or being in the older group increases the likelihood of being happy. The SPSS/PC+ commands required would be

```
get file 'norc84'.
recode age(18 thru 39=1)(40 thru 97=2).
process if age eq 1.
frequencies age.
process if age eq 2.
frequencies age.
```

The output from these commands would include the information shown in Table 5.2.

The first set of percents is for the respondents under age 40. From the PERCENT column we can see that 29.4 percent of them report being very happy. The second set of percents is for the respondents age 40 and over. From the PERCENT column we can see that 39.9 percent of the 40 and over respondents report being very happy. Hence the likelihood of being very happy appears greater for the respondents age 40 and over. Those of you under 40

TABLE 5.2 Happiness by Age for the NORC84 File

PERSONS AGE 18-39

VALUE LABEL	FREQUENCY	PERCENT
VERY HAPPY	210	29.4
PRETTY HAPPY	415	58.0
NOT TOO HAPPY	90	12.6
NA	12	MISSING
TOTAL	727	100.0

PERSONS AGE 40 AND OVER

VALUE LABEL	FREQUENCY	PERCENT
VERY HAPPY	289	39.9
PRETTY HAPPY	340	47.0
NOT TOO HAPPY	95	13.1
DK	1	MISSING
NA	15	MISSING
TOTAL	740	100.0

can take some comfort in the thought that the likelihood of your being very happy will increase as you pass 40.

So far we have seen that one's likelihood of being very happy is improved slightly by being female and over 40. You might complain that these are variables over which you have no control. Fair enough. In the next chapter and afterwards, we will consider the effects of some variables that you can control: educational attainment, income, marital status, and number of children.

5.5 Identifying Variables: VARIABLE LABELS

In SPSS/PC+, variable names are limited to eight or fewer characters. At times you will want to give a variable a label longer than eight characters in order to express more clearly what it is. The VARIABLE LABELS command enables you to attach a label of up to 60 characters to a variable. The label may contain more than one word; it may also contain punctuation. However, most procedures will truncate long labels in the output to only 40 characters.

The label is placed after the variable name and must be enclosed in quotation marks. Either single or double quotation marks may be used. If you use double quotation marks, do not place them within the label; if you use single quotation marks, do not place them within the label.

The following command would give the label YEARS OF EDUCATION to the variable named EDUC:

```
variable labels educ 'YEARS OF EDUCATION'.
```

The VARIABLE LABELS command must begin in column 1 and there must be one space and only one space between the word VARIABLE and the word LABELS.

Two or more variables can be given labels with the same VARIABLE LABELS command. The following example gives VARIABLE LABELS to EDUC, HEALTH, and INCOME:

```
variable labels educ 'YEARS OF EDUCATION'
                health 'SELF-ASSESSMENT OF GENERAL HEALTH'
                income 'TOTAL FAMILY INCOME'.
```

Although more than one variable label can be put on a line, the program is easier to read if each label has its own line. This will also keep the user from splitting the label across two lines which cannot be done without additional special punctuation. (For a discussion of how to split the label across two lines, see the *SPSS/PC+ User's Guide*, p. 42.)

5.6 Identifying Codings: VALUE LABELS

With the VALUE LABELS command, you can label the categories of a variable in the output with more than the number code in the data file. The format for this command is as follows, where labels are being given to categories of the variable SEX:

```
value labels sex 1'Male' 2'Female'.
```

The VALUE LABELS command is similar to the VARIABLE LABELS command with one important exception. *If the VALUE LABELS command contains more than one variable, the variables must be separated by a slash (/). For ex-*

ample, the following command would create value labels for the categories of EDUC, HEALTH, and INCOME:

```
value labels    educ 1 '0 TO 11 Years'
                     2 '12 TO 15 Years'
                     3 '16 Years and Over'/
              health 1 'Excellent'
                     2 'Good'
                     3 'Fair'
                     4 'Poor'/
              income 1 'Under $5,000'
                     2 '$5,000 to $9,999'
                     3 '$10,000 to $14,999'
                     4 '$15,000 to $19,999'
                     5 '$20,000 to $24,999'
                     6 '$25,000 to $34,999'
                     7 '$35,000 to $39,999'
                     8 'Over $40,000'.
```

Most procedures will only print 20 characters of a value label, although like variable labels, up to 60 characters can be in the label.

If you create an SPSS system file, the labels that you define before saving the file will be saved with it. (Saving SPSS system files was described in Chapter 2.)

5.7 The Keyword TO

The keyword TO enables you to refer easily to a large number of adjoining variables on your DATA LIST command. For example, suppose you have a data file corresponding to that of the Happiness Questionnaire in Appendix C, in which ID is the first variable, HAPPY is the second, and (after several other variables) AGE is the last. If you want to refer to the variables from HAPPY through AGE on a FREQUENCIES command, you can give the command FREQUENCIES VARIABLES = HAPPY TO AGE instead of specifying each variable separately.

New variables created through IF and COMPUTE commands are added to the end of the variable list in the order that they are created. So, in the preceding example, if you create a new variable called CLASS before the FREQUENCIES command, it will not be included in the specification HAPPY TO AGE. You will have to specify HAPPY TO CLASS to include it.

5.8 Additional Resources

RECODE is discussed on pages B25–28 and C123–124 of the *SPSS/PC+ V2.0 Base Manual.* COMPUTE is discussed on pages B28–33 and C24–27. IF is discussed on pages B33–36 and C72–74. PROCESS IF is discussed on pages B40 and C122. VARIABLE LABELS is discussed on pages B19–20 and C212. VALUE LABELS is discussed on pages B19–20 and C210–211. TO is discussed on pages B16, B22, C5–6, and C87.

5.9 Summary

The RECODE, COMPUTE, IF, and PROCESS IF commands covered in this chapter enable us to transform data. The RECODE command allows us to regroup categories and change their value codes. COMPUTE enables us to calculate new variables from our old variables. IF allows us to restrict the calculation of new variables to when specified conditions exist. PROCESS IF enables us to make transformations for one statistical procedure without changing the data set for the rest of the job.

VARIABLE LABELS and VALUE LABELS enable us to make our output easier to interpret.

The next two chapters describe the CROSSTABS and BREAKDOWN statistical procedures. These procedures have great utility in themselves, and they also are the preliminary steps for doing more advanced statistical analysis.

RESEARCH PROJECT WORK

1. Write a VARIABLE LABELS command for your research project data file.

2. Write a VALUES LABELS command for your research project data file.

REVIEW QUESTIONS

Review Using RECODE

HINT: Before you can do a RECODE command for a variable, you need to know its missing values.

5.1 For a variable named MARITAL, married people are coded 1, never married people are coded 2, divorced people are coded 3, and widowed people are coded 4. Recode MARITAL so that all three types of unmarried people are coded 2. The missing value for MARITAL is a blank.

5.2 A variable named HEIGHT has each respondent's height coded in inches. Recode HEIGHT so that people under 60 inches are coded 1, people 60 to 70 inches are coded 2, and people over 70 inches are coded 3. The missing value for HEIGHT is a blank.

5.3 A variable named CARS is coded 0 if the family has no car, 1 if the family has one car, 2 if the family has two cars, 3 if the family has three cars, and so on. Recode CARS so that any families with two or more cars will be coded 2. The missing value for CARS is −1.

5.4 A variable named AGE is coded in single year intervals; that is, someone who is 20 years old is given a value of 20, someone who is 66 years old is given a value of 66. The missing value for this variable is −9. Recode AGE into three categories: those under 16, those 16 to 65, and those over 65.

Review Using COMPUTE and IF

5.5 Write a command that will compute a variable named FAMILY$, which is to be WIFE$ (wife's income) plus HUSBAND$ (husband's income).

5.6 Write a command that will divide a variable named SALARY (monthly salary) by 160 to make an estimate of HOURLY$ (average hourly salary) of the subjects.

5.7 Create a new variable named NEWEXEC (new executives), which will be coded 1 when an executive's TENURE with the company, measured in months, is less than 12.

5.8 Write a command that will place a family in category 1 of a variable named IN-COME if their score on a variable named FAMINCOM is greater than a variable named AVEINCOM.

Review Using PROCESS IF

5.9 Using the PROCESS IF and FREQUENCIES commands, write the commands necessary to compare the FREQUENCIES output for women on the variable INCOME with the FREQUENCIES output for men on the same variable for the file NORC84 discussed in Appendix B.

5.10 Using the PROCESS IF and FREQUENCIES commands, write the SPSS/PC+ commands necessary to compare the education of persons age 50 and over to the education of persons ages 25 to 49 in the NORC84 file.

Review Using VARIABLE LABELS and VALUE LABELS

5.11 Write a command that would assign a variable named CHILDS the variable label NUMBER OF CHILDREN.

5.12 Write a command that would assign a variable named INCOME the variable label GROSS INCOME and a variable named NET the variable label NET INCOME.

5.13 Write a command for the variable POLVIEWS that would give the category coded

1 the value label LIBERAL, give the category coded 2 the label MIDDLE OF THE ROAD, and give the category coded 3 the label CONSERVATIVE.

5.14 Write a command for the variable OVERDUE that will create the value label LESS THAN 60 DAYS for the category coded 1 and MORE THAN 60 DAYS for the category coded 2. As part of the same command, for a variable named MILITARY, create the label MILITARY PERSONNEL for category 1 and the label CIVILIAN PERSONNEL for category 2.

ASSIGNMENT QUESTIONS

5.1   RECODE the variable CHILDS in the SPSS file NORC84 so that any families with more than two children will be coded 3.

5.2   RECODE the variable AGE in the SPSS file NORC84 into three categories: those under 16, those 16 to 65, and those over 65.

5.3   Write a command that will compute a variable named RELATIVE which is CHILDS (number of children) plus SIBS (number of siblings).

5.4   Write a command that will divide a variable named INCOME (annual income) by PERSONS (number of persons in the family) to make a new variable named INCOMPER.

5.5   Create a new variable named GRAD which will be coded 1 when EDUC is greater than 15 and 0 otherwise.

5.6   Using the variable INCOME in the SPSS file NORC84 create a variable named UPPER that will be 1 for a family with an income of $25,000 or more and 0 for a family with an income below $25,000.

5.7   For a variable named AGED, write the variable label SHARES HOME WITH PARENTS.

5.8   Using the PROCESS IF and FREQUENCIES commands, write the commands necessary to compare the FREQUENCIES output for blacks on the variable EDUC with the FREQUENCIES output for whites on the same variable for the file NORC84 discussed in Appendix B.

5.9   Using the PROCESS IF and FREQUENCIES commands, write the commands necessary to compare the income of persons any age from 40 to 65 and over to the income of persons any age from 18 to 39 in the NORC84 file.

5.10 For a variable named GRASS, write the variable label FAVOR LEGALIZING MARIJUANA. In the same command, give a variable named CUTSPEND the label FAVOR LESS SPENDING ON EDUCATION.

5.11 For the variable named RELIG, label category 1 PROTESTANT, category 2 CATHOLIC, category 3 JEWISH, category 4 NONE, category 5 OTHER, and category 9 NO ANSWER.

5.12 For the variable named UNEMPLOY, label category 1 YES, category 2 NO, category 8 DO NOT REMEMBER, and category 9 NO ANSWER. In the same command, for the variable named CLASS, label 1 LOWER, 2 WORKING, 3 MIDDLE, 4 UPPER, and 9 NO ANSWER.

6

CROSSTABULATIONS OF TWO OR MORE VARIABLES

New SPSS/PC+ Command:

CROSSTABS

We often begin an analysis suspecting that one variable affects another. For example, students invest time, energy, and money for each additional year of education. One might ask whether this effort pays off in greater happiness. Are people with more education happier than their less-educated peers? This question is "bivariate," meaning it concerns the association between two variables. (The prefix is the Latin word *bi*, meaning two.)

One way to investigate a bivariate question is by doing a crosstabulation. If we crosstabulate a happiness variable with an education variable, the output will reveal the percentage of people in each education category who are in each happiness category. We can then look for differences in happiness levels among the education categories. Such differences would indicate an association between education and happiness. For example, if the likelihood of being very happy for people in the high-education category is greater then the likelihood of being very happy for people in the low-education category, increasing one's education would seem to increase the likelihood of being very happy.

Described verbally, crosstabulations sound confusing. The example in Section 6.1 will clarify the method.

6.1 An Introduction to Crosstabulations

Consider the crosstabulation presented in Table 6.1. It is an analysis of the association between happiness and education using our example data set from Chapter 2.

The three columns in Table 6.1 represent the coding categories for the education variable. (Recall that we recoded 1 to mean 0–11 years of education, 2 to mean 12–15 years of education, and 3 to mean 16 or more years of education.) Column 1 represents the people coded 1 on education. Column 2 represents the people coded 2 on education. Column 3 represents the people coded 3 on education. The total for column 1 is 4, indicating that four respondents were coded 1 on education.

The row numbers under HAPPY correspond to the categories of that variable. Row 1 represents the people who responded "very happy," coded 1. Row 2 represents those who responded "pretty happy," coded 2. Row 3 represents those who responded "not too happy," coded 3.

The upper-left cell of the table (row 1, column 1) is the conjunction of people who were coded 1 on both EDUC and HAPPY. The 50.0 in that cell indicates that 50.0 percent of the people with 0–11 years of education stated they felt very happy. The middle cell of column 1 (that is, row 2) is the conjunction of people who were coded 1 on EDUC and 2 on HAPPY. The 50.0 in that cell indicates that 50.0 percent of the people with 0–11 years of education stated that they felt pretty happy. The bottom cell of column 1 is blank, indicating that none of the people with 0–11 years of education responded that they were not so happy.

It is easy to become mixed up when reading a crosstabulation table, especially one that shows more than two variables. You must think carefully about what the percentages represent and what comparisons are meaningful. In our

TABLE 6.1 Crosstabulation of Happiness by Education

HAPPY	EDUC 1	2	3
VERY HAPPY	50.0	33.3	50.0
PRETTY HAPPY	50.0	55.6	33.3
NOT TOO HAPPY		9.1	16.6
COLUMN TOTAL	4	9	9

example, each percentage has as a base the number of people in that column, and each column is an education category. (Note that for each column, the sum of the percents equals 100. Because the percents in the cells are rounded to three figures, the sum of a column of cells may not equal exactly 100.0. However, SPSS/PC+ will display the sum as 100.00 because that would be the sum of the unrounded cell percents.)

We can compare up and down the columns. In our example, the percent of people in the top cells is greater than the percent of people in the bottom cells, which means that the percent of people who are very happy is greater than the percent of people who are not too happy.

We can also compare across rows. In our example, if we compare across the top row, we find that 50 percent of those with less than 12 years of education (column 1) and 50 percent of those with more than 16 years of education (column 3) are very happy, whereas 33.3 percent of those with 12 to 15 years of education (column 2) are very happy. There is no clear pattern. Among those with the least education and those with the most education, 50 percent stated they were very happy. However, the sample size of our example is small. The association between variables will be clear when we replicate this crosstabulation in Section 6.4 using the larger sample in the NORC84 SPSS system file.

6.2 The CROSSTABS Command

In SPSS/PC+, crosstabulations are produced by the CROSSTABS command. The following CROSSTABS command, using two of its OPTIONS, produced the output in Table 6.1:

```
crosstabs happy by educ/
        options 4.
```

We recommend placing the variable you think is being affected (the dependent variable) before the BY and the variable you think is causing an effect (the independent variable) after the BY. This way the dependent variable will always appear as row categories along the side of your table.

An OPTIONS command can be used with most procedural commands to select alternatives to the default operations and output. For the CROSSTABS command, OPTIONS 4 produces column percents for each cell, which makes the table easier to interpret. Each cell will then contain both the number of cases and the percent that number is of all the cases in that column. At the bottom of the column the total number of cases for that column is given and

what percent that is of the entire table's number of cases. In our text we have
simplified by giving just the column percent for each cell and the column total
number of cases at the bottom.

Placed with the other SPSS/PC+ commands necessary to produce a run
with our example data set, the commands needed to generate the CROSS-
TABS output in Table 6.1 would be

```
data list fixed / id 1-2
                  educ  3-4
                  sex  5
                  happy  6.
begin data.
010912
021223
031521
041222
050611
061612
071522
081612
091821
101412
111321
121611
130922
141212
151221
161821
170821
181222
191613
20142
end data.
missing values educ(99) happy sex (0).
recode educ (0 thru 11=1) (12 thru 15=2) (16 thru 30=3).
crosstabs happy by educ/
         options 4.
```

A problem arises when we do CROSSTABS with a small number of cases.
Some of the cells are empty and, more importantly, the results are not likely to
be generalizable. For example, when we have only four individuals with less

than 12 years of education, we are not confident that they are likely to be typical of all people with less than 12 years of education.

6.3 Using CROSSTABS with an SPSS System File

To illustrate the problem of representativeness and to give you a more accurate impression of the relationship between education and happiness, we now do an identical CROSSTABS for the the entire SPSS system file NORC84, described in Appendix B. The commands needed to do a crosstabulation of the variables HAPPY and EDUC in the NORC84 file are as follows:

```
get file 'norc84'.
recode educ
(0 thru 11=1)
(12 thru 15=2)
(16 thru 30=3).
crosstabs happy by educ/
        options 4.
```

Table 6.2 is constructed from the output produced by these commands. The entire sample size is 1,473 cases. Consequently we now have no empty cells and the percents, based on a much larger sample, are more likely to portray accurately the relationship between education and happiness in the United States.

Along the top of Table 6.2 are the education categories; each column under an education value corresponds to the people in that category. Along the left side of the table are the happiness categories; each row corresponds to the people in that category.

Look at the percent of less-educated people in the very happy category— the upper-left cell (row 1, column 1). The percent is 32 percent (rounded), indicating that about one-third of the people with less than 12 years of education are "very happy." Compare this figure, however, with the percent of people with more education who report being very happy—41 percent. We see that more education increases the likelihood of being very happy.

Interpretation of what causes what, however, is tricky. Perhaps people who are happy tend to stay in school longer. If this is true, happiness increases the likelihood of high educational attainment rather than educational attainment increasing the likelihood of being happy. Perhaps both effects are at work: higher education increases the likelihood of being happy and being happy in-

TABLE 6.2 Crosstabulation of Happiness by Education Using the
NORC84 System File

HAPPY	EDUC 1	2	3
VERY HAPPY	32.3	31.4	41.0
PRETTY HAPPY	48.5	57.1	52.8
NOT TOO HAPPY	19.2	11.5	6.1
COLUMN TOTAL	408	772	262

NUMBER OF MISSING OBSERVATIONS = 31

creases the likelihood of high educational attainment. We should also remember that associations in society are usually far from absolute. Of the highly educated people, 59 percent are not "very happy" (100 percent minus 41 percent) so we might conclude that obtaining more education is far from a good guarantee that one will be very happy.

6.4 Multivariate Analysis with CROSSTABS

We have seen that the probability of respondents reporting that they are happy is linked to their sex and educational achievement. Another question we might ask is whether the association of happiness with education is the same for women as for men. When there are two or more independent variables, the analysis is called "multivariate."

To add a third variable to a CROSSTABS analysis, we simply add the word BY and the name of the third variable. For our example, the CROSSTABS and accompanying commands would become

```
get file 'norc84'.
recode educ (0 thru 11=1)
             (12 thru 15=2)
             (16 thru 30=3)
crosstabs happy by educ by sex/
        options 4/
        statistics 1 2.
```

TABLE 6.3 Output from Multivariate Crosstabulation

CROSSTABULATION OF HAPPY BY EDUC CONTROLLING FOR SEX
SEX   VALUE=1

HAPPY	COL PCT	EDUC 1	2	3	
VERY HAPPY	1	33.5	27.1	38.8	
PRETTY HAPPY	2	45.9	58.9	53.7	
NOT TOO HAPPY	3	20.6	13.9	7.5	
	COLUMN TOTAL	170	280	134	584

CHI-SQUARE   SIGNIFICANCE
  16.5   0.002

     STATISTIC   VALUE
CRAMER'S V   0.12

CROSSTABULATION OF HAPPY BY EDUC CONTROLLING FOR SEX
SEX   VALUE=2

HAPPY	COL PCT	EDUC 1	2	3	
VERY HAPPY	1	31.5	36.4	47.7	
PRETTY HAPPY	2	50.0	53.3	46.9	
NOT TOO HAPPY	3	18.5	10.4	5.5	
	COLUMN TOTAL	238	492	128	858

CHI-SQUARE   SIGNIFICANCE
  21.0   0.000

     STATISTIC   VALUE
CRAMER'S V   0.11

NUMBER OF MISSING OBSERVATIONS = 31

Notice that the control variable is the last in the command sequence. In this analysis, SEX is called the control variable because we will see the effects of education controlling for SEX. If the positions of EDUC and SEX were reversed in the command, we would see the effects of SEX controlling for EDUC.

The subcommand STATISTICS 1 2 will produce two statistics chi-squared (pronounced "kai squared") and Cramer's V. Cramer's V is easy to interpret. It ranges from 0.0 (when there is absolutely no association between two variables) to 1.0 (when there is a perfect association).

Chi-squared (χ^2 is another useful statistic, because it has a known sampling distribution and its significance level is included in the output. Cramer's V is a transformation of χ^2 which standardizes for the number of cells in the crosstabulation table. Consequently, the significance level of Cramer's V is the same as the significance level of χ^2.

The output will be on different pages for each category of the control variable. In our example, the output will be spread over two pages. The first page will contain the HAPPY BY EDUC table for men; the second, the HAPPY BY EDUC table for women.

Table 6.3 is constructed from the output produced by our commands. Notice how the addition of the STATISTICS 1 2 subcommand has produced the chi-squared and Cramer's V statistics at the bottom of each table.

The difference between the least educated and the most educated in the percent very happy is greater for females than for males. For females, the difference in the top row (the very happy respondents) between the respondents with 16 or more years of education (47.7) and the respondents with less than 12 years of education (31.5) is 16.2 percent. The corresponding difference in the table for males is 6.2. This suggests that obtaining a higher level of education improves the likelihood of being very happy more for females than it does for males.

6.5 Additional Resources

CROSSTABS is discussed on pages B93–107 and C33–36 of the *SPSS/PC+ V2.0 Base Manual.*

6.6 Summary

In this chapter we explained how CROSSTABS can be used to produce the crosstabulations of two or more variables. These crosstabulations are useful for examining the associations between variables, particularly nominal variables. We showed how chi-square is used to assess the statistical significance of associations in a crosstabulation. We described Cramer's V, which is a transformation of chi-square so that it ranges on a scale from 0.0 to 1.0. Crosstabulations can be very simple and easy to interpret; they can also be very complex and arduous to interpret. Some of the techniques we cover in Part 2 are methods of searching through complex crosstabulations for the most important associations.

At this point we have seen that, in addition to being female and over 40, we can increase our likelihood of being happy by being more educated. This is the first variable that we have examined over which individuals have any control. We hope that by now your curiosity is aroused over why these variables are associated with happiness. Are more educated people generally happier because they have more money? Are younger people generally happier because they are healthier? These are multivariate questions that we will be able to tackle better with the techniques presented in Part 2 of this text. The never-ending task of the researcher is to try to push our understanding a bit further, knowing full well that answering one question leads immediately to more questions.

RESEARCH PROJECT WORK

1.   a. For the data set you have gathered, replicate the crosstabulations of HAPPY BY EDUC and HAPPY BY EDUC BY SEX done in this chapter.
b. Describe any differences between the results in your sample and the results for the NORC84 file.
c. If there are differences, what do you think caused them?

2.   a. Produce a crosstabulation of HAPPY by another variable in the data set that you think might affect happiness.
b. Discuss whether the results were what you expected.

REVIEW QUESTIONS

6.1   Write the CROSSTABS and OPTIONS commands that would crosstabulate a variable named INCOME with a variable named SEX. Your hypothesis is that the sex variable is causing differences in income.

6.2   Write the CROSSTABS and OPTIONS commands that would crosstabulate a variable named SALES with a variable named DAY. Your hypothesis is that the DAY variable is affecting the SALES variable.

6.3   Write all the commands necessary to crosstabulate EDUC by SEX in our example data set. Assume that SEX is the causal variable and recode EDUC.

6.4   Write the commands that are needed to demonstrate through a crosstabulation the effects of the variable named RELIGION on the variable named POLITICS for the SPSS file NORC84 described in Appendix B.

6.5   Write the CROSSTABS and OPTIONS commands that would produce three crosstabulations demonstrating the association of the variable named EDUC with the variables HAPPY, HEALTH, and INCOME for the SPSS file NORC84 described in Appendix B.

6.6 Write the CROSSTABS and OPTIONS commands that would produce a cross-tabulation demonstrating the association of the variable HAPPY with the variable MARITAL, controlling for the variable SEX.

6.7 What command must be added to the CROSSTABS and OPTIONS commands to produce the chi-square and Cramer's *V* statistics?

6.8 Explain the difference between chi-square and Cramer's *V.*

ASSIGNMENT QUESTIONS

6.1 Write the CROSSTABS and OPTIONS commands that would crosstabulate a variable named AGE with a variable named SEX. Your hypothesis is that there are differences between the sexes in death rates, and therefore in age distribution.

6.2 Write the CROSSTABS and OPTIONS commands that would crosstabulate a variable named HEALTH with a variable named EDUC. Your hypothesis is that the EDUC level of respondents affects the likelihood of good health.

6.3 Write all the commands necessary to crosstabulate HAPPY by SEX in our example data set. Assume that SEX is the causal variable.

6.4 Write the commands that are needed to demonstrate through a crosstabulation the effects of the variable named INCOME on the variable named ATTEND for the SPSS file NORC84 described in Appendix B.

6.5 Write the commands needed to produce three crosstabulations demonstrating the effects of the variable named INCOME on the variables SATFAM, SATFRND, and SATJOB for the SPSS file NORC84 described in Appendix B.

6.6 Write all the commands necessary to crosstabulate INCOME by EDUC controlling for SEX using the NORC84 SPSS file described in Appendix B. Include the command necessary to produce the chi-square and Cramer's *V* statistics.

7

COMPARING MEANS

New SPSS/PC+ Command:

MEANS

We have seen in previous chapters that women, the more educated, and those aged 40 and over are more likely to report being happy. You should be curious about shedding more light on these associations. Many pertinent questions are still unanswered. For example, are women at all income levels happier than men, or is this difference between the sexes restricted to some income categories? We'll address this question as we introduce another analytical procedure: comparing group means.

Crosstabulations, which we discussed in the last chapter, are sometimes difficult to interpret for variables such as income that have many categories. The MEANS command provides an output that is simpler to read, and is a useful tool when the dependent variable is an ordinal or interval measure. To clarify this last point, we need to explain levels of measurement and their role in statistical analysis. Then we'll go on to discuss comparing means with the MEANS command.

7.1 Levels of Measurement

Nominal level of measurement variables have categories that cannot be ranked from lesser to greater. One's religious affiliation is a nominal variable. Another example of a nominal variable is place of birth. It does not make sense to calculate a mean (average) or median (midpoint of a distribution) for such variables. (Nominal variables are also called *categorical* variables.)

Ordinal level of measurement variables have categories that can be ranked. **Interval** level of measurement variables have categories that can be ranked *and* are of equal size. In the example data set presented in Chapter 2, the HAPPY variable is ordinal and the EDUC variable is interval. HAPPY is an ordinal variable because we can rank the categories "very happy," "somewhat happy," and "not too happy" in an order on the dimension of happiness.

The EDUC variable is interval because the categories can be ranked and each interval is of equal size; that is, the distance between 9 years of education and 11 years of education is the same as the distance between 13 years of education and 15 years of education. Some statistical techniques are designed to be used only with interval variables. The assumption of intervals of equal size is often problematic in social science variables when we want to assess their actual impact. Is the interval between 9 years of education and 10 years of education as significant as the interval between 11 years of education and 12 years of education? Probably not, since the latter interval usually brings with it a high school diploma. Is a $10,000 increase in annual income as significant for someone earning $100,000 as it is for someone earning $15,000? Is aging from age 30 to age 40 as significant as aging from age 10 to age 20, or from age 60 to age 70?

Two-category nominal variables such as SEX are called *dichotomous* or *binomial*. They are a special case of nominal variables because, after being coded with numerical values, they can be used in interval-level statistical analyses such as Pearson correlations (see Chapter 8). For a discussion of two-category nominal variables, see Roderick P. McDonald's *Factor Analysis and Related Methods* (Hillsdale, N.J.: Lawrence Erlbaum Associates, 1985), pages 9–11, 198–202.

Further distinctions can be made between levels of measurement, and the classification of a variable's level of measurement is not always clear-cut. At times there are disputes over whether variables are "interval enough" to justify the use of statistics designed for interval measures. Researchers like to use interval measure statistics because they are better than ordinal measure statistics for handling multiple variable analyses and for detecting weak associations between variables. Consequently, there is a tendency to use interval level statistics with ordinal variables. The risk of this practice is that the results may be biased. However, William L. Hays observes in *Statistics for the Social Sci-*

ences, second edition (New York: Holt, Rinehart and Winston, 1973) that at issue here is not really mathematics and statistics, but the good judgment of the researcher in selecting a method for the problem at hand and interpreting the meaning of the results (pages 87–90). There is no simple, hard-and-fast rule about which statistical technique to use for a particular set of variables.

7.2 Comparing Means between Groups: MEANS

An analytical technique that compares group means on a dependent or "criterion" variable is produced by the command MEANS. This technique can only be employed when the mean is a useful measure for the dependent variable. (A dependent variable is one that we think is being affected by another variable in the analysis. The independent variable is the one that is having an effect.)

We can consider, for example, whether there are differences between males and females in happiness. Since we are considering if the sex of a respondent affects the probability of him or her being happy, sex is the independent variable and happiness is the dependent variable. Happiness is an ordinal variable so we can use MEANS.

If the dependent variable is "nominal," a mean or average is not useful since, as you've learned, the categories cannot be ranked from lesser to greater. (Remember our examples of religious affiliation or place of birth as nominal variables.)

The MEANS command would be

```
means happy by sex.
```

Note that MEANS must begin in column 1. Note also that the dependent variable, HAPPY, comes before the BY and the independent variable, SEX, comes after the BY.

Using our example data file described in Chapter 2, the necessary set of SPSS/PC+ commands to do a MEANS would be

```
data list / id 1–2 educ 3–4 sex 5 happy 6.
begin data.
010912
021223
031521
041222
050611
```

```
061612
071522
081612
091821
101412
111321
121611
130922
141212
151221
161821
170821
181222
191613
20142
end data.
missing values educ(-9) happy sex(0).
means happy by sex.
```

Table 7.1 is constructed from the output that would be produced by this MEANS. The top line of the sample output presented in Table 7.1 are the words "Summaries of HAPPY."

The second line of our output indicates that the summary variable HAPPY is by SEX. So you will see what the mean HAPPY score is for each SEX category.

The line with the words "VARIABLE CODE MEAN N" provides the column headings. On the next line, the word SEX indicates the variable name of the independent variable. The "1" under the word CODE indicates that this line is for cases coded 1 on SEX—these are the male cases. The 1.8 is the mean for these cases on the criterion variable. The 8 indicates the number of cases in this category.

The last line provides information for the cases coded 2 on the variable

TABLE 7.1 Output from the MEANS of Happiness by Sex

	SUMMARIES OF HAPPY BY LEVELS OF SEX		
VARIABLE	VALUE	MEAN	CASES
SEX	1	1.8	8
SEX	2	1.5	11

SEX—these are the females. The mean for the females on the criterion variable HAPPY is 1.5. For the HAPPY variable, the happiest category was coded 1 and the least happy category was coded 3. Therefore, the fact that the mean value for women was lower than the mean score for men indicates that on average the women were happier than the men. Although these findings are based on a sample of only 20 respondents, when the analysis was repeated with the entire SPSS file NORC84 with 1,473 respondents, the results were the same to the nearest tenth.

7.3 Using MEANS with an SPSS System File

The SPSS/PC+ commands necessary to do the MEANS of HAPPY by SEX with the NORC84 file described in Appendix B are

```
get file 'norc84.'
means happy by sex.
```

In this analysis the direction of causality is certain: we know that one's level of happiness does not affect the likelihood of being male or female. Exactly why women are more likely to respond that they are "very happy" is one of those thought-provoking questions that leads researchers to call for further study of a subject. Is the health and lifestyle of women more likely than that of men to yield happiness? Are women more reluctant to say that they are not happy? Is the objective situation of women better than that of men? Our analysis does not answer these questions. All it shows is that in general women are more likely than men to tell pollsters that they are happy.

In our next example we consider the question "Does money buy happiness?" Both money and happiness are variables for which a mean score is useful. Our hypothesis, however, is that money affects happiness, so we break down the mean level of happiness for each income category. In other words, happiness is our dependent variable. Using our SPSS file named NORC84, the necessary commands are as follows:

```
get file 'norc84.'
means happy by income.
```

Income was coded from 1 (under $5,000) to 8 (over $50,000). Hence the higher the income category, the higher the income. (See Appendix B for the exact range of each interval.) As before, the happiness variable has three cate-

TABLE 7.2 Output Produced by MEANS HAPPY BY INCOME

SUMMARIES OF HAPPY
BY LEVELS OF INCOME

VARIABLE		MEAN	CASES
FOR ENTIRE POPULATION		1.8	1,320
INCOME	UNDER $5000	2.0	124
INCOME	$5,000 to $9,999	2.0	170
INCOME	$10,000 to $14,999	1.9	197
INCOME	$15,000 to $19,999	1.8	153
INCOME	$20,000 to $24,999	1.8	190
INCOME	$25,000 to $34,999	1.7	206
INCOME	$35,000 to $49,999	1.6	163
INCOME	OVER $50,000	1.6	117

TOTAL CASES = 1,473

MISSING CASES = 153 OR 10.4 PERCENT

gories; the lower the mean score on the variable HAPPY, the happier are the respondents. Table 7.2 contains the overall mean and the mean score for each income group. We can see that the HAPPY level is different for each income category. The higher income categories have higher mean levels of happiness.

In this analysis there is some uncertainty about the problem of deciding the direction of causality. Perhaps naturally happy people are more successful at making money because people like to buy from them or to work with them. That is, maybe being happy earns money rather than money buying happiness.

7.4 Multivariate Analysis with MEANS

Using the MEANS command, as with CROSSTABS, we can do multivariate analyses. For example, we can examine the association between income and happiness to see if it is the same for women as it is for men. The command to produce this analysis would be

```
means happy by sex by income.
```

This command would produce the output presented in Table 7.3. Note that the output is usually easier to read if the control variable is listed before the independent variable. In our example, this is why SEX is placed on the MEANS command before INCOME.

We can see in Table 7.3 that the happiness means are lower (indicating greater happiness) as income goes up for both males and females in the higher income categories. We can also see that the tendency for females to be happier than males is true for all income levels.

The final Assignment Question for this chapter is to answer the second question we poised earlier about whether more educated persons were happier because they had higher income. You can answer this question by analyzing happiness by education controlling for income. (Remember that the sequence of the command would be MEANS HAPPY BY INCOME BY HAPPY.)

TABLE 7.3 Output Produced by MEANS HAPPY BY SEX BY INCOME

SUMMARIES OF HAPPY   GENERAL HAPPINESS
BY LEVELS OF SEX   RESPONDENT'S SEX
             INCOME   TOTAL FAMILY INCOME

VARIABLE	VALUE	LABEL	MEAN	CASES
FOR ENTIRE POPULATION			1.8	1,320
SEX	1	MALE	1.8	556
INCOME	1	UNDER $5,000	2.2	39
INCOME	2	$5,000 TO $9,999	1.9	60
INCOME	3	$10,000 TO $14,999	1.9	84
INCOME	4	$15,000 TO $19,999	1.8	69
INCOME	5	$20,000 TO $24,999	1.9	67
INCOME	6	$25,000 TO $34,999	1.8	95
INCOME	7	$35,000 TO $49,999	1.6	80
INCOME	8	OVER $50,000	1.6	62
SEX	2	FEMALE	1.7	764
INCOME	1	UNDER $5,000	1.9	85
INCOME	2	$5,000 TO $9,999	2.0	110
INCOME	3	$10,000 TO $14,999	1.8	113
INCOME	4	$15,000 TO $19,999	1.7	84
INCOME	5	$20,000 TO $24,999	1.7	123
INCOME	6	$25,000 TO $34,999	1.6	111
INCOME	7	$35,000 TO $49,999	1.6	83
INCOME	8	OVER $50,000	1.6	55

TOTAL CASES   = 1,473

MISSING CASES = 153 OR 10.4 PERCENT

7.5 The STATISTICS Command with MEANS

If we wanted to test for the statistical significance of the mean differences by income we would add the command STATISTICS ALL.

The output produced by the STATISTICS command for FREQUENCIES gives the F ratio from which the statistical significance level for the between group differences is calculated. Furthermore, the association is broken down into its linear and nonlinear components. Note, however, that the statistical significance test is only for the first variable. Therefore, the control variable would have to be dropped from the MEANS command on runs using STATISTICS ALL. Otherwise the statistics would be for the control variable. For example, if we add the STATISTICS ALL command to the previous MEANS without deleting the control variable SEX, the statistical significance test would only be for the association between HAPPY and SEX. The correct commands to examine the statistical significance of the association between HAPPY and INCOME would be

```
means happy by income/
     statistics all.
```

The output produced by the STATISTICS ALL command would include statistics presented in Table 7.4. The SIG abbreviation stands for statistical significance and is the probability that group differences of this magnitude would be due to sampling error. A statistical significance of .000 indicates that the probability is less than .001.

If we wanted to focus on the mean differences between just two groups—an analysis similar to the traditional T test—all we need to do is use a SELECT IF statement to limit the MEANS to those two groups. Once the analysis is complete, taking the square root of the F ratio will give the T value. The

TABLE 7.4 Partial Output of STATISTICS for MEANS Command

	ANALYSIS OF VARIANCE		
SOURCE	D.F.	F	SIG.
BETWEEN GROUPS	7	8.5	.0000
LINEARITY	1	56.6	.0000
DEVIATION FROM LINEARITY	6	0.5	.8200

statistical significance level is the same as for the *F* ratio. Multiple *T* tests, however, are to be avoided because the significance levels for *T* tests are based on individual trials. Looking at a set of *T* scores increases the probability that one will discover one that is "significant."

7.6 Additional Resources

MEANS is discussed on pages B109–115, C88–90, and D15–16 of the *SPSS/ PC+ V2.0 Base Manual.* For more information on levels of measurement, see Hubert Blalock, *Social Statistics,* revised second edition (New York: McGraw-Hill, 1979), pages 15–26.

7.7 Summary

In this chapter we explained how to use MEANS to analyze the differences between groups in their mean score on a variable. The variable for which means are calculated is called the SUMMARY variable, usually thought of as the dependent variable in the analysis.

Using the STATISTICS command with MEANS produces an analysis of variance table that indicates the statistical significance of the differences between group means. Also produced in the table are two advanced statistics that we will explain in Part 2: the significance of the linear regression using the group variable as a predictor and the significance of deviations from the linear model.

The analysis in this chapter showed that reported happiness increases with income. This association remains when we control for SEX. And at all income levels, women are more likely to be happy than men.

RESEARCH PROJECT WORK

In doing the following work, you might want to pool your data file with that of other students in your class so that the group means are based on five or more cases. An alternative would be to recode variables that have too few cases in some categories.

1. Use your research project data file to analyze SATFAM, SATFRND, and SATJOB by INCOME controlling for SEX.

2. Describe the associations you find in Project 1.

3. Discuss what might be causing the associations you find in Project 1.

REVIEW QUESTIONS

7.1 Write a command that would produce the mean scores on a variable named IN-COME for each category of a variable named SEX.

7.2 Write a command that would produce the mean scores on a variable named HEALTH for each category of a variable named EDUC and for each category of a variable named INCOME.

7.3 Write all the commands necessary to produce the mean scores on the variable HAPPY for each category of the variable named EDUC for our example data set given in Chapter 2.

7.4 Write all the commands needed to produce the mean scores on the variable named HAPPY for each category of the variable HEALTH for the SPSS file NORC84 described in Appendix B.

7.5 What is the criterion variable in the MEANS output?

7.6 In a MEANS analysis, does the dependent variable appear before or after the BY on the MEANS command?

7.7 What command would be used to produce the mean scores on income for each category of EDUC controlling for SEX?

7.8 What commands would produce the statistics that would enable the user to judge if the differences in income by education were statistically significant?

7.9 What commands would be needed to determine if the mean income for those with 15 years of education is statistically different from those with 12 years of education?

ASSIGNMENT QUESTIONS

7.1 Write all the commands necessary to produce the mean years of education completed for each of the categories of the variable HAPPY in our example data set in Chapter 2.

7.2 For the SPSS file NORC84, write all the commands necessary to produce the mean score on the variable POLVIEWS for each category of the variable SEX.

7.3 For the SPSS file NORC84, write all the commands necessary to produce the mean score on the variable HAPPY for each category of the variable POLVIEWS.

7.4 For the SPSS file NORC84, write all the commands necessary to produce the mean score on the variable HAPPY for each category of the variable CHILDS.

7.5   For the questionnaire variables in Appendix C, write *only* the MEANS command necessary to produce the mean score on SATJOB for each category of the variable SEX.

7.6   For the questionnaire variables in Appendix C, write *only* the MEANS command necessary to produce the mean score on the variable named HAPPY for each category of the variable named TVHOURS.

7.7   What MEANS command would you need to produce the mean score on the variable HAPPY for each category of the variable named TVHOURS controlling for the variable SEX?

7.8   What commands would be needed to produce statistics indicating the statistical significance of the association between HAPPY and TVHOURS?

7.9   Use the SPSS file NORC84 to analyze happiness by education, controlling for income.

8

CORRELATIONS AND SCATTERPLOTS

New SPSS/PC+ Commands:

CORRELATION
PLOT
SAMPLE

We have seen from frequencies, crosstabulations, and means analyses that the variable HAPPY is associated with SEX, AGE, EDUC, and INCOME. To do these analyses, however, AGE and EDUC were recoded. INCOME also would have been recoded, if the data were not already collapsed into large intervals in the SPSS file NORC84. Whenever we collapse data into large intervals, information is lost and we cannot study the association as precisely as we could before recoding the data. CORRELATION and PLOT provide two analytical methods that do not require collapsing data into a small number of intervals.

In this chapter we use CORRELATION to re-examine the associations of AGE, EDUC, and INCOME with HAPPY and with each other. We use PLOT to present the association between income and age. We add to our analysis the variable HEALTH, which also is in the SPSS file NORC84.

8.1 When and How
to Use CORRELATION

The CORRELATION command gives output that summarizes the strength of an association with the correlation coefficient, which will be in the range from −1.0 to +1.0. One advantage of the correlation coefficient is that it indicates whether the association is positive or negative. A negative coefficient means that when one variable is higher in value, the other variable tends to be lower in value. A positive coefficient means that when one variable is higher, the other variable also tends to be higher. For example, we might expect the correlation between education and income to be positive. On the other hand, you might expect the correlation between education and number of hours watching television to be negative.

The best indicator of the strength of the association between a pair of variables is the correlation coefficient squared. For this reason, a correlation of .20 is four times as strong as a correlation of .10, because $(.20)^2 = .04$ and $(.10)^2 = .01$. Once the correlation is squared, however, it no longer indicates whether the association is positive or negative. This is why tables usually present the coefficient unsquared. There are many different correlation coefficients. The one called the Pearson correlation coefficient or zero-order correlation coefficient is the one most frequently used.

CORRELATION requires the assumption that the variables are associated in a linear manner. For example, if income is low in young adult years, peaks in late middle adult years, and drops off after age 60, the association would not be measured well by a correlation coefficient. There are other types of nonlinear associations that would not be appropriate material for CORRELATION analysis. Two hypothetical examples are given in scatterplots in Figure 8.1.

The first scatterplot in Figure 8.1, for Big Macs sold, illustrates an exponential increase over 25 years. The second scatterplot illustrates the logistic curve of increase in resident population size of a housing development over time. These associations are not appropriate for CORRELATION analysis.

To run CORRELATION we simply list after the command the variables whose associations we want printed. For example, to look at the associations of the interval variables that we have considered so far, use the following commands:

```
correlation happy sex educ income age health.
correlation happy sex age educ income health/
          options 2 5.
```

The complete output is shown in Table 8.1 (see page 106). To find the correlation of sex with happy go down the column headed SEX to the row labeled HAPPY.

FIGURE 8.1 Nonlinear Associations Inappropriate for CORRELATION Analysis

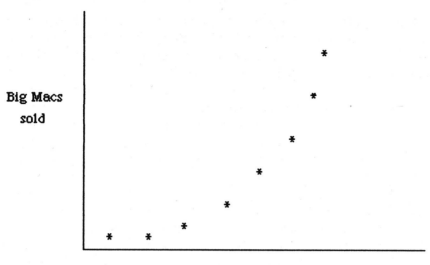

1960-1985

Exponential Increase

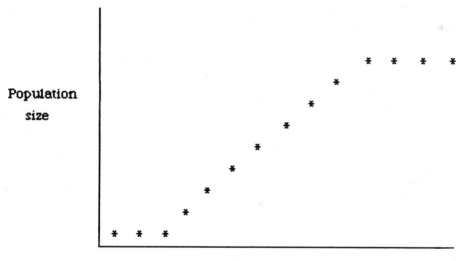

Months

Logistic Curve

TABLE 8.1 Complete Output from CORRELATION   happy sex age educ income
health/ options 2 5

CORRE-LATION:	HAPPY	SEX	AGE	EDUC	INCOME	HEALTH
HAPPY	1.0000	−.0575	−.0921	−.1069	−.1858	.2091
	(0)	(1445)	(1439)	(1442)	(1366)	(1437)
	P= .	P= .014	P= .000	P= .000	P= .000	P= .000
SEX	−.0575	1.0000	.0651	−.0560	−.0734	.0501
	(1445)	(0)	(1467)	(1470)	(1393)	(1461)
	P= .014	P= .	P= .006	P= .016	P= .003	P= .028
AGE	−.0921	.0651	1.0000	−.2862	−.0064	.2662
	(1439)	(1467)	(0)	(1465)	(1389)	(1456)
	P= .000	P= .006	P= .	P= .000	P= .406	P= .000
EDUC	−.1069	−.0560	−.2862	1.0000	.3601	−.3353
	(1442)	(1470)	(1465)	(0)	(1392)	(1458)
	P= .000	P= .016	P= .000	P= .	P= .000	P= .000
INCOME	−.1858	−.0734	−.0064	.3601	1.0000	−.2485
	(1366)	(1393)	(1389)	(1392)	(0)	(1382)
	P= .000	P= .003	P= .406	P= .000	P= .	P= .000
HEALTH	.2091	.0501	.2662	−.3353	−.2485	1.0000
	(1437)	(1461)	(1456)	(1458)	(1382)	(0)
	P= .000	P= .028	P= .000	P= .000	P= .000	P= .

(Coefficient / (Cases) / 1-tailed Significance)

Note. A period (.) is printed if a coefficient cannot be computed.

The correlation coefficient is the top number. In the upper-left corner of the table we can see that for HAPPY with SEX the correlation coefficient is −.058. The (1445) under the pair indicates the number of cases used in calculating the correlation. This number can be different for different pairs because the number of missing cases is not always the same for all variables. The P = .014 shows that a correlation this size would occur because of sampling error only 14 times out of 1,000.

In this analysis, we have added the variable HEALTH to the ones we have seen previously. This variable is the subject's response to the question: "Would you say your own health, in general, is excellent, good, fair, or poor?" The codings for HEALTH range from 1 for excellent to 4 for poor. Therefore, a positive correlation indicates that healthier people tend to be happier. The correlation for HAPPY with HEALTH is .209, the highest for any of the pairs. Only the correlation of HAPPY with INCOME is nearly as high. Although the correlation

---

FIGURE 8.2 Simplified Output from PLOT of income with age (hypothetical data)

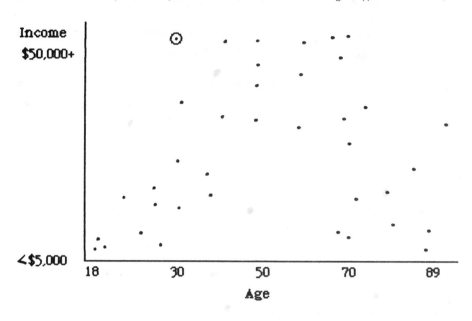

with EDUC is not nearly as strong, it is still greater than a random association that might be expected from random sampling error. So the old folklore that to be healthy, wealthy, and wise brings happiness has some empirical support in our NORC84 survey.

8.2 When and How to Use PLOT

The PLOT command produces a picture of the association between two variables by plotting the point each case would lie on a plane in which each axis corresponds to the intervals of one of the variables. To understand PLOT, one picture is truly worth a thousand words. Look at Figure 8.2. The circled dot represents the case of someone age 30 earning over $50,000 per year. (We should all do so well!) Note that the dot's distance from the vertical axis corresponds to the age interval 30 and its distance from the horizontal axis corresponds to $50,000. You can see that the scatter of cases tends to be higher on the vertical income axis for the older cases (which are more to the right on the age axis). At the oldest ages, however, income once more is at lower levels.

It is difficult to interpret PLOT output when there are fewer than five intervals in either variable. That is why we did not use the variable HAPPY in our example. It is also difficult to interpret PLOT output when there are hundreds of times more cases than there are intervals in the two variables. We can solve the problem of too many cases by taking a sample of our cases before doing the PLOT. This is done with the command SAMPLE followed by the proportion of the cases you want in the sample. In our example we sampled .1 or 10 percent of the cases to use in the scatterplot.

All that is necessary to run PLOT is to use the command followed first by the name of the variable you want on the vertical axis, and then WITH and the name of the variable you want on the horizontal axis. Together the commands obtain the scatterplot of INCOME with AGE given in Figure 8.2. The only SPSS/PC+ commands necessary are

```
sample .1.
plot /plot income with age.
```

A more complete scatterplot for the following code

```
select if (sex eq 1 and age gt 34).
sample .1.
plot /plot income with educ.
```

is shown in Figure 8.3. In our example we sampled .1 or 10 percent of males over the age of 34 to use in the scatterplot of income with education. Figure 8.3 uses actual data from the NORC84 data file. Consequently, the numbers on the vertical axis refer to the income categories in Appendix B. Note also that the scatterplot shows the number of cases that occur at a particular point; rather than a single dot for one case, the program shows the number 1. The program chooses reference numbers by default for the vertical and horizontal axes. If they are not to your liking, you can override the default and choose different numbers. Alternatively, you could delete the reference numbers from your output before you print the scatterplot. Note that this plot of 40 cases requires approximately 5,000 bytes of workspace for execution.

8.3 Additional Resources

CORRELATION is discussed on pages B143–151, C28–30, and D6–7 of the *SPSS/PC+ V2.0 Base Manual.* PLOT is discussed on pages B131–141 and C117–121. SAMPLE is discussed on page B41.

FIGURE 8.3 Complete Output from PLOT of income with education (actual NORC84 data)

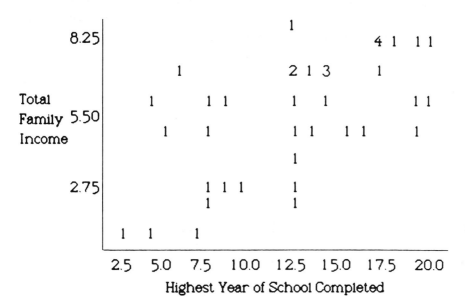

8.4 Summary

In this chapter we explained how to produce scatterplots and correlation coefficients by using the SPSS/PC+ commands PLOT and CORRELATION. Both procedures require interval or ordinal data. Both procedures are well suited for handling variables with a large number of values.

PLOT has the advantage of being able to depict nonlinear relationships accurately, but it has the disadvantage of being unable to handle well those variables with just a few values. CORRELATION does not indicate accurately the association between two variables if the association is not linear.

We also introduced the command SAMPLE, which enables you to select out a randomly selected proportion of your cases when you want to reduce the sample size.

In the next chapter we will discuss the analytical technique known as multiple regression. This will enable you to look at the combined effects of several independent variables. At the same time, you can control for the effects of the independent variables on each other's association with the dependent variable.

RESEARCH PROJECT WORK

1. For your research project data set, do a PLOT of the association between AGE and INCOME.

2. For your research project data set, produce the correlation coefficients of all the variables with each other.

REVIEW QUESTIONS

8.1 Write a command that would produce a scatterplot with INCOME on the vertical axis and EDUC on the horizontal axis.

8.2 Write a command that would produce two scatterplots, one with INCOME on the vertical axis and AGE on the horizontal axis and one with EDUC on the vertical axis and AGE on the horizontal axis. Add the additional command that will produce the correlation coefficient for each scatterplot.

8.3 Write the command that would produce the correlation coefficient of HAPPY with HEALTH.

8.4 Write the commands that would produce the correlation coefficients of INCOME, AGE, FAMSIZE, and CARSIZE in the output format discussed in this chapter.

8.5 Would a scatterplot of number of cars in family on the vertical axis and family income on the horizontal axis be very revealing? If not, why?

8.6 What problem would arise if you produced a scatterplot of income (coded into ten categories) by education using a data file with 10,000 cases? How could you solve the problem?

8.7 What types of variables can be used in a CORRELATION analysis?

8.8 Infant deaths drop off exponentially as the infant's weight increases. Why would it be poor methodology to use CORRELATION to analyze the association between infant death rates and infant weight without transforming one of the variables? Which variable would you transform and how?

8.9 What is the difference between a correlation coefficient of $-.50$ and a correlation coefficient of $+.50$?

8.10 If the correlation coefficient between HEALTH and EDUC was .20 and the correlation coefficient between HEALTH and INCOME was .30, how would you describe the relative strength of the two associations?

ASSIGNMENT QUESTIONS

8.1 Write the SPSS/PC+ commands necessary to produce a scatterplot with IN-COME on the vertical axis and AGE on the horizontal axis. Include the command that will add correlation coefficient to the scatterplot output.

8.2 Write the SPSS/PC+ commands necessary to produce three scatterplots (including correlation coefficients) with EDUC on the vertical axis and MAEDUC, PAEDUC, and SPEDUC on the horizontal axis.

8.3 Write the SPSS/PC+ commands necessary to produce the correlation coefficient for the association between HEALTH and EDUC.

8.4 Write the SPSS/PC+ command necessary to produce the correlation coefficients for all the variables in a data file with each other. Include the command that will produce the nonredundant format used in this chapter.

8.5 Why would a scatterplot of the NORC84 variables HAPPY with HEALTH be inappropriate?

8.6 Would it be correct to use CORRELATION to examine the association between the NORC84 variables HAPPY and MARITAL? Why?

8.7 What is the difference in meaning between positive and negative correlation coefficients?

8.8 If the correlation coefficient between AGE and HAPPY was .20 and the correlation coefficient between HEALTH and HAPPY was .40, what would that mean about their relative strength?

8.9 What distortion would probably occur if the association INCOME and AGE was measured with the correlation coefficient?

8.10 What could be done to make correlation coefficient a better measure of the association between INCOME and AGE?

PART 2

ADVANCED TECHNIQUES

Very useful analyses can be produced using the statistical procedures discussed in Part 1, and you have to use these procedures to clean your data and become familiar with the distributions of your variables and their bivariate associations. There will come a time, however, when you will want to move on to more powerful techniques for analyzing multivariate associations. The procedures we present in Part 2 (multiple regression, analysis of variance, discriminate function analysis, log-linear analysis, and factor analysis) enable you to uncover associations that are difficult or impossible to detect using the techniques discussed in Part 1.

We present the material in Part 2 with the assumption that you now have a basic knowledge of statistics and of SPSS/PC+. The examples present only the statistical procedure commands and assume that you have already used the GET command to access an SPSS system file.

We present a short discussion of the statistical basis of each procedure, but our primary intent is to introduce the SPSS/PC+ commands rather than to teach statistics. For a complete explanation of these statistical techniques, you will need to refer to an advanced statistics book. The Russell Sage Foundation publishes a good series of papers on these methods written for the non-mathematician reader: *Quantitative Applications in the Social Sciences*. In the Additional Resources section at the end of each chapter, we refer you to the appropriate paper from this series.

The statistical procedures discussed in Part 2 require data sets with at least 100 cases for most analyses. Therefore, to use the research project data that was gathered and used in Part 1, you will need to merge together the data files of several students.

9

EXAMINING THE COMBINED EFFECTS OF MANY INDEPENDENT VARIABLES: MULTIPLE REGRESSION

New SPSS/PC+ Command:

REGRESSION

We have seen that health, age, education, income, and sex are all associated with the probability of people reporting they are happy. However, what if we want to examine the effects of each of those variables controlling for the effects of all the other variables in our analysis? A crosstabulation or breakdown would be very difficult to interpret. Multiple regression is a technique that will do what we want and still be easy to interpret. Multiple regression will show us the effects of each variable, controlling for the effects of other variables.

9.1 When to Use REGRESSION

The advantage of multiple regression is that it shows both the combined effects of a set of independent variables and the separate effects of each independent variable controlling for the others. A drawback of multiple regression is that it requires several assumptions about the distribution of each variable and the associations among the variables. Multiple regression applies best to an analysis in which both the dependent variable and the independent variable are normally distributed interval variables. However, ordinal variables are commonly used as well, and moderate deviations from normality do not bias the results greatly.

Multiple regression also assumes that the effects of the independent variables are linear—that is, that the effect of a unit difference in an independent variable is the same at all points in the range of the variable. Another assumption of multiple regression is that the independent variables are not correlated with one another (see Section 9.4). Multiple regression can be used with categorical variables through a technique known as dummy coding (see Section 9.5).

If the relationship between the independent variable and the dependent variable is nonlinear, the independent variable can be transformed (see Section 9.6).

9.2 How to Use REGRESSION

The command that produces multiple regression analyses in SPSS/PC+ is REGRESSION. REGRESSION has three required subcommands. The first subcommand, VARIABLES =, is followed by a list of all the variables that will be used. The second required subcommand, DEPENDENT =, is followed by each variable that you want to use as a dependent variable. For both subcommands, variable names are separated by one or more spaces or commas. A different multiple regression analysis will be produced for each dependent variable. The third subcommand is METHOD = ENTER. (Besides ENTER there are five other methods that are a bit more complex.)

To run REGRESSION with HAPPY as the dependent variable and SEX, AGE, EDUC, INCOME, HEALTH, and MARITAL as independent variables, the following commands are needed. MARITAL was recoded into a dichotomous variable (married = 1, unmarried = 0).

```
regression variables=happy sex age educ income
                health marital/
           dependent=happy/
           method=enter.
```

Note that each subcommand is followed by a slash. Part of the output from these commands is presented in Table 9.1. An example of complete output is given in Table 9.2 at the end of Section 9.5.

TABLE 9.1 Partial Output from REGRESSION Command

MULTIPLE R	.33261
R SQUARE	.11063
ADJUSTED R SQUARE	.10654

F = 27.03512   Signif F = .0000

VARIABLES IN THE EQUATION

VARIABLE	B	SE B	BETA	T	SIG T
MARITAL	-.229	.038	-.174	-6.112	.0000
AGE	-.005	.001	-.129	-4.622	.0000
SEX	-.111	.035	-.084	-3.208	.0014
HEALTH	-.009	.006	-.046	-1.496	.1349
EDUC	.152	.023	.189	6.573	.0000
INCOME	-.025	.010	-.082	-2.570	.0103
(CONSTANT)	2.230	.125		17.834	.0000

9.3 Interpreting REGRESSION Output

In Table 9.1, the multiple R is the correlation between the dependent variable and the entire set of independent variables. The multiple R squared (R^2) is the proportion of variance in the independent variable associated with variance in the independent variables. This proportion is a good indicator of the explanatory power of the regression model.

The adjusted R^2 is corrected for the number of cases. A small number of cases relative to the number of variables in the multiple regression can bias upwards the estimate of R^2. When your sample size is less than ten cases per variable, you will notice that the adjusted R^2 decreases substantially relative to the unadjusted R^2 if the sample size is reduced.

The beta column indicates the values of the standardized regression coefficient. Beta represents the effect that a standard deviation difference in the independent variable would have on the dependent variable in standard deviation (the standardized scores of the dependent variable). The beta for HEALTH is .204, which means a difference of one standard deviation in HEALTH is predicted to cause a difference of .204 standard deviation in HAPPY. Because the coefficient is positive, a person with a lower score on HEALTH is predicted to have a lower score on HAPPY. Recall that the happiest category and the healthiest category are coded 1, the least healthy category is coded 4, and the least happy category is coded 3. So the beta for HEALTH indicates that people who report feeling healthy are more likely to report feeling happy. Based on the betas, differences in health have the greatest impact on happiness, and the differences in marital status have the second greatest impact.

Because the beta coefficient for MARITAL is negative with married people coded 1 and unmarried coded 0, we can conclude that married people tend to be happier than unmarried people.

Another method of evaluating the importance of an independent variable is to observe the change in the R^2 when it is added to or dropped from the analysis. This can be done by using more than one METHOD = ENTER subcommand with independent variables specified after ENTER. The variables specified on each METHOD = ENTER subcommand will be added to the ones already in the analysis. To produce two regressions, one with MARITAL and one without, the commands would be

```
regression variables=happy sex age educ income
                     health marital/
        dependent=happy/
        method=enter sex age educ income health/
        method=enter marital.
```

The T statistic is a measure of the distance of beta from zero in a probability distribution. The SIG T (significance of *t*) is the probability that such deviation from zero would be due to sampling error. For MARITAL, the first predictor variable, the SIG T is .0000, which indicates that a beta this large would occur from sampling error less than one time out of 1,000.

Residuals are the errors in prediction. They are obtained by subtracting the actual score from the predicted score for each case. If the actual score for a case were 3 and the predicted score were 2.5, the residual would be 0.5.

Doing a scatterplot of the standardized residuals by the standardized predicted scores is a convenient test of whether the model violates assumptions about linearity. If the model is good, the residuals will be randomly distributed for each value of the predicted values. At the same time, there should be more predicted values near zero (the mean of a standardized variable) because the dependent variable is assumed to be normally distributed. To obtain this scatterplot, use the subcommand

```
scatterplot (*res *pre)/
```

Like the subcommands given in Section 9.2, SCATTERPLOT must begin after column 1 and is usually aligned with the other subcommands for clarity.

To see a histogram of the residuals, use the subcommand RESIDUAL =

HISTOGRAM. (Recall that a histogram is the graphic representation of a frequency distribution by a series of bars.) The histogram of the residuals should reveal that they have a normal distribution.

9.4 Multicollinearity

A condition when two or more of the predictor variables may be highly correlated with each other is called **multicollinearity**. It results in unstable coefficients. As you will see through this text, there are a number of ways to solve problems associated with multicollinearity. Given an experimental design, one option is to examine the effects of one predictor while the other is held constant. Through regression analysis one can sometimes look at subgroups to remove one of the correlated variables, much as we did (in Chapter 8) when we did a scatterplot of males over the age of 34. Another option is combining the correlated variables into a composite variable; however, then the separate effects of the variables cannot be studied. Factor analysis is one method of linking variables. Averaging standard scores is another. (For more information on this, see the Blalock text referenced in the Additional Resources section at the end of this chapter.)

Before performing a regression analysis, you should perform a FREQUENCIES analysis to determine whether the variables are normally distributed. Theoretically, the variables should be normally distributed. In practice, multiple regression is recognized as a robust technique that can include non-normally distributed variables, if their deviations from normality are not extreme.

You also need to know the intercorrelations among the variables, which can be obtained using the CORRELATION command. Theoretically, the independent variables should be correlated with the dependent variable, but not with one another. In practice, one often sees intercorrelations as high as .60 among independent variables in a regression analysis. Use only one of a group of highly correlated variables or construct an index.

9.5 Dummy Variables

Nominal variables may be used in REGRESSION by employing a coding technique known as **dummy variables.** The simplest dummy variable would be for a two-category variable such as SEX. Simply code one category 0—let this be the males—and code the other category 1—for the females. This variable can be entered in the REGRESSION as an independent variable. A dummy variable should not be used as a dependent variable in regression if one of the categories contains less than 20 percent of the cases, because the assumption of a normally distributed dependent variable would be violated too greatly. Such a violation would tend to produce unreliable estimates of the regression coefficients.

For a nominal variable with more than two categories, a set of dummy variables is used. The number of dummy variables will be one less than the number of categories. For example, the variable RELIG (religious preference) in the NORC84 file has five categories: Protestant, coded 1; Catholic, coded 2; Jewish, coded 3; None, coded 4; and Other, coded 5. To create a set of dummy variables, the following commands could be used:

```
if relig eq 1 d1=1
if relig ne 1 d1=0
if relig eq 2 d2=1
if relig ne 2 d2=0
if relig eq 3 d3=1
if relig ne 3 d3=0
if relig eq 4 d4=1
if relig ne 4 d4=0
```

For each case, except those in the Other category, one dummy variable would equal 1 and the rest would equal 0. For those in the Other category, all the dummy variables would equal 0. A Protestant, for example, would have a score of 1 on D1 and a score of 0 on D2, D3, and D4.

D1 through D4 would then be entered as independent variables in the REGRESSION. To evaluate the total effects of the RELIG variable on the dependent variable, the dummy variables' collective effects would be used by looking at the R^2 with the set of dummy variables included in the REGRESSION and then the R^2 with the dummy variables dropped from the REGRESSION. The difference in R^2 would be one measure of the impact of the RELIG variable.

Another indicator of the importance of RELIG would be if any of the dummy variables had a statistically significant beta coefficient. The beta coefficient for each dummy variable represents how much greater (or lesser if the sign is negative) cases coded 1 on that variable are predicted to score on the dependent variable (in standardized scores) compared to cases in the category for which all the dummy variables are coded 0. The output in Table 9.2 at the end of this section includes RELIG as a dummy variable. Note that at times scientific notation is used for some numbers. In this notation, the decimal should be moved as indicated by the number following the E. Thus the coefficient $-5.15218E-03$ indicates $-.00515218$.

TABLE 9.2 Complete Output from REGRESSION Command

```
                       **** MULTIPLE REGRESSION ****
Listwise Deletion of Missing Data

Equation Number 1     Dependent Variable..     HAPPY     GENERAL HAPPINESS

Beginning Block Number  1.  Method: Enter
```

Variable(s) Entered on Step Number
```
    1..    D4
    2..    HEALTH     CONDITION OF HEALTH
    3..    D3
    4..    SEX        RESPONDENT'S SEX
    5..    MARITAL    MARITAL STATUS
    6..    D2
    7..    AGE        AGE OF RESPONDENT
    8..    EDUC       HIGHEST YEAR OF SCHOOL COMPLETED
    9..    INCOME     TOTAL FAMILY INCOME
   10..    D1
```

```
Multiple R            .35324
R Square              .12478
Adjusted R Square     .11824
Standard Error        .61219
```

Analysis of Variance

	DF	Sum of Squares	Mean Square
Regression	10	71.48974	7.14897
Residual	1338	501.45318	.37478

F =   19.07522   Signif F =   .0000

------------------ Variables in the Equation -------------------

Variable	B	SE B	Beta	T	Sig T
D4	.133964	.157880	.053604	.849	.3963
HEALTH	.163908	.022675	.203980	7.228	.0000
D3	.034640	.197044	.006580	.176	.8605
SEX	-.097991	.034201	-.074147	-2.865	.0042
MARITAL	-.224775	.036831	-.170641	-6.103	.0000
D2	.137044	.148249	.091480	.924	.3554
AGE	-.005198	.001028	-.138673	-5.058	.0000
EDUC	-.011497	.006088	-.056019	-1.888	.0592
INCOME	-.011288	.004534	-.076652	-2.489	.0129
D1	.004695	.146190	.003449	.032	.9744
(Constant)	2.193919	.191145		11.478	.0000

The code used to produce this table is as follows:

```
recode marital (2,3,4,5=0).
if relig eq 1 d1=1
if relig ne 1 d1=0
if relig eq 2 d2=1
if relig ne 2 d2=0
if relig eq 3 d3=1
if relig ne 3 d3=0
if relig eq 4 d4=1
if relig ne 4 d4=0
regression variables=happy sex age educ income health marital
                     d1 d2 d3 d4/
           dependent=happy/
           method=enter.
```

9.6 Nonlinear Effects Corrected through Variable Transformations

When the residual plot reveals nonlinear effects, the researcher can make adjustments by transforming the dependent variable. For example, if the residuals increase in value as the predicted value increases, you can compute the log of the dependent variable and try using that transformed score as the dependent variable to reduce the errors in your predictions.

There are many ways of transforming the predictor variables or the dependent variables to compensate for nonlinear relationships. The SPSS/PC+ COMPUTE functions make it easy to transform variables, thereby facilitating adjustments for nonlinearity. However, the choice of what transformations to make and how to interpret the coefficients is a complex topic beyond the scope of this book. The readings cited in the Additional Resources section at the end of this chapter are a good beginning if you wish to pursue the subject.

9.7 Interaction Effects

An interaction effect exists when the effects of one variable are influenced by scores on another variable. For example, if the effects of income on happiness were greater for high-education respondents than for low-education respondents, there would be an interaction between income and education. Look for interaction effects when knowledge of your research subject suggests that they exist or when you find irregularities in your residuals.

One way to adjust for interaction effects is to include in the analysis a variable that is a composite of the two variables. For our example of income interacting with education, we could adjust by computing a new variable (income multiplied by education) and including this interaction term in the regression as an independent variable along with its two components. If the beta coefficient for the interaction term is statistically significant, it indicates that its variables have a combined effect as well as separate effects.

9.8 Additional Resources

REGRESSION is discussed on pages B197–243 and C125–146 of the *SPSS/ PC+ V2.0 Base Manual.* Multicollinearity is discussed at pages B232–233.

9.9 Summary

In this chapter we discussed multiple regression. This technique is used to evaluate the effects of a set of independent variables on one dependent variable.

The output from REGRESSION indicates the combined effects of a set of independent variables and also each independent variable's separate effects controlling for the other independent variables. The variables are assumed to be interval or ordinal measures; however, nominal variables can be used with a technique known as dummy variable coding.

Multiple regression assumes that the independent variables are normally distributed and not highly correlated with one another.

RESEARCH PROJECT WORK

1.   For your research project data set, perform a REGRESSION using HAPPY as the dependent variable and INCOME, SEX, EDUC, MARITAL, AGE, HEALTH, and TV HOURS as the independent variables. (If your file has fewer than 100 cases, combine it with those of other students to obtain a minimum of 100 cases.)

2.   Interpret the results from Project 1.

REVIEW QUESTIONS

9.1   What types of variables theoretically can be used in a multiple regression analysis?

9.2   Write the commands necessary to do a multiple regression analysis with HEALTH as the dependent variable and INCOME, EDUC, HAPPY, AGE, and SEX as the independent variables.

9.3   Write the commands necessary to do a multiple regression analysis with HAPPY as the dependent variable and INCOME, HEALTH, and RELIG as the independent variables. (Remember to recode religion into dummy variables.)

9.4   What is the meaning of the multiple R at the top of the table in the REGRESSION output (Table 9.1)? How is it related to the predictive strength of the REGRESSION model?

9.5   What does it mean to have multicollinearity problems? How are multicollinearity problems resolved?

9.6   What would it mean if the SCATTERPLOT of standardized residuals by standardized predicted values was not random?

9.7   Add to the commands required for Review Question 9.2 the subcommand necessary to produce the scatterplot of standardized residuals by standardized predicted values.

ASSIGNMENT QUESTIONS

9.1   Write the commands necessary to perform a multiple regression analysis with INCOME as the dependent variable and EDUC, AGE, and SEX as the independent variables.

9.2   Write the commands necessary to do a multiple regression with the NORC84 file using HAPPY as a dependent variable and INCOME and MARITAL as independent variables. Remember to recode MARITAL into either a dichotomous variable or a set of dummy variables.

9.3   What is the difference between the R^2 and the adjusted R^2 at the top of the table in the REGRESSION output (Table 9.1)?

9.4   Which more accurately indicates the proportion of variance in the dependent variable explained in a multiple regression analysis, the R or the R^2?

9.5   What would you need to do if two independent variables in a multiple regression were correlated at the .95 level?

9.6   How can a researcher detect if the assumptions of linear effects on the dependent variables are violated?

9.7   What subcommand must be added to the REGRESSION command to plot the standardized residuals by the standardized predicted values?

10

MULTIVARIATE COMPARISON OF MEANS: ANALYSIS OF VARIANCE AND MULTIPLE ANALYSIS OF VARIANCE

New SPSS/PC+ Command:

MANOVA

We have seen that, in general, the probability of being happy is higher for people who are female, 40 or older, more educated, more affluent, healthy, and married. However, what about interactions among these variables? Are the effects of being older, for example, greater for men than for women? Are the effects of education the same for both sexes? Are the effects of marital status affected by income?

The MEANS procedure allows multivariate comparisons of means. However, MEANS does not calculate the statistical significance or the strength of the association for more than one predictor value at a time. In other words, we cannot learn the statistical significance of one variable controlling for the effects of one or more other variables. Nor is it easy to assess the strength of the interactions among the predictor variables.

Several SPSS/PC+ programs do analysis of variance of one sort or another. Rather then study them all, we examine MANOVA, the most powerful SPSS/PC+ program for addressing these questions.

10.1 Doing Many Types of Analysis of Variance: MANOVA

The MANOVA program does many types of analysis of variance. Analysis of variance (ANOVA) is especially appropriate when the dependent variable is an interval measure and the predicting variables are nominal. In fact, analysis of variance assumes that the dependent variable is interval and that the variances are equal for all groups. ANOVA is also useful when the predicting variables are interval but nonlinear in their effects.

MANOVA allows us to study the effects of nominal variables and interval variables together. In such an analysis, the interval level variables are termed **covariates** and the technique is called **covariate analysis.**

Finally, MANOVA allows us to look at differences on a set of dependent variables, rather than just one. For example, if we have several measures of happiness, we can perform a composite analysis to determine whether groups differ on them. This last application is the actual multiple analysis of variance from which the program received its name—MANOVA.

10.2 One Dependent Variable with Two or More Independent Variables

We begin our study of the MANOVA command with the case of one dependent variable and two or more independent variables. (The case of one dependent variable and one independent variable can be handled more easily with the MEANS command. See Chapter 7.)

Consider the question of whether differences in happiness by marital status are the same for both males and females. The only statistical procedure command we need is

```
manova happy by marital (1,5) sex (1,2).
```

The (1,5) after MARITAL is required to indicate the low and high categories of MARITAL. The (1,2) after SEX is required to indicate the low and high categories of SEX. Missing values should not be included in the range specified

TABLE 10.1 Partial Output from MANOVA

SOURCE OF VARIATION	MEAN SQUARE	F	SIG. OF F
WITHIN CELLS	.41		
MARITAL	7.66	18.8	.000
SEX	.21	.5	.473
MARITAL BY SEX	.41	1.0	.399

on the command. The MANOVA program assumes that there are no empty categories. If MARITAL category 4 were empty, the values would need to be recoded. For example, the cases with a score of 5 could be recoded as 4. (If you are using any value labels, remember to change them as well.)

The output from this command will contain a table of an analysis of variance, partial contents of which are given in Table 10.1.

The WITHIN CELLS row represents the variance that remains within cells after the cases have been partitioned by the MARITAL and SEX categories. This variance may be thought of as unexplained. This row does not convey information about an association; hence it has no F ratio.

The MARITAL row represents the association between HAPPY and MARITAL. The F ratio is the mean of the differences on HAPPY between MARITAL categories squared (7.66) divided by the mean WITHIN CELLS of the differences on HAPPY squared (.41). For MARITAL the F ratio is 18.8, which indicates that, when we control for the effects of SEX, the differences between MARITAL categories are much greater than the differences within the MARITAL categories. The significance level of F is .000, which indicates that a difference this size would occur fewer than 1 time out of 1,000 by random sampling error.

The SEX row reveals a mean sum of squares of .21, an F of .5, and a significance level of .473. The last statistic indicates that, controlling for MARITAL, the differences by SEX are so small that the probability is 473 times out of 1,000 that such differences could occur because of a mere sampling error.

Our purpose in this analysis is to examine the interaction between marital status and sex. In the MARITAL BY SEX row we see that the mean of differences squared by MARITAL and SEX interactions (.41) round to the same as the mean of differences squared within cells (.41). Hence the F is 1, and the significance level of .399 is too high to give us confidence that the MARITAL BY SEX interactions are anything more than sampling error. We would conclude, then, that the effects of marital status are roughly the same for males and females. Similarly, the effects of the variable SEX are the same for all marital statuses.

But marital status is of significant power in HAPPY ind SS.

10.3 One Dependent Variable, Two Group Variables, and One Covariate

At the beginning of this chapter, we raised the question of whether variances in income would affect the MARITAL-HAPPY association. One way to examine this question is to control for income by including it as a covariate; that is, each individual's score will be adjusted for the effects of income. (Depending on the statistical program used and the options specified, the control will be done before, while, or after the group effects are examined. In MANOVA, as we are using it in this chapter, the control for the covariate is done simultaneously with the examination of the group effects. If an association exists between MARITAL and HAPPY only because married couples have more money than unmarried people, then the association between MARITAL and HAPPY will vanish, once we control for income by including it as a covariate.

The statistical procedure command necessary to produce this analysis is

```
manova  happy by marital (1,5) sex (1,2) with income.
```

Note that the covariate is preceded by the word WITH instead of the word BY. Note also that the name of the covariate is not followed by its low and high values.

Part of the output produced by this MANOVA command using the NORC84

TABLE 10.2 Additional Output from MANOVA

* * ANALYSIS OF VARIANCE * *			
SOURCE OF VARIATION	MEAN SQUARE	F	SIG. OF F
WITHIN CELLS	.40		
REGRESSION	11.12	28.03	.000
CONSTANT	850.49	2143.62	.000
MARITAL	3.89	9.80	.000
SEX	.36	.90	.343
MARITAL BY SEX	.36	.91	.454

REGRESSION ANALYSIS FOR WITHIN CELLS ERROR TERM

DEPENDENT VARIABLE .. HAPPY   GENERAL HAPPINESS

COVARIATE	BETA	T-VALUE	SIG. OF T
INCOME	-.14478	-5.294	.000

file is given in Table 10.2. Essentially the output at the top of Table 10.2 resembles that of the MANOVA without the covariate. Note, however, that the mean sum of squares for MARITAL groups has been reduced from 7.66 to 4.38. This result indicates that roughly one third of the differences by marital status disappear when we control simultaneously for the effects of income. Nonetheless, the remaining mean square has an *F* of 10.6 with a significance level below .001. Hence the differences by marital status remain significant even after controlling for the effects of INCOME.

The lower portion of the table allows us to evaluate the impact of the covariate INCOME. We are given its standardized regression coefficient, or beta (−.14478), *t* value, and significance level, all of which indicate that, for cases with higher incomes, the happiness score is lower. (Recall that lower scores on HAPPY indicate greater happiness.) We can see that the effects of income are significant. Note that the error, or within-cells mean square, has been reduced to .40 from the .41 of the previous example, which did not control for income.

10.4 Multiple Dependent Variable and One or More Group Variables

The distinction between MANOVA and other SPSS/PC+ programs is that MANOVA can handle multiple dependent variable analysis of variance. For example, instead of using only one dependent variable, you can use a set of dependent variables such as SATCITY, SATFAM, SATFRND, and HAPPY. One reason for using multiple variables is that a bias creeps into an analysis when there are a large number of tests of group differences. If you perform tests of group differences on several dependent variables, you increase the likelihood that a given-sized difference will occur from sampling error—much as you would increase the likelihood of rolling 12 with a pair of dice if you rolled the dice four times instead of once.

The command to test whether there are differences by marital status or sex on this set of dependent variables would be

```
manova satcity satfam satfrnd happy
        by marital(1,5) sex(1,2).
```

When there are multiple dependent variables, the output from MANOVA will present first a set of tables for the interaction effects, then a set for the last variable in the command, then a set for the next-to-last variable, and so forth. Each set of tables covers a page of output.

The first statistics on each page are multivariate tests of significance, which are measures of whether groups differ significantly in their scores on the set of dependent variables. The most powerful and robust of these measures is Pillai's trace, which is printed first. The last statistics on each page are the univariate F tests, which indicate whether groups differ on each of the dependent variables considered separately, instead of as a set.

Table 10.3 presents the key statistics produced by our example command. Table 10.4 at the end of this section presents an example of complete MANOVA output for our example command. For the interaction effects of MARITAL BY SEX, we can see from the significance level of Pillai's trace that the effects of marital status differ between men and women. The univariate F tests reveal that the differences in effects of marital status are concentrated in satisfaction with family life.

Pillai's trace is also statistically significant for the effects of SEX. The univariate F tests reveal that the differences are concentrated in satisfaction with family and satisfaction with friends.

For the effects of MARITAL, Pillai's trace is again statistically significant. The univariate F tests reveal that the differences are statistically significant on all four dependent measures.

10.5 Additional Resources

MANOVA is discussed on pages B103–151 and C68–82 of *SPSS/PC+ Advanced Statistics V2.0*.

For a more complete discussion of the statistics of analysis of variance, see Gudmund R. Iversen and Helmut Norpoth's *Analysis of Variance* (Beverly Hills, Calif.: Sage Publications, 1976).

TABLE 10.3 Partial Output from MANOVA Multiple Dependent Variable Command

EFFECT .. MARITAL BY SEX

MULTIVARIATE TESTS OF SIGNIFICANCE

TEST NAME	VALUE	APPROX. F	SIG. OF F
PILLAIS	.031	2.8	.000

UNIVARIATE F-TESTS

VARIABLE	HYPOTH. MS	ERROR MS	F	SIG. OF F
SATCITY	1.40	2.04	.7	.601
SATFAM	11.07	1.57	7.0	.000
SATFRND	1.00	1.37	.7	.572
HAPPY	.95	.40	.6	.671

///

EFFECT .. SEX

MULTIVARIATE TESTS OF SIGNIFICANCE

TEST NAME	VALUE	APPROX. F	SIG. OF F
PILLAIS	.013	4.6	.001

UNIVARIATE F-TESTS

VARIABLE	HYPOTH. MS	ERROR MS	F	SIG. OF F
SATCITY	.00	2.04	.0	.977
SATFAM	26.05	1.57	16.5	.000
SATFRND	7.66	1.37	5.6	.018
HAPPY	.55	.40	1.4	.241

///

EFFECT .. MARITAL
MULTIVARIATE TESTS OF SIGNIFICANCE

TEST NAME	VALUE	APPROX. F	SIG. OF F
PILLAIS	.136	12.6	.000

UNIVARIATE F-TESTS

VARIABLE	HYPOTH. MS	ERROR MS	F	SIG. OF F
SATCITY	18.36	2.04	9.0	.000
SATFAM	51.38	1.57	32.6	.000
SATFRND	4.54	1.37	3.3	.010
HAPPY	7.66	.40	19.0	.000

TABLE 10.4 Complete Output from Example MANOVA Command

```
************************       A N A L Y S I S   O F   V A R I A N C E       ************************

1431 CASES ACCEPTED.
   0 CASES REJECTED BECAUSE OF OUT-OF-RANGE FACTOR VALUES.
  42 CASES REJECTED BECAUSE OF MISSING DATA.
  10 NON-EMPTY CELLS.

   1 DESIGN WILL BE PROCESSED.
```

CORRESPONDENCE BETWEEN EFFECTS AND COLUMNS OF BETWEEN-SUBJECTS DESIGN 1

STARTING COLUMN	ENDING COLUMN	EFFECT NAME
1	1	CONSTANT
2	5	MARITAL
6	6	SEX
7	10	MARITAL BY SEX

EFFECT .. MARITAL BY SEX

MULTIVARIATE TESTS OF SIGNIFICANCE (S = 4, M = -1/2, N = 708)

TEST NAME	VALUE	APPROX. F	HYPOTH. DF	ERROR DF	SIG. OF F
PILLAIS	.03105	2.77924	16.00	5684.00	.000
HOTELLINGS	.03175	2.81049	16.00	5666.00	.000
WILKS	.96909	2.79715	16.00	4332.70	.000
ROYS	.02573				

EIGENVALUES AND CANONICAL CORRELATIONS

ROOT NO.	EIGENVALUE	PCT.	CUM. PCT.	CANON. COR.
1	.02641	83.19290	83.19290	.16041
2	.00359	11.32384	94.51674	.05985
3	.00171	5.38369	99.90043	.04131
4	.00003	.09957	100.00000	.00562

DIMENSION REDUCTION ANALYSIS

ROOTS	WILKS LAMBDA	F	HYPOTH. DF	ERROR DF	SIG. OF F
1 TO 4	.96909	2.79715	16.00	4332.70	.000
2 TO 4	.99469	.84095	9.00	3453.62	.578
3 TO 4	.99826	.61770	4.00	2840.00	.650
4 TO 4	.99997	.04492	1.00	1421.00	.832

UNIVARIATE F-TESTS WITH (4, 1421) D. F.

VARIABLE	HYPOTH. SS	ERROR SS	HYPOTH. MS	ERROR MS	F	SIG. OF F
SATCITY	5.61702	2902.96685	1.40426	2.04290	.68738	.601
SATFAM	44.28819	2237.42740	11.07205	1.57454	7.03191	.000
SATFRND	3.98933	1941.69981	.99733	1.36643	.72988	.572
HAPPY	.95107	573.50268	.23777	.40359	.58913	.671

EFFECT .. SEX

MULTIVARIATE TESTS OF SIGNIFICANCE (S = 1, M = 1, N = 708)

TEST NAME	VALUE	APPROX. F	HYPOTH. DF	ERROR DF	SIG. OF F
PILLAIS	.01268	4.55155	4.00	1418.00	.001
HOTELLINGS	.01284	4.55155	4.00	1418.00	.001
WILKS	.98732	4.55155	4.00	1418.00	.001
ROYS	.01268				

EIGENVALUES AND CANONICAL CORRELATIONS

ROOT NO.	EIGENVALUE	PCT.	CUM. PCT.	CANON. COR.
1	.01284	100.00000	100.00000	.11259

DIMENSION REDUCTION ANALYSIS

ROOTS	WILKS LAMBDA	F	HYPOTH. DF	ERROR DF	SIG. OF F
1 TO 1	.98732	4.55155	4.00	1418.00	.001

TABLE 10.4 Continued

```
********** A N A L Y S I S   O F   V A R I A N C E   *********************************
```

UNIVARIATE F-TESTS WITH (1, 1421) D. F.

VARIABLE	HYPOTH. SS	ERROR SS	HYPOTH. MS	ERROR MS	F	SIG. OF F
SATCITY	.00165	2902.96685	.00165	2.04290	.00081	.977
SATFAM	26.05844	2237.42740	26.05844	1.57454	16.54983	.000
SATFRND	7.65518	1941.69981	7.65518	1.36643	5.60231	.018
HAPPY	.55615	573.50268	.55615	.40359	1.37801	.241

EFFECT .. MARITAL

MULTIVARIATE TESTS OF SIGNIFICANCE (S = 4, M = -1/2, N = 708)

TEST NAME	VALUE	APPROX. F	HYPOTH. DF	ERROR DF	SIG. OF F
PILLAIS	.13646	12.54725	16.00	5684.00	.000
HOTELLINGS	.15184	13.44275	16.00	5666.00	.000
WILKS	.86603	13.05460	16.00	4332.70	.000
ROYS	.11565				

EIGENVALUES AND CANONICAL CORRELATIONS

ROOT NO.	EIGENVALUE	PCT.	CUM. PCT.	CANON. COR.
1	.13077	86.12266	86.12266	.34007
2	.01534	10.10438	96.22704	.12293
3	.00534	3.51442	99.74146	.07286
4	.00039	.25854	100.00000	.01981

DIMENSION REDUCTION ANALYSIS

ROOTS	WILKS LAMBDA	F	HYPOTH. DF	ERROR DF	SIG. OF F
1 TO 4	.86603	13.05460	16.00	4332.70	.000
2 TO 4	.97928	3.31606	9.00	3453.62	.000
3 TO 4	.99430	2.03161	4.00	2840.00	.087
4 TO 4	.99961	.55785	1.00	1421.00	.455

UNIVARIATE F-TESTS WITH (1, 1421) D. F.

VARIABLE	HYPOTH. SS	ERROR SS	HYPOTH. MS	ERROR MS	F	SIG. OF F
SATCITY	73.43940	2902.96685	18.35985	2.04290	8.98713	.000
SATFAM	205.50113	2237.42740	51.37528	1.57454	32.62867	.000
SATFRND	18.15035	1941.69981	4.53759	1.36643	3.32076	.010
HAPPY	30.65423	573.50268	7.66356	.40359	18.98843	.000

EFFECT .. CONSTANT

MULTIVARIATE TESTS OF SIGNIFICANCE (S = 1, M = 1, N = 708)

TEST NAME	VALUE	APPROX. F	HYPOTH. DF	ERROR DF	SIG. OF F
PILLAIS	.79593	1382.64165	4.00	1418.00	.000
HOTELLINGS	3.90026	1382.64165	4.00	1418.00	.000
WILKS	.20407	1382.64165	4.00	1418.00	.000
ROYS	.79593				

EIGENVALUES AND CANONICAL CORRELATIONS

ROOT NO.	EIGENVALUE	PCT.	CUM. PCT.	CANON. COR.
1	3.90026	100.00000	100.00000	.89215

DIMENSION REDUCTION ANALYSIS

ROOTS	WILKS LAMBDA	F	HYPOTH. DF	ERROR DF	SIG. OF F
1 TO 1	.20407	1382.64165	4.00	1418.00	.000

UNIVARIATE F-TESTS WITH (1, 1421) D. F.

VARIABLE	HYPOTH. SS	ERROR SS	HYPOTH. MS	ERROR MS	F	SIG. OF F
SATCITY	3815.17176	2902.96685	3815.17176	2.04290	1867.52359	.000
SATFAM	2583.02598	2237.42740	2583.02598	1.57454	1640.49118	.000
SATFRND	2365.25846	1941.69981	2365.25846	1.36643	1730.97420	.000
HAPPY	1747.01570	573.50268	1747.01570	.40359	4328.67957	.000

10.6 Summary

The MANOVA program does many types of analysis of variance. Analysis of variance is especially appropriate when the dependent variable is an interval measure and the predicting variables are nominal. It is also useful when the predicting variables are interval but nonlinear in their effects.

MANOVA allows us to study the combined effects of nominal variables and interval variables. In such an analysis, the interval-level variables are termed covariates, and the technique is called covariate analysis.

Finally, MANOVA allows us to look at differences on a set of dependent variables, instead of just one. For example, if we have several measures of happiness, we can do a composite analysis to determine whether groups differ on them. This last application is the actual multiple analysis of variance for which the MANOVA program is named.

Analysis of variance assumes that the dependent variable is interval and that the variances are equal for all groups.

In multiple analysis of variance, we also assume that the dependent variables are multivariately normally distributed and the covariance matrices are equal for all groups.

RESEARCH PROJECT WORK

1. For your research project data set, replicate the example MANOVA analyses in this chapter, but replace SATCITY with SATJOB for the last example.

2. For your research project data set, reanalyze the effects of INCOME and EDUC on HAPPY. Choose the form of analysis of variance that you think is most appropriate, and explain the reasons for your choice.

REVIEW QUESTIONS

10.1 What are the advantages of using MANOVA instead of MEANS?

10.2 What assumptions does MANOVA make about the dependent and independent variables?

10.3 What command is needed to do an analysis of variance of EDUC by MARITAL by SEX using the MANOVA procedure?

10.4 Would there be any difficulty with the command in Review Question 10.3 if no cases were coded 4 for the MARITAL variable?

10.5 What command is needed to do an analysis of variance of EDUC by MARITAL by SEX with INCOME as a covariate?

10.6 What command is needed to do an analysis of variance using CONFINAN to CONARMY in the NORC84 file as a set of dependent variables and RELIG and SEX as predictor variables?

10.7 What would it mean if the significance of *F* for MARITAL in Review Question 10.3 were .002?

10.8 What would it mean if the significance of *F* for MARITAL BY SEX in Review Question 10.3 were .000?

10.9 Would marital status be a significant variable in the analysis if the interaction effects of MARITAL BY SEX were significant but the effects of MARITAL were not?

10.10 When there are multiple dependent variables, what statistic indicates whether there are group differences among the predictor groups in their scores on the set of dependent variables?

ASSIGNMENT QUESTIONS

10.1 When is MANOVA preferred over REGRESSION as an analytical technique?

10.2 Would it be appropriate to do an analysis of variance using MANOVA in which MARITAL from the NORC84 file was the dependent variable and the predictor variables were SEX and AGE?

10.3 Write the MANOVA command to do an analysis of variance of INCOME by MARITAL by RELIGION.

10.4 Write the MANOVA command to do an analysis of variance of INCOME by MARITAL by RELIGION using AGE as a covariate.

10.5 Write the MANOVA command to do an analysis of variance using SATCITY to SATHEALT from the NORC84 file as a set of dependent variables and REGION by MARITAL as predictor variables.

10.6 What would it mean if the Pillai's trace in the output from the command in Assignment Question 10.4 were significant at the .005 level for the REGION effect?

10.7 What would it mean if, in output for the REGION effect from Assignment Question 10.5, the univariate *F* test for SATCITY had a significance of .545?

11

DISCRIMINANT FUNCTION ANALYSIS

New SPSS/PC+ Command:

DSCRIMINANT

Our regression analysis in Chapter 9 indicated that, when the effects on reported happiness of the variables sex, age, education, income, health, and marital status are considered simultaneously, the most important variable is health, followed by marital status and income. All the variables had statistically significant effects. However, as we discussed, regression requires the assumption that, for each value of the predictor variable, scores on the dependent variable be normally distributed with equal variances. We might be concerned that this assumption is not met adequately by our happiness measure. Or an examination of the residuals might reveal that the assumption is seriously violated. What could we do then?

The discriminant function analysis produced by the command DSCRIMINANT does not require assumptions about the variance of the dependent variable. In fact, it is designed to work with nominal dependent variables. DSCRIMINANT is a convenient technique for seeing the associations between a large set of independent variables and dependent variables. One of its limitations, however, is that it cannot handle well a dependent variable with a large number of values. Interval variables such as income or education must be recoded into a small number of categories, which involves a loss of detailed information. Hence you would want to use REGRESSION with interval dependent variables, unless they deviate sharply from a normal distribution.

11.1 What Discriminant Function Analysis Is and When to Use It

Discriminant function analysis is a technique for deciding into which category of a variable a case is most likely to fall. For example, you might want to know whether a job applicant is more likely to succeed in a particular position or is more likely to quit or be fired. Or you might want to know whether a home-mortgage applicant is a good risk or is more likely to default on the loan. Perhaps the least popular user of discriminant analysis is the dreaded Internal Revenue Service (IRS). IRS employs the technique to determine the probability that you cheated in filing your income tax return.

The greatest advantage of discriminant function analysis over regression analysis is that the dependent variable can be a nominal measure. Regression analysis can be used for a dichotomous (two-category) nominal dependent variable, if at least 20 percent of the cases are in the smallest category. However, discriminant analysis has the great advantage of being able to classify cases into three or more nominal categories—a task that regression analysis cannot handle. With discriminant analysis, we can judge better whether a person will be a Democrat, Republican, or Independent. We can predict whether one's vacation preference will most likely be Hawaii, Alaska, or Europe.

Discriminant analysis is best served when the independent variables being used to predict the correct classification of cases are interval measures and normally distributed. However, as in regression analysis, nominal independent variables often can be used through dummy variable codings with acceptable results.

11.2 How to Use DSCRIMINANT

Let's consider what occurs in discriminant analysis by replicating our regression analysis of Chapter 9. The dependent variable will still be HAPPY. The discriminant function analysis will predict for each case which of the three happiness scores is most likely. For classification variables we will use sex, age, education, income, marital status, and parenthood.

Our example uses variables from the SPSS/PC+ system file NORC84.

It considers the task of classifying cases into one of the three categories of HAPPY using as predictors the variables SEX, AGE, EDUC, INCOME, and MARITAL. (CHILDS will be added later.)

The SPSS/PC+ commands would be

```
recode marital (2 thru 5=0).
dscriminant groups=happy (1,3)/
           variables=sex age educ income health
                     marital/
           priors=size/
           statistics=13.
```

The GROUPS = subcommand indicates the dependent variable for which group membership is being predicted. The numbers in parentheses following the variable name indicate the low and high values of the dependent variable.

The VARIABLES = subcommand is followed by a list of the predictor variables.

The PRIORS = SIZE subcommand is needed when we want the cases to be classified using prior knowledge to the proportion in each category in the sample. For example, if 15 percent of the cases in the sample are in category 1, then the analysis uses this knowledge in making the predicted classifications.

When group sizes are very unequal, small groups can have a low percentage of correct classifications even though the overall correct classification percentage is high. Using PRIORS = SIZE can worsen this problem by causing the classification of a disproportionately large number of cases into the category that has the highest proportion of the cases.

The STATISTICS = 13 command produces a table showing the accuracy of the DSCRIMINANT analysis in classifying cases.

11.3 The Accuracy of Discriminant Analysis

We use discriminant analysis to predict group membership; therefore, an obvious measure of our success is the percentage of cases that are classified correctly. Table 11.1 shows a portion of the actual output from our commands of the preceding section. The simplest summary statistic to look at is the percent of cases correctly classified, which is given at the end of the table. In our example, 57.44 percent of cases are correctly classified. Let's compare this result to how many cases would be correctly classified by random assignment.

With two groups of equal size, we would expect 50 percent of the classifi-

TABLE 11.1 Partial Output of DSCRIMINANT

	NO. OF	PREDICTED	GROUP	MEMBERSHIP
ACTUAL GROUP	CASES	1	2	3
GROUP 1 VERY HAPPY	456	160 35.1%	292 64.0%	4 .9%
GROUP 2 PRETTY HAPPY	689	96 13.9%	588 85.3%	5 .7%
GROUP 3 NOT TOO HAPPY	166	16 9.6%	145 87.3%	5 3.0%
UNGROUPED CASES	18	4 22.2%	14 77.8%	0 .0%

PERCENT OF "GROUPED" CASES CORRECTLY CLASSIFIED: 57.44%

cations to be correct by chance. However, when the groups are not of equal size and when each group is randomly assigned the number of cases equal to its size, the expected percent of correct classifications is found by squaring the proportion in each group and then summing the squares. In our example, this expected percent would be

$$(.34)^2 + (.52)^2 + (.12)^2 + (.01)^2 \times 100 = 40\%$$

We can evaluate our model by comparing its proportion of errors $(1 - .57 = .43)$ to the proportion of errors that would occur if cases were classified randomly $(1 - .42 = .58)$. Therefore, our model enabled us to reduce the proportion of errors by

$$[(.58 - .43)/.58] \times 100 = 26\%$$

This amount is the random-error proportion minus the model-error proportion, and then divided by the random-error proportion so that the reduction in error is expressed as a proportion of the original-error proportion.

Returning to the classification results given in Table 11.1, note that each horizontal row represents the actual group membership. The first column heading is ACTUAL GROUP. Under this heading the 1 identifies the row of group 1's statistics, 2 identifies the row of group 2's statistics, and so on. Proceeding to the NO. OF CASES column, we see that group 1 has 456 cases, group 2 has 689 cases, and group 3 has 66 cases.

The next three columns indicate the predicted group memberships. In this table, the correct predictions are given by the diagonal percents from the upper-left number, 35.1%, to the bottom-right number, .0%. The number above each percentage is the actual number of cases predicted to have that group membership.

11.4 Classifying Unknown Cases

Thus far we have discussed how to derive a predictive discriminant model from a set of cases for which we know the score on the dependent variable. What if, after we have the predictive discriminant model, we want to use it to predict the group membership of cases for which we do not have that information?

The simplest method is to use the SELECT subcommand to choose the cases used for calculating the discriminant function. The STATISTICS = 13 command will produce two sets of classification statistics—one for the SELECT cases and one for the remaining cases. The STATISTICS = 14 command will produce each case's predicted group membership and the probability of its being in that group.

Suppose, for example, we want to predict happiness levels for a sample of people for whom we have data for the predictor variables but not for the dependent variable, HAPPY. We first would create a variable that separated the cases with known HAPPY data from those with unknown HAPPY data. Let's assume that the unknown cases are for the year 1985 and that a variable YR is coded 84 for the known cases and 85 for the unknown cases. If we add the SELECT subcommand to the DSCRIMINANT command, our example will read

```
recode marital (2 thru 5=0)
dscriminant groups=happy (1,3)/
         variables=sex age educ income health
                 marital/
         priors=size/
         select=yr (84)/
         statistics = 13 14.
```

11.5 Evaluating the Importance of Variables: The Discriminant Function Coefficients

To determine the contribution of a particular variable to the accuracy of the discriminant analysis classifications, you can repeat the analysis but drop or add the variable in question from the VARIABLES = subcommand. The change in the percent of cases classified correctly when the variable is dropped or added represents the variable's contribution.

Contribution = percent correct with variable − percent correct without

variable

Another method of assessing the importance of a particular variable is to look at its discriminant function coefficient. Discriminant analysis produces discriminant function coefficients for each predicting variable. For each case the score on a variable is multiplied by the variable's discriminant function coefficient. For each case the multiplication is done for all its variable scores and the products are summed. This sum is the case's **discriminant function score.** The discriminant function coefficients are calculated to maximize the differences between the groups in discriminant function scores. In other words, the ratio of between-groups variance to within-groups variance is maximized.

The set of standardized discriminant function coefficients for the predicting variables is produced as part of the DSCRIMINANT output. The standardized coefficients for our example are given in Table 11.2.

The term *standardized* indicates that each variable score is standardized before it is multiplied by the coefficient. In standardizing a variable score, the

TABLE 11.2 Standardized Coefficients with DSCRIMINANT

STANDARDIZED CANONICAL DISCRIMINANT FUNCTION COEFFICIENTS

	FUNCTION 1	FUNCTION 2
SEX	0.27	0.06
AGE	0.40	−0.67
EDUC	0.15	0.63
INCOME	0.26	0.13
HEALTH	−0.59	0.32
MARITAL	0.54	0.04

mean for that variable is subtracted from the score, and then the difference is divided by the standard deviation of the variable. For AGE the mean is 34 and the standard deviation is 8. Thus, for a case with a score of 40 on AGE, the standardized score would be

$$(40 - 34)/8 = .75$$

Algebraically the formula is

$$\frac{X - \overline{X}}{S_x}$$ where X equals a case score on a variable,

$\overline{X}$ is the mean for the variable, and

S_x is the standard deviation for the variable.

Standardized variables have a mean of 0 and a standard deviation of 1.

Standardized coefficients are used to remove the effects of differing means and differing standard deviations in the predicting variables. Otherwise, variables with smaller standard deviations would tend to have larger coefficients, making it difficult to assess the relative importance of the predicting variables.

The coefficients for the first function are the most important. As in our regression analysis example in Chapter 9, the variable with the biggest effect on happiness is health, followed by marital status and age. The signs of the coefficients in discriminant analysis have no special meaning. Because the dependent variable is treated as a nominal measure, we cannot think in terms of positive or negative associations.

As in regression analysis, correct assessment of each predictor variable's importance depends on having all the relevant variables in the equation.

The DSCRIMINANT program does not produce an estimate of the statistical significance of each predictor variable. To approximate the contribution of a particular variable to the statistical significance of a discriminant analysis, you will need to drop the variable in question, repeat the analysis, and then compare the statistical significance of the analyses with and without the variable. The variable's contribution is the reduction in the statistical significance, which is the likelihood that the group differences are the result of sampling probability error. (The statistical significance of an analysis is given by the Wilks' lambda, discussed in the next section.)

11.6 Evaluating the Importance of Functions: Eigenvalue, Canonical Correlation, and Wilks' Lambda

Discriminant analysis maximizes the between-groups differences on discriminant scores and minimizes the within-groups differences. Hence, one measure of how well a discriminant analysis worked is to compare the between-groups variance to the within-groups variance. The **eigenvalue,** which in DSCRIMINANT output is the between-groups variance divided by the within-groups variance, is one statistic for evaluating the worth of a discriminant analysis. An eigenvalue of 0 means that the discriminant analysis had no discriminating value, whereas an eigenvalue above 0.40 is considered excellent. (The discriminant analysis eigenvalue has no upper limit.) The eigenvalues for our example are given in the second column of Table 11.3.

The **canonical correlation** squared is the ratio of the between-groups variance in scores on the function to the total variance in scores. It is a good measure of how well the function discriminates between groups on a scale that ranges from 0.0 to 1.0.

Wilks' lambda (also called the *U* statistic) is the within-groups sum of squares divided by the total sum of squares. This ratio can vary from 0.0 to 1.0. The lower Wilks' lambda is, the better the discriminating power of the model. The Wilks' lambdas for our example are given in Table 11.3. In the AFTER FUNCTION column, the 0 indicates what the Wilks' lambda in that row is for when all the functions are in the analysis. The lambda of 0.88 indicates that differences between groups account for 12 percent of the variance in the predicting variables. The lambda for AFTER FUNCTION 1 indicates what percent of the variance is accounted for by group differences after the effects of function 1 are removed. The lambda of 0.99 indicates that the proportion of accounted-

TABLE 11.3 Measurement of Accuracy with DSCRIMINANT

CANONICAL DISCRIMINANT FUNCTIONS

FUNCTION	EIGENVALUE	CANONICAL CORRELATION
1	0.12	0.33
2	0.01	0.11

AFTER FUNCTION	WILKS' LAMBDA	CHI SQUARE	SIGNIFICANCE
0	0.88	170.4	0.0000
1	0.99	17.3	0.0039

for variance remaining after the effects of function 1 are removed is .01. We can see, therefore, that the effects of function 1 are much greater than the effects of function 2.

Table 11.3 also shows that, when none of the functions have been dropped from the analysis, the statistical significance is 0.0000 and, when the first function is dropped from the analysis, the statistical significance is 0.0039.

11.7 Pooled Within-Groups Correlations with Functions

A statistic for examining a variable's association with a discriminant function is the Pearson correlation coefficient between a variable and that function. The DSCRIMINANT output produces this statistic for each of the variables (see Table 11.4).

The first function accounted for 12 percent of the "explained" variance (its canonical correlation squared) in the predictor variables, compared to 1 percent for the second function. Therefore, the correlations with the first function are more important than the correlations with the second function.

Variables that correlate below 0.20 with a function have only a weak association with it, and their effects tend to be unstable. The standardized discriminant function coefficients are better than the correlations for assessing a variable's impact on the discriminant function scores of cases and their predicted classification.

We can also judge the impact of an individual variable by adding or drop-

TABLE 11.4 Correlations with DSCRIMINANT

STRUCTURE MATRIX:
POOLED WITHIN-GROUPS CORRELATIONS BETWEEN DISCRIMINATING VARIABLES
    AND CANONICAL DISCRIMINANT FUNCTIONS
(VARIABLES ORDERED BY SIZE OF CORRELATION WITHIN FUNCTION)

	FUNC 1	FUNC 2
MARITAL	0.62	0.07
INCOME	0.59	0.35
HEALTH	−0.58	−0.11
SEX	0.16	0.00
AGE	0.19	−0.76
EDUC	0.32	0.76

ping it from the analysis and observing changes in the percent of cases classified correctly, the eigenvalues, the canonical correlations, and the Wilks' lambda. Table 11.5 at the end of this section gives the complete output from DSCRIMINANT when CHILDS is added to the analysis. The code used to produce this table is as follows:

```
recode marital (2 thru 5=0).
dscriminant groups=happy(1, 3)/
           variables=sex age educ income health marital
                       childs/
           priors=size.
```

(The sample changes slightly because there were 11 cases with missing values on CHILDS who were not dropped from the analysis.) When CHILDS is included in the analysis, the percentage of correctly classified cases actually drops, as does the canonical correlation coefficient. CHILDS's standardized discriminant coefficient for function 1 is the lowest for any of the predictor variables (-0.09). All the evidence suggests that parenthood is not having an impact on happiness.

11.8 Multicollinearity Problems

As you may recall from Chapter 9, multicollinearity—when two or more of the predictor variables may be highly correlated with each other—results in unstable coefficients. One way to deal with multicollinearity is to combine the highly correlated variables into a composite variable. A second way to eliminate multicollinearity is to drop one of the two highly correlated variables.

Before doing a discriminant analysis, produce a correlation coefficient matrix and examine the correlations among the predictor variables. If any of the correlations between two predictor variables is above 0.70, consider carefully the possibility of dropping one of the variables from the analysis or combining the variables.

If the group membership variable has only two categories, the higher the correlation between a predictor variable and the dependent variable, the better. Just be sure you do not have a tautological relationship; that is, be sure you are not using one measure of an attribute to predict another measure of the same attribute. For example, it would not be reasonable to use years of education to predict whether or not a person is a college graduate. If the group membership variable has more than two nominal categories that cannot be ranked, its cor-

TABLE 11.5 Complete Output from Example DSCRIMINANT Command

D I S C R I M I N A N T   A N A L Y S I S

ON GROUPS DEFINED BY HAPPY   GENERAL HAPPINESS

1473 (UNWEIGHTED) CASES WERE PROCESSED.
 173 OF THESE WERE EXCLUDED FROM THE ANALYSIS.
  18 HAD MISSING OR OUT-OF-RANGE GROUP CODES.
 145 HAD AT LEAST ONE MISSING DISCRIMINATING VARIABLE.
  10 HAD BOTH.
1300 (UNWEIGHTED) CASES WILL BE USED IN THE ANALYSIS.

NUMBER OF CASES BY GROUP

	NUMBER OF CASES		
HAPPY	UNWEIGHTED	WEIGHTED	LABEL
1	451	451.0	VERY HAPPY
2	685	685.0	PRETTY HAPPY
3	164	164.0	NOT TOO HAPPY
TOTAL	1300	1300.0	

ANALYSIS NUMBER   1

DIRECT METHOD: ALL VARIABLES PASSING THE TOLERANCE TEST ARE ENTERED.

MINIMUM TOLERANCE LEVEL.............   0.00100

CANONICAL DISCRIMINANT FUNCTIONS

MAXIMUM NUMBER OF FUNCTIONS............   2
MINIMUM CUMULATIVE PERCENT OF VARIANCE......   100.00
MAXIMUM SIGNIFICANCE OF WILKS' LAMBDA.......   1.0000

PRIOR PROBABILITIES

GROUP	PRIOR	LABEL
1	0.34692	VERY HAPPY
2	0.52692	PRETTY HAPPY
3	0.12615	NOT TOO HAPPY
TOTAL	1.00000	

TABLE 11.5 *Continued*

D I S C R I M I N A N T   A N A L Y S I S

CANONICAL DISCRIMINANT FUNCTIONS

FUNCTION	EIGEN-VALUE	PERCENT OF VARIANCE	CUMULATIVE PERCENT	CANONICAL CORRELATION	: AFTER : FUNCTION	WILKS' LAMBDA	CHI-SQUARE	D.F.	SIGNIFICANCE
					: 0				
1*	0.12520	87.68	87.68	0.3335760	: 1	0.8733569	175.22	14	0.0000
2*	0.01760	12.32	100.00	0.1315086		0.9827055	22.575	6	0.0010

* MARKS THE 2 CANONICAL DISCRIMINANT FUNCTIONS REMAINING IN THE ANALYSIS.

STANDARDIZED CANONICAL DISCRIMINANT FUNCTION COEFFICIENTS

	FUNC 1	FUNC 2
SEX	0.27448	0.04831
AGE	0.43428	-0.44218
EDUC	0.13995	0.42995
INCOME	0.22672	0.12290
HEALTH	-0.59839	0.31491
MARITAL	0.57623	0.13901
CHILDS	-0.09066	-0.53120

STRUCTURE MATRIX:

POOLED WITHIN-GROUPS CORRELATIONS BETWEEN DISCRIMINATING VARIABLES
AND CANONICAL DISCRIMINANT FUNCTIONS
(VARIABLES ORDERED BY SIZE OF CORRELATION WITHIN FUNCTION)

	FUNC 1	FUNC 2
MARITAL	0.62334*	0.06193
HEALTH	-0.58351*	-0.07599
INCOME	0.57782*	0.30161
SEX	0.16060*	-0.04068
CHILDS	0.07290	-0.74606*
AGE	0.18091	-0.68500*
EDUC	0.31873	0.65358*

CANONICAL DISCRIMINANT FUNCTIONS EVALUATED AT GROUP MEANS (GROUP CENTROIDS)

GROUP	FUNC 1	FUNC 2
1	0.41776	-0.09231
2	-0.11326	0.11816
3	-0.67576	-0.23966

CLASSIFICATION RESULTS -

ACTUAL GROUP	NO. OF CASES	PREDICTED GROUP MEMBERSHIP		
		1	2	3
GROUP 1 VERY HAPPY	451	158 35.0%	288 63.9%	5 1.1%
GROUP 2 PRETTY HAPPY	685	103 15.0%	569 83.1%	13 1.9%
GROUP 3 NOT TOO HAPPY	164	18 11.0%	139 84.8%	7 4.3%
UNGROUPED CASES	18	4 22.2%	14 77.8%	0 0.0%

PERCENT OF "GROUPED" CASES CORRECTLY CLASSIFIED: 56.46%

CLASSIFICATION PROCESSING SUMMARY

    1473 CASES WERE PROCESSED.
       0 CASES WERE EXCLUDED FOR MISSING OR OUT-OF-RANGE GROUP CODES.
     155 CASES HAD AT LEAST ONE MISSING DISCRIMINATING VARIABLE.
    1318 CASES WERE USED FOR PRINTED OUTPUT.

relation coefficients with other variables are useless, even though the program will calculate them (see the discussion in Chapter 7 of levels of measurement).

11.9 Group Centroids

The **group centroid** is the point corresponding to the mean score of the group on each function. In Table 11.5 (given at the end of Section 11.7), the mean score for the very happy cases on function 1 is 0.42, and their mean score on function 2 is −0.09. In classifying cases, the predicted group membership is the one whose centroid is closest to the case's discriminant function scores. For two functions, the group centroids can be plotted on a plane with each function serving as an axis. A case will be classified into the group that has the centroid closest to the case's own point when plotted on the grid formed by the two functions.

11.10 The Number of Functions

When there are more than two groups in a discriminant analysis, more than one discriminant function can be calculated. If the number of groups is K, then $K - 1$ discriminant functions can be computed. Thus with three groups, two discriminant functions can be calculated. With four groups, three discriminant functions can be calculated, and so on.

The first function has the maximum ratio of between-groups variance to within-groups sums of squares. The second function will be uncorrelated with the first function and will maximize the remaining between-groups variance to within-groups sums of squares, subject to the constraint that the functions are uncorrelated.

The output from the multigroup discriminant analysis will include an analysis of variance for each function. We may decide to use in the analysis only those functions that have a substantial between-groups F ratio. To limit the number of functions used in the analysis, use the FUNCTIONS subcommand as illustrated (indent it at least one space if it begins a line).

```
functions=1
```

Note that the number of functions to be used is specified after the equals sign. In our example it is 1.

11.11 Additional Resources

The DSCRIMINANT command is discussed on pages B1–39 and C13–23 of *SPSS/PC+ Advanced Statistics V2.0*.

For a more complete discussion of the statistics of discriminant function analysis, see William R. Klecka's *Discriminant Analysis* (Beverly Hills, Calif.: Sage Publications, 1980).

11.12 Summary

In a discriminant analysis we are concerned with predicting correctly to which of two or more groups each case belongs.

Information in the DSCRIMINANT output lets us know

- the percent of cases we predict correctly,
- how much better our model is than random assignment (this relationship must be calculated), and
- how much of the variance in the predicting variables is accounted for by each function, and whether this amount is statistically significant.

DSCRIMINANT does not directly provide a statistic showing how much each predictor variable contributes to our ability to classify correctly and whether this contribution is statistically significant. We can, however, approximate the contribution of an individual variable by repeating the analysis without the variable and noting the change in the percent of cases classified correctly and the change in the statistical significance of the analysis.

RESEARCH PROJECT WORK

1. For your research project data set, perform a discriminant function analysis of HAPPY using AGE, EDUC, HEALTH, INCOME, MARITAL, and SEX as predictor variables.

2. Discuss the possibility of spuriousness (when a variable appears to cause something but does not) for each of the predictor variables in Project 1. That is, might they be affected by HAPPY instead of, or in addition to, affecting HAPPY? Might both HAPPY and the predictor variable be affected by a third variable and hence be associated without being causally related?

REVIEW QUESTIONS

11.1 Write the SPSS/PC+ command necessary to produce a discriminant analysis with CLASS as the group (dependent) variable and SEX, RACE, AGE, INCOME, EDUC, DEFENSE, and SPEND as predictor variables.

11.2 Using the SPSS/PC+ system file NORC84, write all the SPSS/PC+ commands necessary to access the file and produce the following discriminant analysis. Create the group variable FAMWORK, a combination of family status (CHILDS) and work status (WRKSTAT). Code FAMWORK 1 for women who do not work for pay and who do not have children, 2 for women who do not work for pay and who have children, 3 for women who work for pay and who do not have children, 4 for women who work for pay and who have children. Do the analysis for women only. Use as predictor variables RACE, EDUC, INCOME, AGE, MAWORK, CLASS.

11.3 How can you evaluate whether a discriminant analysis was effective?

11.4 How can you determine the number of cases that would be misclassified by random assignment?

11.5 How can you determine whether a discriminant analysis is statistically correct?

11.6 How can you determine how much an individual function adds to your ability to classify cases correctly?

11.7 How do you determine the statistical significance of a particular function?

11.8 How do you determine the contribution of a particular variable to the correct classification of cases?

11.9 How do you determine the statistical significance of a particular variable?

11.10 Once you have the final discriminant function (or functions) to use for classifying new cases, how do you use it (or them) to classify new cases?

ASSIGNMENT QUESTIONS

11.1 Write the SPSS/PC+ commands necessary to access the file NORC84 and to do a discriminant analysis using UNEMP as the group variable and SEX, AGE, MARITAL, RACE, CHILDS, HEALTH, and HAPPY as the predictor variables.

11.2 What subcommand would you need to add following the VARIABLES = subcommand if the probability of being unemployed was not equal to the probability of being employed? (Let the probability of being unemployed equal .1 and the probability of being employed equal .9.)

11.3 If you ran two discriminant analyses, one with SEX and the other without SEX, in order to determine the importance of SEX in predicting unemployment correctly, how would you interpret the following results?

a. Percent unemployed classified correctly with SEX: 15%

b. Percent unemployed classified correctly without SEX: 12%

c. Statistical significance with SEX = .003

d. Statistical significance without SEX = .060

11.4 How much did the variable SEX affect the statistical significance of the discriminant analysis in Assignment Question 11.3? In other words, how much did the variable SEX reduce the likelihood that the predictions were due simply to probability error?

11.5 How would you evaluate how much the discriminant functions improved your ability to predict whether a person would be unemployed in Assignment Question 11.3?

11.6 Look at the following table. How would you evaluate the decision to include all these variables in a discriminant analysis of being employed versus being unemployed? (Assume that the variables have all been coded as internal or dichotomous variables, and focus your evaluation on the correlation coefficients.)

Pearson Correlation Coefficient Matrix for Assignment Question 11.6

	TRAINING	AGE	SEX	MARITAL	EDUC	DIPLOMA	RACE
TRAINING	1.00						
AGE	- .31	1.00					
SEX	.20	.05	1.00				
MARITAL	.70	.85	.20	1.00			
EDUC	.75	.25	.25	- .20	1.00		
DIPLOMA	.80	.15	.30	- .35	.90	1.00	
RACE	- .15	- .15	.15	- .15	.30	.10	1.00
EMPLOY	.40	.55	- .10	.60	.40	.55	- .30

12

LOG-LINEAR MODELS

New SPSS/PC+ Command:

HILOGLINEAR

We have seen that happiness is affected by income, age, and sex. We have questioned whether the effects of these variables are the same for all groups. For example, perhaps income is more important at some ages than at others. Maybe the effects of age are not the same for men as for women. Answers to these questions may be found in crosstabulation tables, but the tables are so complex and have so many cells that it is a tedious task to evaluate all the possible interactions among the variables.

The log-linear analyses that can be done with the SPSS/PC+ command HILOGLINEAR swiftly untangle the information in a crosstabulation table. The output reveals which associations are most important and whether or not they are statistically significant. With a little additional work, we can state very precisely how interactions among certain variables affect the likelihood that a subject will be in a particular category on another variable.

12.1 When to Use HILOGLINEAR

The program produced by the HILOGLINEAR command is a way of summarizing and highlighting the associations in a complex crosstabulation table. Log-linear models such as HILOGLINEAR are called for when your analysis involves three or more variables and when the variables are nominal, highly skewed in their distribution, or nonlinear in their effects.

Often nominal variables are dummy coded and treated as interval variables in regression or analysis of variance. The more skewed the variable is to one category, the more this practice leads to biased coefficients. For example, if over 80 percent of the labor force is employed, married, and nonmigrant, dummy coding any of these variables in a study of worker satisfaction in the United States could distort the results.

The greatest disadvantage of log-linear models is that they need a large number of cases. A rough rule of thumb is that your sample size should be at least five times the number of cells in the table.

One way researchers reduce the number of cells in the analysis (and hence the number of cases they need) is by collapsing categories or ordinal or interval variables that are being used in a log-linear model. For example, instead of having the exact age of each respondent, one can code age into ten-year intervals. In recoding the categories, some precision is lost; we assume that the effects of the variable do not differ significantly within these categories. Collapsing of categories is a practice to be adopted only from necessity.

12.2 How to Use HILOGLINEAR

As with other advanced techniques, begin a HILOGLINEAR analysis by checking the frequency distribution of all the variables you intend to use to ensure they are coded correctly and to familiarize yourself with their distribution. Because we have already done this initial work on the NORC84 data file in earlier chapters, we can move on to an actual log-linear analysis.

Let's see what more can be learned about happiness using the log-linear analysis produced by the HILOGLINEAR command. (Other log-linear techniques are available with SPSS/PC+; however, HILOGLINEAR is the simplest to use, requires the least computer time, and uses the least CPU memory space.) To use HILOGLINEAR, you must assume that the log-linear effects are hierarchical. This means that if a variable is in the model as a third-order effect, it must be in the model as a second-order effect. (A second-order effect involves the interaction of two variables, a third-order effect involves the interaction of three variables, and so on.) In most analyses this assumption is not bothersome, because the researcher would not conceptualize a variable as having important higher-order effects unless the lower-order effects were also important.

We have reason to believe that happiness is affected by a person's sex and age. Perhaps the effects of age will be different for males than for females. Further along in the analysis, we will be adding more variables (and thus more cells), so we will recode age into ten-year intervals to ensure that we have enough cases. (98 and 99 are missing value codes. Therefore, we cannot use the keyword HI in our RECODE command.) Likewise, we can consider the interactions of INCOME with the other variables, but we need to recode it into a smaller number of categories. Our RECODE statements will be

```
recode age  (18 thru 29=1)  (30 thru 39=2)  (40 thru 49=3)
            (50 thru 59=4)  (60 thru 69=5)  (70 thru 97=6).
recode income (1,2=1)  (3,4=2)  (5,6=3)
            (7,8=4).
```

This recoding of variables leaves us with 120 cells in our crosstabulation table. We find this number by multiplying together the number of categories in each variable

$$(\text{HAPPY} * \text{SEX} * \text{AGE} * \text{INCOME} = 3 * 2 * 6 * 4 = 120)$$

Our NORC84 sample size of 1,473 is far more than $5 * 120 = 600$. (Recall that the sample size should be at least five times the number of cells.)

The simplest approach to using the HILOGLINEAR command in SPSS/PC+ is with the subcommand PRINT ALL: This subcommand produces a table that shows the chi-square and probabilities of each order effect. Recall that a chi-square statistic is based on the difference between what you would expect to find in each cell, if there were no associations, versus what was actually found.

The first-order effects test the assumption that each category of a variable has the same number of cases. This assumption is rarely true, and, because it tells us nothing about associations among the variables, we are not very interested in this statistic.

The two-way, or second-order, effects test the assumption that the variables are independent. The likelihood ratio chi-square for this model can be treated as a total error term that can be partitioned in parts associated with each variable. These effects are the bivariate associations controlling for the effects of the other variables.

The three-way and higher-order effects are interaction effects. These effects are usually small and difficult to interpret. Essentially, an interaction effect means that a variable has one effect for one group but a different effect for another group. For example, if the effects of age on the likelihood of being happy were different for men than for women, this effect would be third-order.

The HILOGLINEAR command and accompanying PRINT ALL subcommand needed for our analysis of the effects of happiness of age controlling for sex and income are

```
hiloglinear sex (1,2) age (1,6) income (1,4)
              happy (1,3) /
              print all.
```

Note that the PRINT ALL subcommand is preceded by a slash indicating the variable specifications have ended. The printout is easier to read if the dependent variable is listed last. When placed in the context of the SPSS/PC+ commands needed to recode AGE and INCOME, our set of commands is

```
recode age (18 thru 29=1) (30 thru 39=2) (40 thru 49=3)
              (50 thru 59=4) (60 thru 69=5) (70 thru 97=6).
recode income(1,2=1) (3,4=2) (5,6=3)
              (7,8=4).
hiloglinear  sex (1,2) age (1,6) income (1,4)
              happy (1,3) /
              print all.
```

12.3 Interpreting HILOGLINEAR Output

The output from the preceding set of commands will include information given in Table 12.1. In the first row of the table, the 1 indicates that this row contains the information on the first-order effects. This information tests the hypothesis that the cases are equally distributed throughout the cells. We are not inter-

TABLE 12.1 Output on Effects from HILOGLINEAR

TESTS THAT K-WAY EFFECTS ARE ZERO.

K	DF	L.R. CHISQ	PROB
1	11	593.2	.000
2	41	263.4	.000
3	62	84.5	.019
4	29	29.9	.579

ested in testing this hypothesis, because we do not expect to have the same number of males as females or the same number of older people as younger people in our sample.

In the second row, the 2 indicates that these effects are second-order. These effects are of interest because we want to know whether the variables SEX, AGE, and INCOME are associated with HAPPY. The 41 in the DF column indicates that there are 41 degrees of freedom when all the second-order effects are considered. The next number to the right, 263.4 in the L.R. CHISQ column, is the likelihood ratio chi-square for the second-order effects. If there were no associations among the variables, this measure would be 0.0. The next number to the right, .000 in the PROB column, is the probability that the chi-square for this row differs from 0.0 because of sampling error. We can see that it is unlikely—less than 1 time out of 1,000—that the associations we find in this row are due to sampling error.

The row beginning with 3 in the K column pertains to third-order effects. The probability of .019 tells us that the third-order effects are **statistically significant**, meaning that they are unlikely to be caused by sampling error.

The final row reflects the fourth-order effects. These effects have a sampling error probability of .579. Fourth-order effects might indicate that the effects of income on happiness for older males are different from the effects of income for older females or that the effects of age on happiness are different for wealthy males than for poor males. It is helpful to know that there are significant fourth-order effects in our analysis, but we are still faced with the task of working through a crosstabulation table to locate them precisely.

The next table of special interest in the output shows partial associations (see Table 12.2). This table gives the partial chi-square and the probabilities for all the associations except the highest-order association. (Information for the highest-order association was given in the preceding table.)

Examine Table 12.2 carefully. The left column, entitled EFFECT NAME, designates each association examined in the analysis. The top row, SEX * AGE * INCOME, shows the association between sex, age, and income. In that row, we can see the following statistics: there are 15 degrees of freedom in this association, the partial chi-square is 21.4, and the probability that an association this large could occur by sampling error is .125. The third-order effect that is most statistically significant is AGE * INCOME * HAPPY, which has a probability of .022 resulting from sampling error. This suggests that the effects of income differ by age, or the effects of age differ by income, or both.

With the exception of the association between age and sex, all the second-order effects are significant, below the .05 level.

The chi-squares for the single variables are all significant; however, this result merely means that there were not an equal number of cases in each of the cells. It tells us nothing about associations between the variables.

TABLE 12.2 Output of Partial Associations from HILOGLINEAR

TESTS OF PARTIAL ASSOCIATIONS.

EFFECT NAME	DF	PARTIAL CHISQ	PROB
SEX*AGE*INCOME	15	21.4	.125
SEX*AGE*HAPPY	10	5.7	.839
SEX*INCOME*HAPPY	6	8.9	.176
AGE*INCOME*HAPPY	30	47.6	.022
SEX*AGE	5	5.0	.413
SEX*INCOME	3	19.8	.000
AGE*INCOME	15	149.0	.000
SEX*HAPPY	2	8.8	.012
AGE*HAPPY	10	33.2	.000
INCOME*HAPPY	6	76.8	.000
SEX	1	32.6	.000
AGE	5	190.6	.000
INCOME	3	25.9	.000
HAPPY	2	344.0	.000

We return to our original question of whether the effects of age on happiness differ for men and women. The SEX * AGE * HAPPY row shows that the differences are so small that 839 times out of 1,000 they could result from sampling error.

Are the effects of income on happiness different for men than for women? The SEX * INCOME * HAPPY row indicates that there are most likely some differences, but they are so small that 176 times out of 1,000 such differences would occur from sampling error.

The output from HILOGLINEAR includes the initial proportion shown in Table 12.3. We can use this table to describe each association more precisely. For example, we can compare the odds of a male over age 70 with income of $10,000 to $19,000 reporting being very happy with the odds of a male under age 30 with the same income being very happy. (Recall that very happy respondents were coded 1 on HAPPY.) To make this comparison, we examine the OBS. COUNT (observed count) column of the table. In Table 12.3 the numbers for the four middle categories of age are omitted for brevity. More complete output is given in Table 12.4 at the end of this section. The code used is as follows:

```
hiloglinear sex (1,2) age(1,6) income(1,4) happy(1,3)/
          print all
```

We can see that 12 of our 55, or 22 percent, of the under-30 males report being very happy. (55 is the total of 12 + 32 + 11.) For the males over age 70, 6

TABLE 12.3 Partial Output on Proportions from HILOGLINEAR

OBSERVED, EXPECTED FREQUENCIES AND RESIDUALS

FACTOR	CODE	OBS. COUNT
SEX	1	
AGE	1	
INCOME	2	
HAPPY	1	12
HAPPY	2	32
HAPPY	3	11
AGE	6	
INCOME	2	
HAPPY	1	6
HAPPY	2	7
HAPPY	3	2

out of 15, or 40 percent, report being very happy. Thus, in this income range the likelihood that a male over age 70 will be very happy is almost twice as great as the likelihood for a male under age 30.

The HILOGLINEAR output gives a staggering amount of information. A sensible approach is to look at the summary statistics on the associations to see which are most important. Then dig into the table of observed counts to see the details of the association.

One also has the option of printing out coefficients and significance levels for each cell. Unfortunately, the present form of HILOGLINEAR output for these statistics is not easy to interpret. Researchers will probably use log-linear models to detect the presence or absence of a model. Afterwards, "it may be easier to measure the strength of association with other statistics." (H.T. Reynolds, *Analysis of Nominal Data* (Beverly Hills, Calif.: Sage Publications, 1977, p. 65.) For example, doing a crosstabulation of HAPPY by AGE controlling for SEX and INCOME would allow us to see easily the percentage of men who were very happy compared to the percentage of women who were very happy in each income group. (See Chapter 6 for a discussion of crosstabulations.)

12.4 Additional Resources

HILOGLINEAR is discussed on pages B183–202 and C39–45 in *SPSS/PC+ Advanced Statistics V2.0.*

For a more complete discussion of log-linear analysis, see David Knoke

TABLE 12.4 More Complete Output from HILOGLINEAR

```
******************       H I E R A R C H I C A L   L O G   L I N E A R       ******************

DATA INFORMATION
     1319 UNWEIGHTED CASES ACCEPTED.
        0 CASES REJECTED BECAUSE OF OUT-OF-RANGE FACTOR VALUES.
      154 CASES REJECTED BECAUSE OF MISSING DATA.
     1319 WEIGHTED CASES WILL BE USED IN THE ANALYSIS.

FACTOR INFORMATION
 FACTOR    LEVEL    LABEL
 SEX         2      RESPONDENT'S SEX
 AGE         6      AGE OF RESPONDENT
 INCOME      4      TOTAL FAMILY INCOME
 HAPPY       3      GENERAL HAPPINESS

DESIGN 1 HAS GENERATING CLASS

     SEX*AGE*INCOME*HAPPY

THE ITERATIVE PROPORTIONAL FIT ALGORITHM CONVERGED AT ITERATION 1.
THE MAXIMUM DIFFERENCE BETWEEN OBSERVED AND FITTED MARGINAL TOTALS IS      .000
AND THE CONVERGENCE CRITERION IS    .250
```

OBSERVED, EXPECTED FREQUENCIES AND RESIDUALS.

FACTOR	CODE	OBS. COUNT & PCT.	EXP. COUNT & PCT.	RESIDUAL	STD. RESID.
SEX	MALE				
AGE	1				
INCOME	1				
HAPPY	1	10.00 (.76)	10.00 (.76)	.000	.000
HAPPY	2	20.00 (1.52)	20.00 (1.52)	.000	.000
HAPPY	3	8.00 (.61)	8.00 (.61)	.000	.000
INCOME	2				
HAPPY	1	12.00 (.91)	12.00 (.91)	.000	.000
HAPPY	2	32.00 (2.43)	32.00 (2.43)	.000	.000
HAPPY	3	11.00 (.83)	11.00 (.83)	.000	.000

INCOME	3						
HAPPY	1	13.00	(.99)	13.00	(.99)	.000	.000
HAPPY	2	25.00	(1.90)	25.00	(1.90)	.000	.000
HAPPY	3	1.00	(.08)	1.00	(.08)	.000	.000
INCOME	4						
HAPPY	1	9.00	(.68)	9.00	(.68)	.000	.000
HAPPY	2	13.00	(.99)	13.00	(.99)	.000	.000
HAPPY	3	3.00	(.23)	3.00	(.23)	.000	.000
AGE	2						
INCOME	1						
HAPPY	1	1.00	(.08)	1.00	(.08)	.000	.000
HAPPY	2	12.00	(.91)	12.00	(.91)	.000	.000
HAPPY	3	2.00	(.15)	2.00	(.15)	.000	.000
INCOME	2						
HAPPY	1	8.00	(.61)	8.00	(.61)	.000	.000
HAPPY	2	19.00	(1.44)	19.00	(1.44)	.000	.000
HAPPY	3	4.00	(.30)	4.00	(.30)	.000	.000
INCOME	3						
HAPPY	1	9.00	(.68)	9.00	(.68)	.000	.000

. .

GOODNESS-OF-FIT TEST STATISTICS

LIKELIHOOD RATIO CHI SQUARE = .00000   DF = 0   P = 1.000
PEARSON CHI SQUARE = .00000   DF = 0   P = 1.000

TESTS THAT K-WAY AND HIGHER ORDER EFFECTS ARE ZERO.

K	DF	L.R. CHISQ	PROB	PEARSON CHISQ	PROB	ITERATION
4	29	29.866	.4207	26.858	.5794	NA
3	91	114.382	.0493	114.080	.0512	NA
2	132	377.831	.0000	385.269	.0000	NA
1	143	970.997	.0000	1101.051	.0000	0

TABLE 12.4 *Continued*

********************************** H I E R A R C H I C A L   L O G   L I N E A R ***********************************

TESTS THAT K-WAY EFFECTS ARE ZERO.

K	DF	L.R. CHISQ	PROB	PEARSON CHISQ	PROB	ITERATION
1	11	593.166	.0000	715.782	.0000	0
2	41	263.449	.0000	271.190	.0000	0
3	62	84.516	.0303	87.221	.0191	0
4	29	29.866	.4207	26.858	.5794	0

TESTS OF PARTIAL ASSOCIATIONS.

EFFECT NAME	DF	PARTIAL CHISQ	PROB	ITER
SEX*AGE*INCOME	15	21.390	.1248	4
SEX*AGE*HAPPY	10	5.711	.8389	3
SEX*INCOME*HAPPY	6	8.949	.1764	4
AGE*INCOME*HAPPY	30	47.643	.0215	5
SEX*AGE	5	5.025	.4128	5
SEX*INCOME	3	19.757	.0002	5
AGE*INCOME	15	149.014	.0000	4
SEX*HAPPY	2	8.780	.0124	5
AGE*HAPPY	10	33.179	.0003	4
INCOME*HAPPY	6	76.839	.0000	3
SEX	1	32.618	.0000	2
AGE	5	190.649	.0000	2
INCOME	3	25.886	.0000	2
HAPPY	2	343.995	.0000	2

and Peter J. Burke's *Log-Linear Models* (Beverly Hills, Calif.: Sage Publications, 1980) and H. T. Reynolds's *Analysis of Nominal Data* (Beverly Hills, Calif.: Sage Publications, 1977).

12.5 Summary

Log-linear models are a way of summarizing and highlighting the associations in a complex crosstabulation table. Log-linear models such as HILOGLINEAR are called for when your analysis involves three or more variables, all of which are either nominal, highly skewed in their distribution, or nonlinear in their effects.

The greatest disadvantage of log-linear models is that they require a large number of cases. A rough rule of thumb is that your sample size should be at least five times the number of cells in the table.

RESEARCH PROJECT WORK

For your research project data file, replicate the example analysis of this chapter. Describe any differences between the outcome of your analysis and the outcome of our example, and discuss the possible causes of these differences.

REVIEW QUESTIONS

12.1 What assumptions are made for regression analysis that are not required for log-linear models?

12.2 What advantages are there to doing a log-linear analysis instead of a crosstabulation?

12.3 How many cases would normally be required to do a log-linear analysis of health (four categories) by marital (five categories) by religion (five categories)?

12.4 Write the SPSS/PC+ commands that would produce a hierarchical log-linear analysis of the variables HEALTH, MARITAL, and RELIGION. Treat HEALTH as the dependent variable. Include the subcommand necessary to produce a printout of associations.

12.5 What would the first-order effects in the analysis of Review Question 12.4 indicate?

12.6 What would the second-order effects from Review Question 12.4 indicate?

12.7 What would the third-order effects from Review Question 12.4 indicate?

12.8 The chi-square and probability of the highest-order effects are omitted from the HILOGLINEAR output for TESTS OF PARTIAL ASSOCIATIONS. How can these statistics be found?

12.9 How would you interpret a probability of .023 for the partial chi-square of the effect HEALTH * MARITAL?

12.10 If your output from HILOGLINEAR indicates that a particular association is significant, what is the simplest way to determine the strength of the association?

ASSIGNMENT QUESTIONS

12.1 What assumptions are made in analysis of variance that are not required in log-linear analysis?

12.2 Write the HILOGLINEAR command and subcommands needed to analyze SEX by RELIGION by MARITAL by SATFAM in the NORC84 file making SATFAM the dependent variable.

12.3 If the following table resulted from the commands in Assignment Question 12.2, what would these statistics mean?

TESTS THAT K-WAY AND HIGHER ORDER EFFECTS ARE ZERO.

K	DF	L.R. CHISQ	PROB
4	14	5.4	.452
3	26	8.2	.220
2	37	40.7	.043
1	45	607.7	.000

12.4 What would the following portion of output from Assignment Question 12.2 indicate?

TESTS OF PARTIAL ASSOCIATIONS

EFFECT NAME	DF	PARTIAL CHISQ	PROB
SEX * RELIG * SATJOB	24	13.654	.354
SEX * MARITAL * RELIG	16	34.234	.463
SEX * MARITAL * SATJOB	70	73.004	.453
SEX * MARITAL	5	5.929	.312
SEX * RELIG	2	2.141	.343
SEX * SATJOB	24	13.654	.050
MARITAL * RELIG	16	34.234	.463
MARITAL * SATJOB	70	73.004	.003
SATJOB * RELIG	5	5.929	.312
SEX	10	2.141	.343

MARITAL	1	33.433	.000
RELIG	5	129.233	.000
SATJOB	2	404.293	.000

12.5 What would the following portion of output from Assignment Question 12.2 indicate?

OBSERVED, EXPECTED FREQUENCIES AND RESIDUALS.

FACTOR	CODE	OBS.	COUNT & PCT.
SEX	1		
MARITAL	1		
RELIGION	1		
SATJOB	1		11.00
SATJOB	2		25.00
SATJOB	3		33.00
SATJOB	4		24.00
SATJOB	5		23.00
SATJOB	6		33.00
SATJOB	7		23.00
SEX	2		
MARITAL	1		
RELIGION	1		
SATJOB	1		22.00
SATJOB	2		50.00
SATJOB	3		66.00
SATJOB	4		48.00
SATJOB	5		46.00
SATJOB	6		66.00
SATJOB	7		46.00

13

FACTOR ANALYSIS

New SPSS/PC+ Command:

FACTOR

Looking at the variables in the NORC84 file, we can see many that may affect happiness that are not yet in our analysis, including SIBS, CHILDS, HELPFUL, FAIR, CONEDUC, CONPRESS, CONLEGI, SATFAM, SATFRND, and SATJOB. On closer inspection, we see that some of these variables together appear to be measuring a more general variable. For example, HELPFUL, FAIR, CON- EDUC, CONPRESS, and CONLEGI may all measure trust in others. SATFAM, SATFRND, and SATJOB may all be indicators of satisfaction with one's social position. SIBS, CHILDS, and MARITAL (which is already in our analysis) may be measures of the extensiveness of one's family network.

Working with a large number of variables is tedious. If the variables are really just different measures of another more general variable, we can facilitate and simplify our work by constructing a measure of the general variable and using that measure in our analysis. **Factor analysis** is a way of measuring a general variable, or **factor**, underlying a large set of variables. This method also helps in dealing with the problem of multicollinearity, discussed in earlier chapters.

13.1 What Factor Analysis Is and When to Use It

Often a researcher has several variables that appear to be related to one another because they are different ways of measuring one general variable or factor.

Factor analysis is a technique for condensing many variables into a few underlying constructs. For example, we might have a 100-item test that we think measures three distinct abilities: verbal, mathematical, and analytical. Using factor analysis we could try to obtain a "factor score" for each of these abilities. Our analysis would reveal whether there were fewer than or more than three distinct factors. Our analysis would also reveal which variables were most closely associated with each factor and would weigh those variables most heavily in calculating the factor scores.

Factor analysis is not necessary when one already knows (1) which variables measure each factor and (2) the variables' relative importance—for example, one may have predetermined that all the variables will be weighted equally.

Before performing a factor analysis, you should examine a correlation matrix of the variables. Because you are assuming that underlying factors account for the variance in all the variables, it is questionable to include any variable whose correlations with the other variables are all below 0.4 in absolute value.

Factor analysis is sometimes used when the researcher has a large set of variables and suspects that they could be summarized more concisely by a few underlying factors but is not certain what these factors would be. This use of factor analysis would be termed *exploratory*.

13.2 How to Use FACTOR

To do a factor analysis for the variables mentioned at the beginning of this chapter as possible influences on happiness, we would use the following commands:

```
factor variables=sibs marital childs helpful fair
              coneduc conpress conlegi satfam
              satfrnd satjob.
```

By default, FACTOR in SPSS/PC+ uses a technique called **principal components** to extract factors. Several other extraction techniques are available; however, principal components is the most frequently used. (See *SPSS/PC+*

Advanced Statistics V2.0, page C-33, for a list of the SPSS/PC+ extraction techniques available and the subcommands used to initiate them.)

First the principal-components method calculates a factor that will explain the maximum variance in all the variables. Then a second factor is calculated that explains the maximum amount of the remaining variance. However, the second factor has the restriction that it cannot be correlated with the first factor. Another way of stating that two factors are not correlated with each other is to say they are **orthogonal**.

The process can be continued until all the variance in the variables has been explained. Normally this point is reached when the number of factors equals the number of variables. Such a solution is not helpful, however, because we are striving for greater simplicity. Having as many factors as there are variables does not simplify anything. Most researchers use the eigenvalue statistic, discussed in the next section (and which you may remember from Chapter 11), to decide how many factors to use in their analysis.

13.3 Output from FACTOR

The first part of the factor analysis will be a table of initial statistics as shown in Table 13.1. The far left column gives the names of all variables used in the factor analysis. To the right of the names is a column of COMMUNALITY statistics. The **communality** statistic for each variable is the proportion of variance in the variable explained by all the factors. The communality of a variable can range

TABLE 13.1 Initial Statistics Output from FACTOR

INITIAL STATISTICS:

VARIABLE	COMMUNALITY	*	FACTOR	EIGENVALUE	PCT OF VAR
		*			
SIBS	1.0	*	1	2.05	18.6
MARITAL	1.0	*	2	1.48	13.4
CHILDS	1.0	*	3	1.33	12.1
HELPFUL	1.0	*	4	1.07	9.7
FAIR	1.0	*	5	.91	8.3
CONEDUC	1.0	*	6	.88	8.0
CONPRESS	1.0	*	7	.83	7.6
CONLEGI	1.0	*	8	.69	6.2
SATFAM	1.0	*	9	.67	6.1
SATFRND	1.0	*	10	.66	6.0
SATJOB	1.0	*	11	.44	4.0

TABLE 13.2 Factor Matrix Output from FACTOR

FACTOR MATRIX:

	FACTOR 1	FACTOR 2	FACTOR 3	FACTOR 4
SIBS	.10	.51	-.52	.26
MARITAL	-.37	.48	-.00	-.18
CHILDS	-.16	.61	-.29	.41
HELPFUL	.47	.36	-.22	-.40
FAIR	-.52	-.20	.15	.58
CONEDUC	.33	.35	.53	.01
CONPRESS	.10	.28	.54	.15
CONLEGI	.40	.33	.51	.13
SATFAM	.67	-.33	-.07	.40
SATFRND	.68	-.04	-.23	.26
SATJOB	.44	-.16	-.11	-.14

TABLE 13.3 Final Statistics Output from FACTOR

FINAL STATISTICS:

VARIABLE	COMMUNALITY	*	FACTOR	EIGENVALUE	PCT OF VAR
		*			
SIBS	.61	*	1	2.05	18.6
MARITAL	.40	*	2	1.48	13.4
CHILDS	.65	*	3	1.33	12.1
HELPFUL	.56	*	4	1.07	9.7
FAIR	.67	*			
CONEDUC	.51	*			
CONPRESS	.40	*			
CONLEGI	.55	*			
SATFAM	.73	*			
SATFRND	.59	*			
SATJOB	.25	*			

[communalities here is how much of the variable is explained by all four factors]

from 0.0, indicating absolutely no association, to 1.0, indicating a perfect association. When a principal-components extraction is done, the communality of each variable in the initial statistics will be 1.0, which results from the initial analysis having as many factors as there are variables.

The third column gives the factor numbers. All the statistics to the right of the factor number apply to that factor number—not to the variable named on the far left. Accordingly, the column of eigenvalue statistics pertains to the factors, not the variables. For example, the eigenvalue 2.04 in the first row indicates the amount of variance underlying all the variables associated with factor 1. The sum of the eigenvalues equals the number of variables; hence, an eigenvalue of 2.04 in an analysis of 11 variables shows that the proportion of the variance explained by factor 1 is 2.04 divided by 11, or 18.6 percent, as indicated in the PCT OF VAR (percent of variance) column on the right.

Table 13.2 provides more information about the first extraction. In the factor matrix are the loadings of each variable on each factor. The **factor loading** is the correlation of a variable with a factor. For example, the factor loading of SIBS on factor 1 is .10. The factor loading of SIBS on factor 2, factor 3, and factor 4 are .51, −.52, and .26, respectively. A factor loading of .10 means that $(.10)^2$ or 1 percent of the variance in SIBS is accounted for by factor 1.

The next portion of FACTOR output is shown in Table 13.3. Note that the communalities no longer equal 1. The final statistics are based only on factors with an eigenvalue greater than 1. In our example, only the first four factors had an eigenvalue greater than 1 (see Table 13.1). Although the communalities no longer equal 1, meaning that not all the variance in the variables is accounted for, we have simplified our data from 11 variables to 4 factors. For example, with SIBS we have accounted for $(.61)^2$ or 37 percent of its variance using the first four factors.

13.4 Rotating Factors

Rotating factors is a method of simplifying factors so that each variable tends to load highly on only one factor. Remember that the first factor was calculated to maximize the total amount of variance it could explain. In using this procedure, the factor may have distorted somewhat in order to accommodate some of the variance of variables that are not really part of the factor. Rotating the factors helps correct this distortion.

An important decision we have to make is whether to do an **orthogonal rotation**, which means that the factors will remain uncorrelated, or an **oblique rotation**, which means that the factors will be allowed to correlate with one another. The choice is up to the researcher. If we thought the factors were truly distinct and unassociated with one another, we would do an orthogonal rotation. For example, we might be doing a profile of consumers in which one factor is rustic preferences and a second factor is luxury designer preferences. If we decide that these two factors are not associated with each other, we can do an orthogonal rotation.

TABLE 13.4 Partial Output from FACTOR: Orthogonal Rotation

ROTATED FACTOR MATRIX:

	FACTOR 1	FACTOR 2	FACTOR 3	FACTOR 4
SIBS	.05	.16	-.10	.76
MARITAL	-.57	.07	.07	.25
CHILDS	-.15	-.12	.07	.78
HELPFUL	.04	.72	.08	.17
FAIR	-.05	-.81	-.05	.07
CONEDUC	.01	.15	.70	-.03
CONPRESS	-.07	-.11	.62	-.01
CONLEGI	.13	.10	.72	.02
SATFAM	.85	.01	.09	-.00
SATFRND	.69	.25	.08	.22
SATJOB	.35	.33	-.03	-.12

As another example, we might be doing a profile of diet preferences that has a sweet food factor and a fatty food factor. If we decide these two factors are associated, we will want to do an oblique rotation.

A varimax orthogonal rotation is produced by default, so no additional commands are needed. In a **varimax rotation**, the calculations are done to maximize the tendency of each variable to load highly on only one factor. Other orthogonal rotation techniques are available; however, the varimax is the most frequently used. (See *SPSS/PC+ Advanced Statistics V2.0* for a list of other rotation techniques available.)

The final portion of output from the FACTOR command would be the rotated factor matrix presented in Table 13.4. In this factor matrix after the rotation, the variables tend to be more extreme in their loadings. Interpretation of the results is simplified because each factor is more clearly identified by a subset of variables that load high on it but low on other factors. Note, for example, that HELPFUL loads .04 on factor 1 and .72 on factor 2. Before the rotation, its loading was .47 on factor 1 and .36 on factor 2 (see Table 13.2).

An orthogonal rotation does not change the communalities of the variables. Just as much variance is explained after the rotation as before. Likewise, an orthogonal rotation does not change the eigenvalues of the factors. Each factor explains the same proportion of the variance as it did before the rotation. Furthermore, after an orthogonal rotation, the correlation between the factors remains 0.0, as it was before the rotation.

Now let's do an oblique rotation of the same data. An oblique rotation allows for some correlation between factors. To do an oblique rotation, we must add the subcommand ROTATION = OBLIQUE preceded by a slash. The SPSS/PC+ commands for our example will now be

```
factor variables=sibs marital childs helpful fair
                 coneduc conpress conlegi satfam
                 satfrnd satjob/
     rotation=oblique.
```

The default method of oblique rotation employed by SPSS/PC+ is called **oblimin.** When an oblique rotation is done, the output differs somewhat from an orthogonal rotation. Instead of a factor matrix, an oblique rotation produces both a **factor pattern matrix** and a **factor structure matrix.**

The factor pattern matrix contains the regression coefficients of each variable for each factor produced when the variable is regressed on the factors (see Chapter 9 for a discussion of regression). These regression coefficients are not the same as the correlations of the variables with the factors, because a regression coefficient is affected by intercorrelations among the factors. On the other hand, a correlation between a variable and a factor is not affected by intercorrelations among the variables. This distinction is not necessary prior to rotation or after an orthogonal rotation, because there are zero correlations among all the factors until we do an oblique rotation.

As an example of a factor pattern matrix coefficient, look at the first variable, SIBS, in the left-hand column of Table 13.5. To the right of this variable, in the FACTOR 1 column, is the coefficient .09, which is the regression coefficient, or factor loading, of SIBS on factor 1. The loadings of SIBS on factor 2, factor 3, and factor 4, respectively, are .76, −.12, and −.12. These loadings indicate the relative importance of the factors in accounting for variance in SIBS.

Looking at the factors, we can see that factor 1 has high pattern matrix coefficients for satisfaction with family (.87) and friends (.69) and a moderately high coefficient for marital status (.58). We might label this the good relationships factor. Factor 2 has high loadings on SIBS (.76) and CHILDS (.78) and might be labeled the relative factor. Factor 3 has high loadings for CONEDUC (.70), CONPRESS (.62), and CONLEGI (.72) and might be labeled the confidence in public institutions factor. Factor 4 has high coefficients for HELPFUL (−.73) and FAIR (.83) and could be labeled the trust factor. In Section 13.6 we discuss how these factors can be used as variables in further analyses.

The second half of Table 13.5 is the factor structure matrix. The coefficients in this matrix are the correlation of each variable with each factor. The correlation of SIBS with factor 1 is .03. The correlations of SIBS with factor 2, factor 3, and factor 4 are .75, −.08, and −.19, respectively. These correlation coefficients differ from the regression coefficients in the factor pattern matrix because they do not adjust for correlations among the factors.

13.5 Factor Correlation Matrix

The factor correlation matrix printed only after an oblique rotation shows the correlation of the factors with one another (see Table 13.6). Prior to rotation, the factors are orthogonal; that is, their correlation with one another is 0.0. Low correlations indicate that the factors are distinct.

Complete output from FACTOR is shown in Table 13.7 (see page 180). The code used is as follows:

```
factor variables=sibs marital childs helpful
                 fair coneduc conpress
                 conlegi satfam satfrnd satjob.
```

TABLE 13.5 Partial Output from FACTOR: Oblique Rotation

PATTERN MATRIX:

	FACTOR 1	FACTOR 2	FACTOR 3	FACTOR 4
SIBS	.09	.76	-.12	-.12
MARITAL	-.58	.21	.06	-.12
CHILDS	-.08	.78	.06	.15
HELPFUL	-.04	.14	.05	-.73
FAIR	.06	.11	-.02	.83
CONEDUC	-.01	-.04	.70	-.13
CONPRESS	-.05	-.02	.62	.13
CONLEGI	.12	.02	.72	-.06
SATFAM	.87	.05	.08	.09
SATFRND	.69	.25	.06	-.16
SATJOB	.31	-.12	-.04	-.31

STRUCTURE MATRIX:

	FACTOR 1	FACTOR 2	FACTOR 3	FACTOR 4
SIBS	.03	.75	-.08	-.19
MARITAL	-.58	.29	.07	-.01
CHILDS	-.20	.78	.08	.11
HELPFUL	.11	.20	.11	-.73
FAIR	-.14	.04	-.07	.81
CONEDUC	.04	-.01	.70	-.17
CONPRESS	-.07	.00	.61	.10
CONLEGI	.14	.03	.72	-.14
SATFAM	.85	-.05	.09	-.12
SATFRND	.70	.19	.09	-.34
SATJOB	.39	-.13	-.02	-.37

13.6 Factor Score Coefficients

We are now faced with the task of calculating the score for each case on each factor. (Remember, the factor pattern coefficients and the factor structure coefficients are concerned with the association between *variables* and factors, not *cases* and factors.) To calculate the factor score of each case for each factor, we use yet another type of coefficient: **factor score coefficients.**

The score on a particular variable is multiplied by the factor score coefficient of that variable for that factor. We do this multiplication for each score of the case on each variable and then sum the products.

The factor scores for each case can be saved. Each set of factor scores can then be treated as a new variable. For example, suppose we extracted four factors and wanted to save the factor scores for all four. We would decide on a variable name and then use the subcommand SAVE. (Although we have seen SAVE as a command in earlier chapters, in this context it is a subcommand that must begin after column 1.) For our example, let's use the name FACTVAR. The SAVE subcommand would be

```
save (all factvar)
```

The first factor's scores would be saved under the variable name FACTVAR1, the second factor's scores under the name FACTVAR2, and so on. Be careful to allow space for the digits at the end of the variable name; you must not exceed the eight-character limit.

Once the variables based on factor scores are saved, we can do other analyses that include these factors as variables. For example, to use FACTVAR1 (our good relationships factor), FACTVAR2 (our relatives factor), FACTVAR3 (our trust factor), and FACTVAR4 (our confidence in public institutions factor), the complete commands to calculate the factors and do a regression with HAPPY as the dependent variable are

TABLE 13.6 Factor Correlation Matrix Output from FACTOR

```
FACTOR CORRELATION MATRIX:
```

	FACTOR 1	FACTOR 2	FACTOR 3	FACTOR 4
FACTOR 1	1.00			
FACTOR 2	-.11	1.00		
FACTOR 3	.01	.04	1.00	
FACTOR 4	-.23	-.08	-.07	1.00

TABLE 13.7 Complete Output from FACTOR

F A C T O R   A N A L Y S I S

ANALYSIS NUMBER   1 LISTWISE DELETION OF CASES WITH MISSING VALUES

EXTRACTION   1 FOR ANALYSIS   1, PRINCIPAL-COMPONENTS ANALYSIS (PC)

INITIAL STATISTICS:

VARIABLE	COMMUNALITY	*	FACTOR	EIGENVALUE	PCT OF VAR	CUM PCT
SIBS	1.00000	*	1	2.04620	18.6	18.6
MARITAL	1.00000	*	2	1.47710	13.4	32.0
CHILDS	1.00000	*	3	1.33152	12.1	44.1
HELPFUL	1.00000	*	4	1.06501	9.7	53.8
FAIR	1.00000	*	5	.91254	8.3	62.1
CONEDUC	1.00000	*	6	.88336	8.0	70.1
CONPRESS	1.00000	*	7	.83155	7.6	77.7
CONLEGI	1.00000	*	8	.68556	6.2	83.9
SATFAM	1.00000	*	9	.66929	6.1	90.0
SATFRND	1.00000	*	10	.65776	6.0	96.0
SATJOB	1.00000	*	11	.44012	4.0	100.0

PC EXTRACTED   4 FACTORS.

FACTOR MATRIX:

	FACTOR 1	FACTOR 2	FACTOR 3	FACTOR 4
SIBS	.09589	.50814	-.52274	.26073
MARITAL	-.36800	.48463	-.00148	-.18096
CHILDS	-.15767	.60811	-.28938	.41338
HELPFUL	.46903	.36488	-.21893	-.40163
FAIR	-.51515	-.19906	.14624	.58198
CONEDUC	.32944	.34793	.53189	.01488
CONPRESS	.09725	.27619	.53820	.15455
CONLEGI	.39874	.32668	.51446	.12864

180

```
SATFAM     .67100    -.33404    -.07248     .40422
SATFRND    .68452    -.03924    -.22716     .26439
SATJOB     .44224    -.15585    -.10537    -.13946
```

FINAL STATISTICS:

VARIABLE	COMMUNALITY	*	FACTOR	EIGENVALUE	PCT OF VAR	CUM PCT
		*				
SIBS	.60864	*	1	2.04620	18.6	18.6
MARITAL	.40304	*	2	1.47710	13.4	32.0
CHILDS	.64928	*	3	1.33152	12.1	44.1
HELPFUL	.56237	*	4	1.06501	9.7	53.8
FAIR	.66508	*				
CONEDUC	.51271	*				
CONPRESS	.39929	*				
CONLEGI	.54693	*				
SATFAM	.73046	*				
SATFRND	.59161	*				
SATJOB	.25041	*				

VARIMAX   ROTATION   1,   EXTRACTION   1,   IN ANALYSIS   1   -   KAISER NORMALIZATION.

VARIMAX CONVERGED IN   6 ITERATIONS.

ROTATED FACTOR MATRIX:

	FACTOR 1	FACTOR 2	FACTOR 3	FACTOR 4
SIBS	.05439	.15959	-.10027	.75509
MARITAL	-.57397	-.07073	.06689	.25322
CHILDS	-.14804	-.12379	.07349	.77887
HELPFUL	-.04064	.72382	.08276	.17307
FAIR	-.05307	-.80952	-.04666	.06906
CONEDUC	.01175	.14508	.70062	-.02558
CONPRESS	-.06701	-.11069	.61841	-.01067
CONLEGI	.12867	.10070	.72088	.02392
SATFAM	.85015	.00650	.08756	-.00081
SATFRND	.69074	.24557	-.08108	.21819
SATJOB	.35353	.33049	-.03128	-.12340

```
factor variables=sibs marital childs helpful fair
                 coneduc conpress conlegi satfam
                 satfrnd satjob/
      rotation=oblique
      save (all factvar)/
regression variables=happy factvar 1 factvar 2 factvar 3
          factvar 4/
          dependent=happy/
          method=enter.
```

If we wanted, we could include other variables from our file as independent variables in the regression along with the four factors.

Factor analysis has many variations. The SPSS/PC+ program contains seven extraction techniques, four rotation techniques, and three possible calculations of factor scores. We have presented the most commonly used approaches. The *SPSS/PC+ Advanced Statistics V2.0* manual gives the commands for the other methods but without much discussion of the various assumptions and advantages of each method. To understand better the various methods of factor analysis, you will need to devote considerable study to the subject.

13.7 Additional Resources

FACTOR is discussed on pages B41–70 and C24–38 in *SPSS/PC+ Advanced Statistics V2.0.*

For a more complete discussion of factor analysis, see Jae-On Kim and Charles W. Mueller's *Introduction to Factor Analysis: What It Is and How to Do It* (Beverly Hills, Calif.: Sage Publications, 1978).

13.8 Summary

A factor is a composite variable underlying the variance in a set of variables. A factor loading is a measure of the association between a variable and the factor of which it is a component. Factor loadings range from −1.0 to 1.0. No association is indicated by 0.0; a perfect association is indicated by 1.0. The sign of the loading indicates whether the association is positive or negative.

The eigenvalue is a measure of variance in the set of variables in the analysis.

The communality of a variable is the proportion of its variance accounted for by the variables in the analysis. The communality is 0.0 for no association and 1.0 for a perfect association. The communality of all the variables will be 1.0 when the number of factors equals the number of variables.

A factor score is the value of the factor for a particular case.

In an orthogonal rotation, the correlation between the factors in the analysis is kept at 0.0. In an oblique rotation, some correlation is permitted among the factors in the analysis.

RESEARCH PROJECT WORK

Do an exploratory factor analysis on your research data set, including all the variables except ID. Before you execute the analysis, hypothesize which variables you think will cluster together. If your hypotheses prove incorrect, discuss why the findings were different from what you expected.

REVIEW QUESTIONS

13.1 What is a factor?

13.2 What is a factor loading?

13.3 What is the eigenvalue in factor analysis?

13.4 What is the communality of a variable in factor analysis?

13.5 What is a factor score?

13.6 How is an orthogonal rotation different from an oblique rotation?

13.7 What is the factor extraction technique used by default in FACTOR?

13.8 What is the default rotation done by FACTOR if no technique is specified?

13.9 What type of oblique rotation is done by FACTOR if the ROTATION = OBLIQUE subcommand is given without specifying a technique?

13.10 What command would be needed to produce a factor analysis with an orthogonal rotation of the 13 variables CONFINAN through CONARMY in the SPSS system file NORC84, described in Appendix B?

ASSIGNMENT QUESTIONS

13.1   What does the following output indicate about the factors produced by the command in Review Question 13.10?

INITIAL STATISTICS:

VARIABLE	COMMUNALITY	*	FACTOR	EIGENVALUE	PCT OF VAR
CONFINAN	1.0	*	1	3.93	30.2
CONBUS	1.0	*	2	1.32	10.2
CONCLER	1.0	*	3	1.18	9.1
CONEDUC	1.0	*	4	.99	7.6
CONFED	1.0	*	5	.84	6.4
CONLABOR	1.0	*	6	.78	6.0
CONPRESS	1.0	*	7	.74	5.7
CONMEDI	1.0	*	8	.69	5.3
CONTV	1.0	*	9	.61	4.7
CONJUDG	1.0	*	10	.53	4.1
CONSCI	1.0	*	11	.52	4.0
CONLEGI	1.0	*	12	.47	3.6
CONARMY	1.0	*	13	.42	3.2

13.2   What does the following output indicate about the factors produced by the command in Review Question 13.10?

FACTOR MATRIX:

	FACTOR 1	FACTOR 2	FACTOR 3
CONFINAN	.63	-.03	.35
CONBUS	.50	-.21	.26
CONCLER	.43	-.21	.43
CONEDUC	.51	.00	.14
CONFED	.61	-.02	-.36
CONLABOR	.48	.44	-.20
CONPRESS	.44	.55	.01
CONMEDI	.58	-.36	.19
CONTV	.45	.59	.23
CONJUDG	.60	-.21	-.52
CONSCI	.57	-.46	-.15
CONLEGI	.69	.09	-.40
CONARMY	.61	.06	.26

13.3 What does the following output indicate about the factors produced by the command in Review Question 13.10?

FINAL STATISTICS:

VARIABLE	COMMUNALITY	*	FACTOR	EIGENVALUE	PCT OF VAR
		*			
CONFINAN	.51	*	1	3.93	30.2
CONBUS	.36	*	2	1.32	10.2
CONCLER	.41	*	3	1.18	9.1
CONEDUC	.28	*			
CONFED	.50	*			
CONLABOR	.46	*			
CONPRESS	.49	*			
CONMEDI	.50	*			
CONTV	.60	*			
CONJUDG	.67	*			
CONSCI	.55	*			
CONLEGI	.64	*			
CONARMY	.44	*			

13.4 What does the following output indicate about the factors produced by the command in Review Question 13.10?

PATTERN MATRIX:

	FACTOR 1	FACTOR 2	FACTOR 3
CONFINAN	.66	.19	.01
CONBUS	.59	-.03	-.05
CONCLER	.69	-.04	.14
CONEDUC	.40	.17	-.12
CONFED	.05	.13	-.64
CONLABOR	-.07	.56	-.31
CONPRESS	.03	.67	-.08
CONMEDI	.62	-.16	-.19
CONTV	.21	.74	.13
CONJUDG	-.02	-.07	-.84
CONSCI	.37	-.29	-.54
CONLEGI	.01	.26	-.70
CONARMY	.54	.27	-.04

STRUCTURE MATRIX:

	FACTOR 1	FACTOR 2	FACTOR 3
CONFINAN	.69	.32	-.28
CONBUS	.60	.09	-.27
CONCLER	.63	.07	-.11
CONEDUC	.48	.27	-.30
CONFED	.32	.28	-.69
CONLABOR	.16	.61	-.41
CONPRESS	.20	.69	-.23
CONMEDI	.67	.00	-.40
CONTV	.31	.75	-.10
CONJUDG	.28	.09	-.82
CONSCI	.52	.10	-.62
CONLEGI	.33	.41	-.76
CONARMY	.61	.39	-.30

13.5 What does the following output indicate about the factors produced by the command in Review Question 13.10?

FACTOR CORRELATION MATRIX

	FACTOR 1	FACTOR 2	FACTOR 3
FACTOR 1	1.00		
FACTOR 2	.05	1.00	
FACTOR 3	-.25	-.04	1.00

14

ANALYZING CENSUS DATA TAPES WITH SPSS×

New SPSS× command:

FILE TYPE

SPSS/PC+ does not access tape drives, nor does it handle hierarchical files. As we will demonstrate, these are valuable tools in working with census data. Consequently, we recommend using SPSS× for such projects. The U.S. Bureau of the Census does not ask any attitudinal questions in its decennial census nor in its current population surveys. Therefore, we cannot extend our analysis of reported happiness to the data gathered by the Bureau of the Census. On the other hand, SPSS× is well equipped to cope with some of the difficulties posed by census data files. You may very likey want to use one of these files someday.

An introduction to the many variables in the census data files is beyond the scope of this book, but we will describe the two basic types of files and the requirements for working with them. These files are the Public Use Microdata Sample (PUMS) files and the Summary Tape File (STF) datafiles.

Also beyond the scope of this book, and simply impossible, is a description of the operating system commands or hardware limitations of the numerous types of computer installations around the country. In this chapter we describe the necessary SPSS× commands.

14.1 Individual Level Census Data: PUMS Files

The distinguishing characteristic of the PUMS files is that the basic case units are individuals. With over 200 million individuals in the United States, even computer technology does not enable the typical user to work with every individual, so the Bureau of the Census releases samples (on tape) from its decennial census for the public to use. For the 1980 census, the codebook for these tapes is *Census of Population and Housing: 1980 Public Use Microdata Samples Technical Documentation* (Washington D.C.: U.S. Government Printing Office, 1982). For the 1990 census, new technology, including compact disc random access memory (CD-ROM), is being planned.

Other useful documentation available about census data includes:

- *1980 Census of Population and Housing Users' Guide* (available from the U.S. Government Printing Office)
- *Telephone Contacts for Data Users* (available from the Bureau of the Census)
- *Data User News* (available from the Bureau of the Census)
- *Directory of Data Files* (available from the Bureau of the Census)

The smallest of these documents, and often the most useful, is the *Telephone Contacts for Data Users*, a free four-page brochure.

State data centers with regional branches provide the census data tapes at nominal cost and are also a convenient source of expertise on how to use them. If you are having trouble locating a state data center or an office of the Bureau of the Census to help you, call the Bureau's Data User Services at 1-301-763-4100.

The major difficulty with the PUMS files is that household information is on one record, followed by one or more records containing the information on the persons living in the household, with one record for each individual. If you want to use household information only, there is no problem. Simply give a SELECT IF command that specifies 'H' (in single quotation marks) for the variable RECTYPE. This alphanumeric variable, in the same location for both types of records, is coded P for individuals and H for households. Likewise, if you want to use individual information, use a SELECT IF command that specifies 'P' for the record type variable.

More likely you will want to use information from both the household and the individual records so that each individual is connected with the attributes of his or her household. In this case, you will be dealing with what is called a **nested hierarchical file** and will need to use the command FILE TYPE. For example, to do an analysis using the variable FAMINCOM from the household records and linking it with the variables SEX, MARITAL, and AGE from the individual records for each household, we would use the following set of SPSS^x commands:

```
file type nested file-pums80 record-rectype 1  (a)
record type 'h'
data list / famincom 112-116
record type 'p'
data list / sex 7 marital 11 age 33-34
end file type
```

Note that several other commands and subcommands must accompany the FILE TYPE command. First is the subcommand NESTED, which indicates that we want the data from the first record type "spread" to the records of the second record type. In our example, the data from each record of type H will be spread to each P record that follows it, until the next H record is encountered.

The next subcommand in the FILE TYPE command is FILE = PUMS80, which specifies the name we gave to the file in our operating system commands (which are not shown here). On the same line is the subcommand RECORD = RECTYPE 1(A), which indicates that the record type will be identified by the variable RECTYPE, which is in column 1. (The A in parentheses indicates that this variable is alphanumeric.)

RECORD TYPE 'H' indicates that the first record type is identified by having the value H for the variable and location specified by the RECORD = subcommand on the first line. So, if the value in column 1 for the variable RECTYPE is H, then the DATA LIST command following RECORD TYPE 'H' applies.

DATA LIST FAMINCOM 112–116 applies to the type H records, because this command follows the RECORD TYPE 'H' command. Likewise RECORD TYPE 'P' indicates that the DATA LIST following it applies to records with the value P in column 1.

END FILE TYPE indicates that the set of commands specifying the file type has been concluded.

After the more complicated set of commands surrounding the DATA LIST phase of your data definition process, you can proceed as usual with other SPSS^x commands.

In the STF data files, however, the units of analysis are geographic units and the data are aggregate statistics. These files present a different set of challenges, which we discuss in the next section.

14.2 Aggregate Data by Geographic Area: STF Data Files

The STF data files consist of tables of data organized by geographic units. Each case is a geographic area, but the areas might be anything from a neighborhood block group to a state. The geographic level is specified by the value of SUMRYLV, a variable whose location varies depending on which type of STF file you are using. You'll need to check your codebook to locate SUMRYLV and to learn the values that correspond to each level. You do not have to treat these files as nested for most analyses, because the same variables are used for each geographic level.

A simple DATA LIST command will suffice to define your data. Often, however, you will want to print out the information for just some of the levels. You can do so by using a SELECT IF command with the SUMRYLV variable after the DATA LIST command. There is also a variable RECOIND for some of the STF files that indicates whether the aggregated statistics are for the total population or a particular ethnic/racial group within it. Using a SELECT IF command with RECOIND enables you to select out the total population or just those subgroups of the total that you wish to examine.

A tricky aspect of STF data files is that each cell in a table must be thought of as a variable. If you have the population by age in five-year intervals, each of those five-year intervals must be given a variable name. (The SPSS^x convention of defining a set of variables with the same prefix by using the keyword TO is most useful. With it we can define 18 variables by using the words AGE1 TO AGE18 on the DATA LIST command followed by the columns these adjacent variables span.) For example,

```
data list / age 1 to age 18 20-109
```

To produce a table when each cell has its own variable name, use a LIST command that specifies each variable name. Use the VARIABLE LABELS command to identify the cell to which each variable label corresponds. If you make AREANAME (a variable containing the first name of each geographic unit) the first variable named on the LIST command, the output will indicate which area the table represents.

Another problem in working with the STF data file is that a zero sometimes indicates that the information is being suppressed, whereas other times a zero is a legitimate value. (The Bureau of the Census suppresses some information when there are so few cases that confidentiality would be jeopardized.) To solve this problem, certain variables indicate whether the information for another variable is being suppressed or not. For example, the first **suppression variable** on one of the STF data files is coded 1 when the total population count is being suppressed because fewer than 30 persons live in the area. For this file you would need to use an IF command to change values of the total population variable from zero to missing value when the suppressor variable has a value of 1.

There are five STF data files (STF1, STF2, STF3, STF4, and STF5), and for each file there is a document from a series entitled *Census of Population and Housing, 1980: Summary Tape File Technical Documentation.* These documents are available from the U.S. Bureau of the Census, in Washington, D.C. (1983). They contain information on codings, the structure of the file, and its geographic coverage.

Another useful resource for the STF data files is the Geographic Identification Code Scheme (GICS). This set of tables gives the codes and names of the political and geographic areas used for the 1980 census, so that you can select out from a tape just the data from areas that interest you.

14.3 Additional Resources

The SPSS/PC+ manuals do not discuss using census data tapes. A sophisticated discussion can be found in *SPSS Processing of U.S. Census Data* (Chicago: SPSS Inc., 1984).

14.4 Summary

The PUMS (Public Use Microdata Sample) files have households and individuals as the basic case units.

The major difficulty with the PUMS files is that household information is on one record, followed by one or more records containing the information on the persons living in the household—one record for each individual. If you want to use information from both the household and the individual records such that each individual is connected with the attributes of his or her household, you need to use the FILE TYPE command.

The STF (Summary Tape File) data files consist of tables of data organized by geographic units. Each case is a geographic area, but the areas might be anything from a block group to an SMSA. The geographic level is specified by the value of SUMRYLV, a variable whose location varies depending on which type of STF data file you are using.

For STF data files, each cell in a table must be thought of as of as a variable. Another problem in working with the STF data files is that a zero may indicate either suppressed information or a legitimate value. To solve this problem, certain variables indicate whether the information for another variable is being suppressed.

REVIEW QUESTIONS

14.1 What is the basic difference between PUMS files and STF data files?

14.2 Could you use a PUMS file if you wanted to determine the correlation among individuals between family income and educational attainment?

14.3 Could you use an STF data file if you wanted to determine the correlation among individuals between family income and educational attainment?

14.4 When is it necessary to use a FILE TYPE command with a PUMS file?

14.5 In using an STF data file, if you wanted to produce tables for the county geographic level only, what would you do?

14.6 In using an STF data file, if you wanted to produce tables for the total population and for the Spanish-origin populations only, what would you do?

14.7 Suppose that using an STF data file you want to produce for SMSAs the table of number of households in each household-value category. Why would you need a variable name for each category in the distribution of household values?

14.8 Why are the 0 values in an STF data file problematic?

ASSIGNMENT QUESTIONS

14.1 For the PUMS80 file used in the example in Section 14.1, what SPSS^x commands would be necessary to produce a FREQUENCIES run of the variable MARITAL for individuals only?

14.2 For the PUMS80 file, what SPSS^x commands would be necessary to produce a FREQUENCIES run of the variable FAMINCOM for households only?

14.3 For the PUMS80 file, what SPSS^x commands would be necessary to produce a CROSSTABS of FAMINCOM by MARITAL?

14.4 Assuming that the following commands are correct and that no information has been suppressed, what additional SPSS^x commands would be needed to produce a table showing the name and total population size (POPSIZE) for each county? (The VALUE LABEL information in the following commands shows how SUMRYLV and RECOIND are coded.)

```
data list  file-stf  records=6
     /1  sumrylv 10-11  recoind 16-17 (a)    popsize 107-108
         areaname 145-174 (a)
value labels  sumrylv 8  'smsa' 17  'county' 24 'census tract'
              recoind 0 'total' 1  'white' 2 'black' 3 'hispanic'
```

14.5 What SPSS^x commands would you need to add to produce a table of the total population, the black population, and the area name for SMSAs?

15

THE SPSS/PC+ INTERFACE WITH MICROSOFT CHART

SPSS/PC+ allows a convenient interface with several popular graphing programs. In this chapter we discuss how to use Microsoft Chart from within
SPSS/PC+. These instructions assume that you have Microsoft Chart installed
in your SPSS directory and that you also have installed SPSS/PC+ GRAPHICS,
which is the interface program linking SPSS/PC+ and Microsoft Chart. This
chapter discusses a direct approach for graphing data in an SPSS file, but explains only a few of the Microsoft commands and options. Unfortunately, the
user manual that accompanies Microsoft Chart is primarily a command reference guide and not a systematic introduction to using the program. To learn
more about Chart, special order the Microsoft Chart Version 3.0 Training Work-
book directly from Microsoft.

An initial warning! You will be using both SPSS/PC+ and Microsoft Chart
and the effect of pressing the Enter and Arrow keys is different in each program. Pay attention when you shift from one program to another and remember what the procedures are for each program.

15.1 Entering the Chart Program and Producing a Graph from SPSS/PC+

When you are in SPSS/PC+ and press the Enter key (this key is designated by ↵ or Return on some keyboards), you may "paste" unwanted portions of commands into the scratch pad at the bottom of your screen. If that happens, save time by ignoring the scratch pad errors until you are ready for the final editing of your commands.

To graph data from SPSS/PC+ using Microsoft Chart, first you need to create an active SPSS file. (You can do this using a GET, IMPORT, or DATA LIST command.) As an example, we again use the NORC84 file and assume that you have this SPSS file. The same procedures, however, would work with other SPSS files. To activate the NORC84 file, after entering SPSS/PC+, shift to the Edit mode by holding the Alt key down and pressing the E key. Type *GET FILE 'NORC84'.* on the scratch pad. Press the F10 key and then the Enter key to execute the GET command.

Return to the Menu mode by holding down the Alt key while pressing M.

FIGURE 15.1 The Graph Data Menu

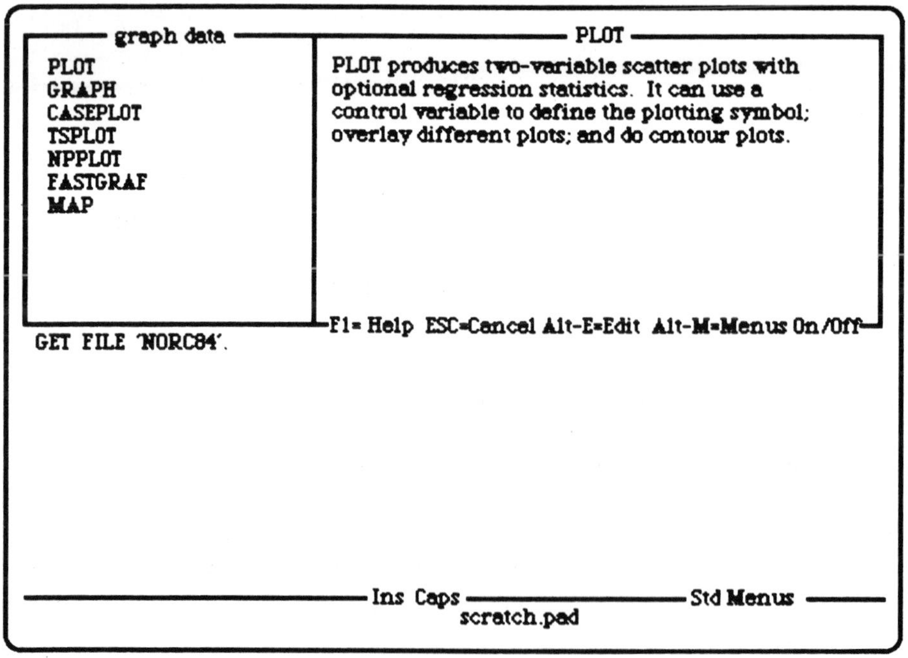

FIGURE 15.2 The Graph Chart Type Menu

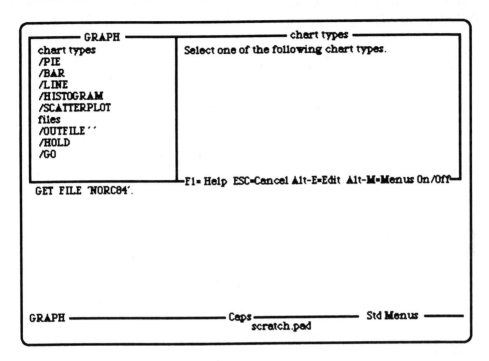

Next highlight the "graph data" line from the Main Menu in the upper-left corner of the screen by pressing the G key. (In SPSS/PC+ UpArrow and Down-Arrow keys can also be used to move the highlight.) Then press the RightArrow key. This will bring up the Graph Data Menu (see Figure 15.1).

On the Graph Data Menu, highlight the "graph" line by pressing the G key. Then press the RightArrow key to bring up the Graph Chart Type Menu (see Figure 15.2). On the Graph Chart Type Menu, the chart type choices are PIE, BAR, LINE, HISTOGRAM, and SCATTERPLOT.

Using the DownArrow key to move the highlight down the page gives a brief description of each chart type in the box on the right as you highlight each name. Under the files subheading are the options OUTFILE, HOLD, and GO. We are not concerned with using them in this book; however, if you are curious, highlight them to see a description of their use.

If you are a novice at constructing charts, you will probably find the bar chart to be your best choice. A bar chart uses wide vertical lines to illustrate the number or percentage of cases in each category; for example, the number of people in each age group. It allows you to display frequency distributions and graph frequency distributions in terms of a second variable to illustrate bivariate relationships.

As another option, the data in a bar chart could be put in a pie chart (and vice versa). A pie chart is a circle divided into wedges like the pieces of a pie. This type of chart is especially well suited for illustrating proportions; for example, the percentages of a budget spent on each category or the percentages of students with each major.

Let's run through an example. Select /BAR by pressing the B key, and then press the RightArrow key. The /BAR Menu appears on the screen (see Figure 15.3).

On the /BAR Menu, the words *frequency counts* are highlighted and the box on the right explains that this is the selection to show the number of cases in each category of a variable. Highlighting the other choices provides explanations of their functions. With "frequency counts" highlighted, press the Right-Arrow key. This calls up the Frequency Counts Menu (see Figure 15.4). This is the final menu that you need to produce a bar chart. Study it carefully.

Highlighted on the Frequency Counts menu is the subcommand COUNT BY. The description in the right box indicates that this command will show the number of cases in each category of a variable and provides an example of the command syntax. (The example is a bit misleading since what follows BY is a

---

FIGURE 15.3 The /Bar Menu

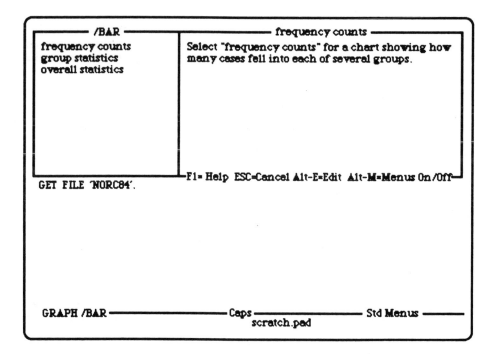

FIGURE 15.4 The Frequency Counts Menu

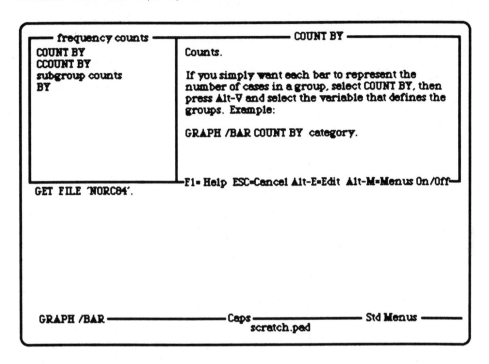

variable name, not a category.) Highlighting the CCOUNT subcommand reveals that this is for a cumulative count. Highlighting the subgroup heading brings up an explanation in the right box about how the keyword BY can be used to produce subcategory breakdowns of the frequencies by a second variable. Examples are also provided.

At this point, highlight the COUNT subcommand and press the Enter key. This will paste in the command GRAPH /BAR COUNT BY to the scratch pad. Shift to Edit by holding down the Alt key and pressing E. Then type *HAPPY* after the word *BY.* Your scratch pad should now look like

```
get file 'norc84'.
graph /bar count by happy.
```

If there are errors, make the necessary corrections. If you have forgotten the name of the variable you wish to use, hold down the Alt key and press V while in the Menu mode. This will cause the list of variables in the active file to appear in a menu at the top of the screen. Use the Arrow keys to highlight the variable of your choice and press Return. The result will be that the highlighted variable is pasted into the scratch pad.

CHART 15.1 Default Printing of Happiness Chart

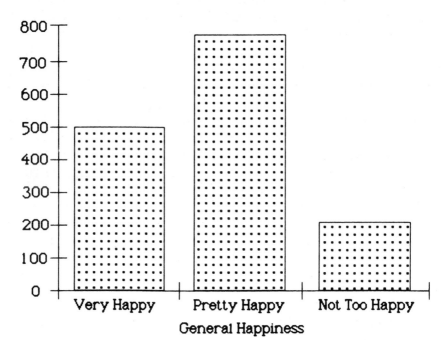

To execute the GRAPH command, move the cursor to the GRAPH /BAR COUNT BY HAPPY. line. Then press the F10 key followed by the Enter key. The computer calls up the CHART program and the bar chart for HAPPY appears on the screen (see Chart 15.1).

15.2 Operating within the Chart Program

Now you have shifted from the SPSS/PC+ program to the Chart program. *Read the next two paragraphs carefully!* They will keep you from getting lost in Chart. In Chart the arrows no longer move the highlight as they do in SPSS/PC+. Sorry about that, it's one of life's inconsistencies. For the time being, don't touch the arrows; we'll explain their various functions as this chapter progresses.

In the Chart program you will be using command menus that appear at the bottom of the screen. Pressing a letter will execute the command beginning with that letter. For example, at the bottom of the screen displaying the chart of happiness you produced, you can choose commands from the Chart Menu. (Chart is the name of the program and the name of one of its menus.) Pressing the F key would execute the FORMAT command.

Sometimes when a command is executed, a Specification Menu appears. Pressing the first letter of a specification choice will highlight that choice but not execute the command until you press the Enter key. This allows you to make other specifications before the root command is executed. (More about this in the next section.)

If you enter the wrong command, an unwanted menu will appear. You can return to the Main Menu without executing a menu command by pressing the Esc key. Two exceptions to this are if you accidentally execute the ENTRY or LIST commands. These commands bring up different screens, and to exit them you must press the C key to execute the CHART command from their menus. (The Entry and List screens are explained later in the chapter.)

The next few sections describe how to execute commands that allow you to customize your chart.

15.3 Changing the Size or Position of a Chart

The bars on Chart 15.1 are too wide for an aesthetic appearance. A selection of commands given at the bottom of the screen allows you to perform operations on the chart. These are

COMMANDS: Alpha Delete Entry Format Gallery Help Insert List Move

Options Print Quit Range Split Transfer

To change the width or height of the chart, first press F to execute the FORMAT Menu command. Now the Format Menu is at the bottom of the screen. Pressing S executes the SIZE command. The width and height of the table are given at the bottom of the screen and you are also informed that the dimensions of the table can be changed using the Arrow keys. Pressing the LeftArrow key causes a line box to outline the figure, and holding down the LeftArrow key causes the box to become narrower and narrower. Hold down the key until the right line of the box reaches the Y in the PRETTY HAPPY category label. The size of the line box will be the new size of the chart. Using the other Arrow keys you can make the box shorter, taller, or wider. If you try to change the dimension beyond the screen limits, Chart emits a warning beep. Sometimes you will

CHART 15.2 Chart with Columns Reduced

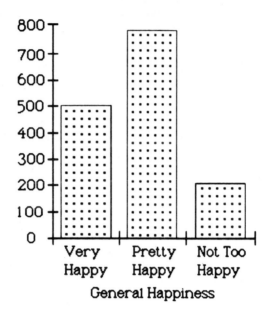

need to reposition a chart before you can expand its dimensions. For example, you may have to move its location down before you can make it taller. As you'll see in a moment, you can do this with the MOVE command.

To change the height of the box, you need to move the highlight to the HEIGHT command on the menu at the bottom of the screen by pressing the Tab key.

When the chart has the appearance you want, press Enter, and the chart will be reformatted and drawn on the screen with the new shape (see Chart 15.2).

When the chart does not fill the screen, you may wish to reposition the chart on the screen. To do this, press M to execute the MOVE command from the menu and bring up the Move Menu. Now the position of the chart is given at the bottom of the screen and you are told that you can move the chart using the Arrow keys. Pressing the RightArrow key causes a line box to outline the chart. Holding down the RightArrow key moves the line box to the right. The other Arrow keys move the line box in their respective directions around the screen. When the line box is where you want the chart to be, press the Enter key. The chart will be redrawn and positioned where the line box was on the screen.

15.4 Changing the Labels of a Chart

The title given to the chart was GENERAL HAPPINESS, because that was the variable label for HAPPY in the SPSS file. To change the title of the chart, press the DownArrow until the words *LABEL—Master Series Point* are at the bottom left of the screen. Then press the RightArrow key until the words *LABEL— GENERAL HAPPINESS* appear in the bottom left of the screen. Then press the A key to execute the ALPHA command. Now type *Level of Happiness* and then press the Enter key.

Other labels can be changed by pressing the RightArrow key until the label you desire to change or delete appears after LABEL at the bottom left of the screen. Type the A key, then the new label (or a blank if you want to delete the old label) and press the Enter key.

The labels also can be moved using the MOVE command as described in the previous section when the label you want to move appears after LABEL at the bottom of the screen.

The exceptions to these procedures are for the horizontal category labels and the vertical axis labels. To change the category labels, quit the Chart program. This action will return you to SPSS/PC+. Then execute a VALUE LABELS command and reenter Chart. Unfortunately, this throws you back to square one in formatting your Chart. An alternative is to make changes in the Entry screen as described in Section 15.9.

15.5 Printing a Chart

When the chart has the appearance you want, it can be printed by pressing the P key to activate the PRINT command. The Print Menu appears on the screen. The first time you use the Chart program, before printing you will have to indicate which printer you will be using. From the Print Menu, press S to execute the SETUP command. The name of a printer will appear at the bottom of the screen. If it is not the printer you are using, press the RightArrow key, and a list of the available printers will appear on the screen. Using the Arrow keys, highlight the printer you want to use and then press the Enter key. If the communication device specified to the right of the printer specification is incorrect, use the Tab key to move the highlight to that specification and type in the correct communication device name. Execute SETUP by pressing the Enter key. Once the SETUP is correct for your printer or plotter, you do not have to repeat this command in future runs.

The Print Menu will return to the bottom of the screen after you execute

SETUP. Turn on the printer, press P to execute the PRINTER command and the chart on the screen will be printed. Other commands will not execute while this command is in process.

15.6 Saving and Retrieving a Chart

Another option you have in the Print Menu is to save the chart that you have created. If you are pleased with the appearance of a chart, in addition to printing it, you will want to save it so that you can reproduce it in the future without going through all the work of the first production. From the Chart Menu, press T to execute the TRANSFER command which brings up the Transfer Menu. Then type S to execute the SAVE command. This causes Chart to ask you the name under which you want your chart information stored. The primary file name cannot have more than eight characters, although these eight may be followed by a period and a three-character suffix. (Using DOS conventions, you can store the file on another directory or disk.)

To retrieve the chart you have stored, from the opening Chart Menu press T to execute the TRANSFER command; this brings up the Transfer Menu. Then type L to execute the LOAD command. Chart then asks you the name of the file you want to retrieve. If you do not remember the name, press the RightArrow key to bring up the names of files in your active directory. Putting in the name of another directory before pressing the RightArrow key will bring up the names of files in that directory. If the file is on another directory, you will have to use its prefix in a DOS format to access that file.

15.7 Adding a Control Variable to a Chart

To add a control variable to the analysis, use another BY on the SPSS/PC+ command. For example,

```
get file 'norc84'.
graph /bar count by happy by race.
```

If you still have the chart from Section 15.6 on the screen, return to SPSS/PC+ by pressing the Q key to execute QUIT. A question of your intentions will appear on the screen. Then press the Y key to indicate that you really mean to do

CHART 15.3 Happiness by Race

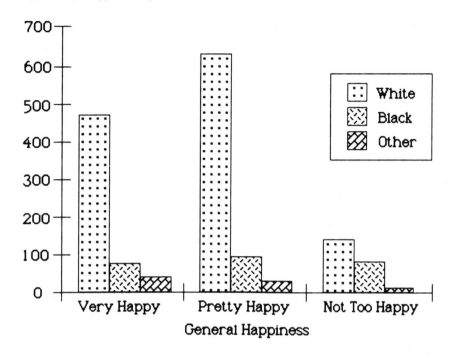

this. Chart will return you to where you were in SPSS/PC+. Go into Edit mode by holding down the Alt key while pressing E. Add BY RACE to the GRAPH command in the scratch pad. Then with the cursor on this line, press F10, and then Enter. Since you have already done a run, the GET command is not necessary in this run because you already have NORC84 as your active file. The result should be as illustrated in Chart 15.3.

15.8 Converting to Percentages

When you have charted HAPPY BY RACE, you will notice that this results in much taller columns for whites: the largest race category. To control for the size of each group and thereby obtain a better graphic comparison, you need to shift to the List screen. Do this by pressing the L key to execute the command LIST. This calls up the List screen (see Figure 15.5). You will see a line for each of your variables. The cursor can be moved up and down the rows with the Arrow keys. The column the cursor is in originally is titled the Incl. column (for

FIGURE 15.5 The List Screen

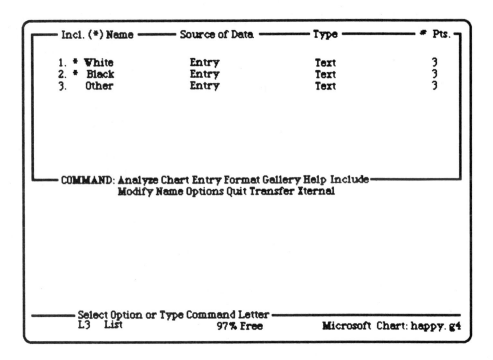

```
 ┌── Incl. (*) Name ──── Source of Data ──── Type ──────── # Pts. ─┐
 │                                                                │
 │  1. * White          Entry              Text           3       │
 │  2. * Black          Entry              Text           3       │
 │  3.   Other          Entry              Text           3       │
 │                                                                │
 │                                                                │
 │                                                                │
 │  COMMAND: Analyze Chart Entry Format Gallery Help Include      │
 │           Modify Name Options Quit Transfer Xternal            │
 │                                                                │
 │                                                                │
 │── Select Option or Type Command Letter ──────────────         │
 │   L3   List                    97% Free       Microsoft Chart: happy. g4
 └────────────────────────────────────────────────────────────────┘
```

CHART 15.4 Percent in Happiness Categories by Race

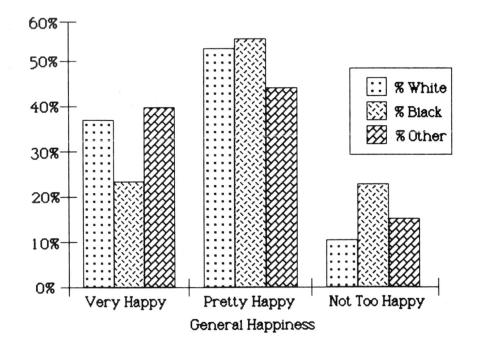

Include) as indicated at the top. Any command that you give will affect the row in which the cursor is. With the cursor in the top row, press the A key and the ANALYZE command will execute, giving you several choices. At this point, press the P key to create a new data series, which is percentage of WHITES. Moving the cursor down to the appropriate rows, do the same procedures for the BLACK and OTHER data series.

Now move the cursor up the Incl. column. Type an asterisk (*) for the rows of labeled percentages and a minus sign (-) for the other rows. Press the C key to execute the CHART command and the chart will be redrawn with the percentages instead of the untransformed frequencies (see Chart 15.4).

15.9 Deleting Columns

If you want to delete some of the columns of percentages to produce a less cluttered chart, you first need to make copies of the percentages series. (The first set of percentages is linked to the series they were derived from, and Chart will not allow you to change them.)

To produce the copies, press L to return to the List screen. Press the A key to execute the ANALYZE command then press C to make a copy. A new series will be created titled COPY OF PERCENTAGE WHITE. Do this for each of the percentage data series.

The title COPY OF PERCENTAGE WHITE would look absurd in the legend. This title can be renamed by pressing N to execute the NAME command while the cursor is on the COPY OF PERCENTAGE WHITE data series row. The various elements that you can rename will appear at the bottom of the screen. Highlighted will be the series name COPY OF PERCENTAGE WHITE. We'll rename it % White to distinguish it from PERCENTAGE WHITE, the series from which it was copied. Type % *White* and press Return.

Now you can change the number of columns. Suppose you want to keep only the Very Happy column in the table. Move the cursor to the % White row and then press the E key to execute the ENTRY command. This will shift you to the Entry screen for that series (see Figure 15.6). Using the DownArrow, move the cursor down to the PRETTY HAPPY row. Then delete this row and the one below it by pressing the M key, which executes the MODIFY command. Follow up by pressing the D key to execute the DELETE command. When asked how many lines you want to delete, press the number 2. The bottom two categories for the series will be deleted.

Return to the LIST screen by pressing the L key, and repeat the procedure just described for % BLACK and % OTHER. Be sure that asterisks are displayed

FIGURE 15.6 The Entry Screen

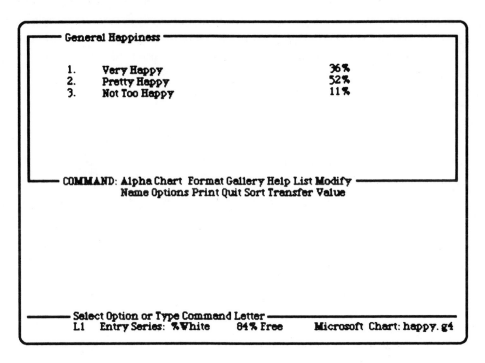

CHART 15.5 Percent Very Happy by Race

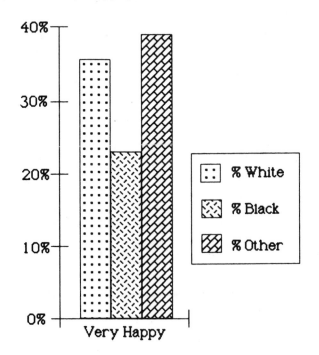

for each of the % rows and minus signs are displayed for each of the other rows, including the PERCENTAGE rows. Then press the C key to execute the CHART command. The new chart—with three columns instead of nine—will appear in the Chart screen (see Chart 15.5). You can now print or save this chart.

15.10 Adding a Second Control Variable

It is not possible to add a second control variable (for example, education) to the GRAPH command, but such an analysis can be performed by creating a separate chart for each educational category. (Here we explain how to merge the data from two charts onto one chart. For more information, you may want to review Sections 15.8 and 15.9.)

The SPSS/PC+ commands for the chart for people with less than 12 years of education would be

```
process if (educ lt 12).
graph /bar count by happy by race.
```

Save this chart by pressing the S key to execute SAVE from the Command Menu. When asked what to name the file type HAPPY1 and press the Enter key. This will save the file under the name HAPPY1.

Then press Q to execute the QUIT command. Press Y when asked if you really want to exit Chart, and you will be returned to SPSS/PC+.

Now create another chart for those with 12 or more years of education with the commands

```
process if (educ ge 12).
graph /bar count by happy by race.
```

At this point you should have the chart on the screen for the more than twelve years of education group. Convert the data series to percentages and label the data series to indicate that it is for people with 12 or more years of education. Print the chart, and if you are satisfied with the format, save it under the name HAPPY2 to distinguish it from the previous chart. The data for happiness by race by education would now be on two charts.

What about if instead of two charts, you want to merge the data onto one chart? In this case, you'd go through the steps of creating and saving HAPPY1,

CHART 15.6 Happiness Level by Race by Education

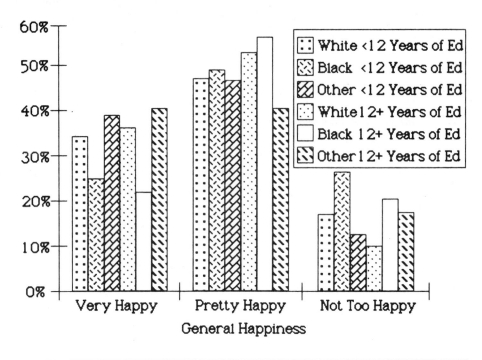

CHART 15.7 Percent Very Happy by Race by Education

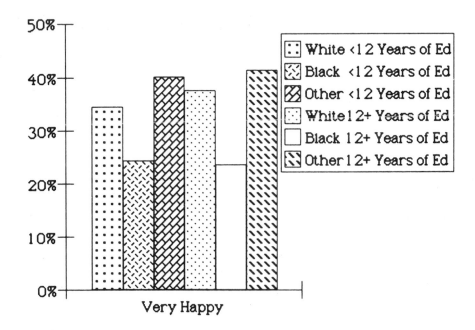

then creating HAPPY2. From the Chart screen press the T key to execute the TRANSFER command, followed by M to execute the MERGE command. What appears on the screen is the HAPPY1 chart again. If, however, you press the L key to bring up the List screen, you will see that the HAPPY2 data series is still there, but not entered in the chart because there are minus signs in their rows of the Include Series columns. Change these minuses to asterisks in the rows of data series you want entered. Press the C key to bring up the Chart screen, which now contains happiness by race by education (see Chart 15.6). You'll notice that in Chart 15.6 (and in Chart 15.7) the legend divides categories as <12 years of education and 12+ years of education. The category designated as 12+ is used for those with 12 or more years of education.

If you want a less cluttered table, some of the data columns can be deleted as in Chart 15.7. (For a refresher on deleting columns, see section 15.9.)

15.11 Changing the Font and Size of Label Type

Changing the font and size of the type used for labels in Chart is rather tricky. To begin with, what you see on the screen is not necessarily what will be the output of your printer. When I use an Epson printer, my output matches the screen fairly well. But when I use a Hewlett-Packard LaserJet II printer, the default screen font is printed much smaller than it appears on the screen. To make the screen reflect more accurately what will be printed, execute the OPTIONS command from the Chart screen. This action will bring up a menu with a Display specification on the right. Move the highlight to Display specification by pressing the Tab key, highlight Device by pressing the D key and press the Enter key. The screen will reformat with what is usually a more accurate representation of what will be printed.

The default font cannot be changed in size. Therefore, to change font size you must change the font type as well. From the Chart screen, press the Down-Arrow until the specification Label appears at the lower left. Then press the RightArrow until the label for which you want to change the font appears. Press F to execute the FORMAT command. When the new Command Menu appears, press T to execute the TYPE command. Press the Tab key to move the highlight around the specifications until you reach Font at the bottom left. Press the RightArrow key until the font type you want appears in the highlight. (The Modern B font has a pleasant appearance on the screen and has a wide range of sizes.) Next press the Tab key to move the highlight to the Size specification. The current font size will be displayed. If you want a larger font size, press the

RightArrow key; if you want a smaller font size, press the LeftArrow key. Chart will list step by step the font sizes available for the font you have selected. When you have highlighted the font size you want, press the Enter key and the screen will be reformatted with the font type and size that you chose.

To change the font type or size for axis categories or values, from the Chart screen press the DownArrow until the words *AXIS CATEGORY* or *AXIS VALUE* appear at the bottom left of the screen. (Once one of the two has appeared, pressing the RightArrow will switch you between AXIS CATEGORY and AXIS VALUE.) The categories are for the horizontal axis and the values are for the vertical axis. You have to make changes for categories and values separately. If you want to change the font for categories, when AXIS CATEGORY is at the bottom left, press the F key to execute the FORMAT command. Press the T key to execute the TYPE command. Using the Tab key, move the highlight through the specifications until you reach Tick Label Font. Press the RightArrow key to see a sequential list of your choices; when the font you want appears in the highlight, press the Tab key to move to the size specification. Use the Right-Arrow and LeftArrow keys to highlight the font size you want, and then press the Enter key. The Chart will be redrawn using the new font type and size for the category labels.

To change the size, position, or font of the chart legend, go to the Chart screen and press the DownArrow until the word *LEGEND* appears at the lower left. Press the F key to execute the FORMAT command or the M key to execute the MOVE command. Then follow the same procedures as described for these commands concerning other objects on the screen.

15.12 Summary

In the Chart program you move between three types of screens: Chart, List, and Entry. Think of these as three rooms. In each room you have equipment available that allows you to perform operations that you cannot perform in the other rooms.

The Chart screen shows your chart and allows you to change its appearance. The List screen controls what data series goes into the Chart screen for display, and allows you to perform some statistical transformations of the data. The Entry screen allows you to see the data entered in each series and also to change a data entry, if you so desire. Just as you would have to go from room to room to operate different machines, you must go from screen to screen to run their respective commands.

To use Chart without SPSS/PC+, you enter the program with the command CHART. At this point you will have called up the List screen. You can enter a chart you have previously saved with the TRANSFER command followed by the LOAD command.

From the List screen you can also enter a new data series. Select MODIFY and then from the MODIFY Command Menu, select INSERT. After the prompt, enter the number of the data series you will be using. To name a data series, move the highlight to the series row, press Enter, and after the prompt enter the name that you wish it to have. To enter data, press the E key to move to the Entry screen. In that screen, press N for the prompt to label the data series. Enter the label you want the first series to have, then press the RightArrow key to move to the value column and enter the numbers that you want. Press the L key to return to the List screen and repeat the procedure for the other data series.

The sections in this chapter demonstrated how to combine the power of Microsoft Chart and SPSS/PC+ to move data and charts freely between the two programs. I hope that this knowledge of these research and analytical tools will give you a good beginning to understanding research, whether you conduct research in the future or simply evaluate research done by other people.

APPENDIX A
SPECIAL TOPICS

A.1 COUNT Command

The COUNT command allows you to create a new variable by counting the number of times a given value occurs for a set of variables. For example, we could count the number of times a respondent gave the most positive response to the first five questions of the Happiness Questionnaire in Appendix C. We create the new variable SAT#MAX as follows:

```
count sat#max=happy
             health
             satfam
             satfrnd
             satjob (1).
```

More than one value can be used in the COUNT command. We could, therefore, count the number of times a respondent gave one of the two most positive responses on the same questions.

```
count sat#pos=happy
             health
             satfam
             satfrnd
             satjob (1,2).
```

More than one variable can be created with one COUNT command. Separate the new variables with a slash. For example, we could have created the two variables SAT#MAX and SAT#POS with one command.

```
count sat#max=happy
               health
               satfam
               satfrnd
               satjob (1)/
         sat#pos=happy
               health
               satfam
               satfrnd
               satjob (1,2).
```

If all the data are missing for the variables being used in the COUNT command, the new variable will have a value of 0. If you want to eliminate cases with all missing data, use a SELECT IF command before the COUNT command. The keywords LO, HI, and THRU can be used with the COUNT within the parentheses to specify the values to be counted.

A.2 FREE Format

In FREE format the user does not need to place the data for each variable in specific columns. All that is necessary is that the data be entered in the correct sequence with one or more blanks between the entries. For example, say we want to enter the income and education of a set of persons. The first person had income of $35,000 and 16 years of education, the second had $9,000 income and 9 years of education, and the third had $130,000 income and 20 years of education. The data entries would be

```
35000   16
9000    9
130000  20
```

The subcommand FREE is added to the DATA LIST command before the variable names.

Using string variables in a FREE format statement requires that you place an A and the maximum number of columns for the variable in parentheses after the variable name. For example, to access a variable NAME—a string variable—and a variable INCOME—not a string variable—with a FREE format, the following command could be used:

```
data list free / name (A23) income
```

The greatest advantage of the FREE format is that you do not have to pay attention to column position when entering data. The greatest disadvantage is that you may not notice when you omit the data for a variable.

A.3 Multiple Record Files

If the data are spread over more than one record, insert a slash on the DATA LIST command to indicate the beginning of a new record:

```
data list / id 1-4
           sex 6
         / marital 5.
```

Suppose that marital status is located in column 5 of the second record. The slash before MARITAL indicates that the next variable will be on the second record.

A.4 PROCESS IF Command

PROCESS IF instructs SPSS/PC+ to carry out the instructions that follow until the next data analysis command is reached. The advantages are that processing time is not wasted on cases that do meet the initial conditions and recoding statements do not have to be written for categories that are not of interest. For example, suppose you want to analyze the traits of immigrants to the United States who are coded 2 on the variable NATIVE. The following commands would recode the variable YRIMMIG for immigrants only; it would not apply to nonimmigrants. The IF commands create a new variable, CLASS, that is coded 1 for cases that have over 25,000 on the variable INCOME and is coded 0 for others. (These variables are from a census public use sample, not NORC84.)

```
process if native eq 2.
recode yrimmig (lo to 1959  =1)
               (1960 to 1969=2)
               (1970 to 1979=3)
               (1980 to hi  =4).
if   income gt 25000  class=1.
if   income le 25000  class=0.
frequencies  crosstabs  income by yrimmig
             options  4 13.
```

In this example, the RECODE and FREQUENCIES would not be done for cases for which NATIVE did not equal one. In addition to processing time, the

PROCESS IF commands save the programmer considerable time by doing transformations with fewer commands. Without the PROCESS IF command, the transformations done in the one recode command would require four IF commands. When many transformations are involved, this succinctness is a great advantage.

Two commands that can be used with the PROCESS IF commands are ELSE IF and ELSE. ELSE IF refers to another subset of the file not specified by the PROCESS IF specifications. ELSE refers to all the remaining cases not specified on the DO IF command or any ELSE IF commands in the PROCESS IF sequence. The following commands elaborate this section's first example using ELSE IF and ELSE.

```
process if native eq 2.
recode yrimmig (lo to 1959  =1)
               (1960 to 1969=2)
               (1970 to 1979=3)
               (1980 to hi   =4).
else if native eq 1.
recode  birthpl (lo to 15=1)
                (16 to 29=2)
                (30 to 40=3)
                (41 to hi=4).
if   income gt 25000  class=1.
if   income le 25000  class=0.
frequencies  crosstabs  income by yrimmig birthpl
             options  4 13.
```

A.5 SAMPLE Command

The SAMPLE command can be used two ways. The first is by indicating the proportion of cases to be sampled. For example,

```
sample .25.
```

would cause 25 percent of the cases to be selected randomly. If you had a specific number of cases you wanted drawn, an alternative method is a format that first states the sample size and then the size of the population that you are sampling. For example,

```
sample 500 21000.
```

would sample 500 cases from 21,000. If there were fewer than 21,000 cases, the sample would be reduced. If there were more than 21,000 cases, the sample would only be drawn from the first 21,000 cases.

A.6 String Variables

String variables may contain nonnumeric characters. To indicate that a variable is a string variable, on the DATA LIST command place an A in parentheses after the column numbers for the variable. For example, if we had a string variable called NAME on columns 1–20 of a single record file, the following DATA LIST command would allow us to access NAME:

```
data list  name 1-20  (a).
```

A string variable cannot be used if multiplication, division, or other arithmetic operations will be performed. A string variable can be used as the variable in MEANS for which other variable means are calculated. For example, one could use MEANS INCOME BY SECTION, where INCOME is not a string variable but SECTION is.

When using FREE formats, the A in parentheses is followed by the maximum number of columns the variable uses (see Section A.2).

A.7 The Keyword TO

The keyword TO enables you to refer easily to a large number of adjoining variables on your DATA LIST command. For example, suppose you have a data file corresponding to that of the Happiness Questionnaire in Appendix C, in which ID is the first variable; HAPPY is the second; and, after several other variables, AGE is the last. If you want to refer to the variables from HAPPY through AGE on a FREQUENCIES command, you can give the command FREQUENCIES VARIABLES = HAPPY TO AGE instead of specifying each variable separately.

New variables created through IF and COMPUTE commands are added to the end of the variable list in the order that they are created. So, in the preceding example, if you create a new variable called CLASS before the FREQUENCIES command, it will not be included in the specification HAPPY TO AGE. You will have to specify HAPPY TO CLASS to include it.

APPENDIX B
THE SPSS SYSTEM FILE
NORC84

The SPSS system file NORC84 contains data from the 1984 General Social Survey. The General Social Survey is an annual survey conducted by the National Opinion Research Center. A probability sample of 1,473 persons was taken in 1984 using multistage cluster sampling.

Following is a list of the variable names in alphabetical order. In this list, a more descriptive variable label is given on the same line as the variable name. The question number of the variable and the column number(s) of the variable in the file are also given. You can use the question number to look up more complete information in the questionnaire that follows this list and the next one (of variables by column number).

Alphabetical Listing of Variables

Variable Name	Variable Label	Question Number	Column Number
ABDEFECT	Abortion if birth defect likely	60	65
ABHLTH	Abortion if mother's health in danger	61	66
ABNOMORE	Abortion if no more children wanted	62	67
ABPOOR	Abortion if family is poor	63	68
ABRAPE	Abortion if pregnancy from rape	64	69
ABSINGLE	Abortion if unmarried	65	70
AGE	Age of respondent	1	1–2
ANOMIA1	Conditions getting worse	55	60
ANOMIA2	Not fair to bring child into world	56	61
ANOMIA3	Officials neglect average man	57	62

Alphabetical Listing of Variables (*continued*)

Variable Name	Variable Label	Question Number	Column Number
ATTEND	Frequency of religious attendance	16	21
CAPPUN	Feelings about capital punishment	25	30
CHILDS	Number of children	8	13
CLASS	Social class identification	17	22
COMMUN	Feelings about Communism	28	33
CONFINAN	Confidence in banks	40	45
CONBUS	Confidence in major companies	41	46
CONCLER	Confidence in organized religion	42	47
CONEDUC	Confidence in educational institutions	43	48
CONFED	Confidence in presidency	44	49
CONLABOR	Confidence in organized labor	45	50
CONPRESS	Confidence in press	46	51
CONMEDI	Confidence in medicine	47	52
CONTV	Confidence in television	48	53
CONJUDG	Confidence in Supreme Court	49	54
CONSCI	Confidence in scientific community	50	55
CONLEGI	Confidence in congress	51	56
CONARMY	Confidence in military	52	57
DEGREE	Highest school degree of respondent	9	14
DRUNK	Sometimes drink too much	53	58
EDUC	Years of education of respondent	4	7–8
FAIR	Fairness of people	34	39
FINALTER	Changes in financial situation	58	63
GETAHEAD	Get ahead by hard work	59	64
GRASS	Favor legalizing marijuana	27	32
GUNLAW	Favor gun permits	26	31
HAPPY	Is respondent happy	29	34
HEALTH	Respondent's health	30	35
HELPFUL	Helpfulness of people	33	38
INCOME	Family income	3	5–6
MARITAL	Current marital status	7	12
MAWORK	Was your mother employed	12	17

Alphabetical Listing of Variables (*continued*)

Variable Name	Variable Label	Question Number	Column Number
NATEDUC	Nation spending enough on education	19	24
NATFARE	Nation spending enough on welfare	20	25
PARTYID	Political party identification	31	36
POLVIEWS	Political ideology	32	37
PRESTIGE	Prestige of occupation	5	9–10
RACE	Race of respondent	11	16
REGION	Region of interview	13	18
RELIG	Religious preference	15	20
SATCITY	Satisfaction with city	35	40
SATFAM	Satisfaction with family	36	41
SATFRND	Satisfaction with friendships	37	42
SATJOB	Satisfaction with job	38	43
SATHEALT	Satisfaction with health	39	44
SEX	Sex of respondent	10	15
SIBS	Number of siblings	2	3–4
SMOKE	Do you smoke	54	59
SPKATH	Allow speakers against churches	22	27
SPKCOM	Allow Communists to speak	23	28
SPKHOMO	Allow homosexuals to speak	24	29
SRCBELT	Size of residential city	14	19
TAX	Paying fair federal income tax	21	26
UNEMP	Ever unemployed in past ten years	18	23
WRKSTAT	Employment status currently	6	11

The following is a list of the NORC84 variables by column number.

Variables by Column Number

AGE 1–2	UNEMP 23	FAIR 39	CONSCI 55
SIBS 3–4	NATEDUC 24	SATCITY 40	CONLEGI 56
INCOME 5–6	NATFARE 25	SATFAM 41	CONARMY 57
EDUC 7–8	TAX 26	SATFRND 42	DRUNK 58
PRESTIGE 9–10	SPKATH 27	SATJOB 43	SMOKE 59
WRKSTAT 11	SPKCOM 28	SATHEALT 44	ANOMIA1 60
MARITAL 12	SPKHOMO 29	CONFINAN 45	ANOMIA2 61
CHILDS 13	CAPPUN 30	CONBUS 46	ANOMIA3 62
DEGREE 14	GUNLAW 31	CONCLER 47	FINALTER 63
SEX 15	GRASS 32	CONEDUC 48	GETAHEAD 64
RACE 16	COMMUN 33	CONFED 49	ABDEFECT 65
MAWORK 17	HAPPY 34	CONLABOR 50	ABNOMORE 66
REGION 18	HEALTH 35	CONPRESS 51	ABHLTH 67
SRCBELT 19	PARTYID 36	CONMEDI 52	ABPOOR 68
RELIG 20	POLVIEWS 37	CONTV 53	ABRAPE 69
ATTEND 21	HELPFUL 38	CONJUDG 54	ABSINGLE 70
CLASS 22			

In the NORC84 questionnaire, the column numbers of the variable are given in parentheses under the variable name, and the question number appears to the right at the beginning of the question.

Questions by Column Number

AGE
(1–2)

1. Age (determined by asking date of birth)
   18–90. Actual age
   98. Don't know (DK)
   99. No answer (NA)

SIBS
(3–4)

2. How many brothers and sisters did you have? Please count those born alive but no longer living, as well as those alive now. Also include stepbrothers and stepsisters and children adopted by your parents.
   0–20. Actual number
   98. DK
   99. NA

INCOME
(5–6)

3. Into which of the following groups did your total FAMILY income, from ALL sources, fall last year—before taxes, that is?
    1. Under $5,000
    2. $5,000 to $9,999
    3. $10,000 to $14,999
    4. $15,000 to $19,999
    5. $20,000 to $24,999
    6. $25,000 to $34,999
    7. $35,000 to $49,999
    8. $50,000+
    9. Refused
    98. DK
    99. NA

EDUC
(7–8)

4. Number of years of formal education.
    0–20. Actual number
    98. DK
    99. NA

PRESTIGE
(9–10)

5. Hodge/Siegel/Rossi prestige scale score for respondent's occupation.
    0. No score due to no job
    12–89. Prestige scale score for job

WRKSTAT
(11)

6. Last week were you working full-time, working part-time, going to school, keeping house, or what?
    1. Working full-time
    2. Working part-time
    3. With a job, but not at work because of temporary illness, vacation, strike
    4. Unemployed
    5. Retired
    6. In school
    7. Keeping house
    8. Other

MARITAL
(12)

7. Are you currently married, widowed, divorced, separated, or have you never been married?
    1. Married
    2. Widowed
    3. Divorced
    4. Separated
    5. Never married

CHILDS
(13)

8. How many children have you ever had? Please count all that were born alive at any time (including any you had from a previous marriage).
0–7. Actual number
8. Eight or more
9. NA

DEGREE
(14)

9. Highest degree.
0. Less than high school
1. High school
2. Associate/junior college
3. Bachelor's
4. Graduate
8. DK
9. NA

SEX
(15)

10. Sex (coded by interviewer).
1. Male
2. Female

RACE
(16)

11. What race do you consider yourself?
1. White
2. Black
3. Other

MAWORK
(17)

12. Did your mother ever work for pay for as long as a year, after she was married?
0. Did not live with mother
1. Yes
2. No
8. DK
9. NA

REGION
(18)

13. Region of interview.
1. New England
2. Middle Atlantic
3. East North Central
4. West North Central
5. South Atlantic
6. East South Central
7. West South Central
8. Mountain
9. Pacific

SRCBELT   14. Size/type of residence location.
(19)   1. Central city of one of 12 largest Standard Metropolitan
                         Statistical Areas (SMSAs)
                      2. Central city of remainder of the 100 largest SMSAs
                      3. Suburbs of one of 12 largest SMSAs
                      4. Suburbs of the remainder of the 100 largest SMSAs
                      5. Other urban (counties having towns of 10,000 or more)
                      6. Other rural (counties having no towns of 10,000 or
                         more)

RELIG   15. What is your religious preference? Is it Protestant, Catho-
(20)   lic, Jewish, some other religion, or no religion?
                      1. Protestant
                      2. Catholic
                      3. Jewish
                      4. None
                      5. Other
                      9. NA

ATTEND   16. How often do you attend religious services?
(21)   0. Never
                      1. Less than once a year
                      2. About once or twice a year
                      3. Several times a year
                      4. About once a month
                      5. 2–3 times a month
                      6. Nearly every week
                      7. Every week
                      8. Several times a week
                      9. DK/NA

CLASS   17. If you were asked to use one of four names for your social
(22)   class, which would you say you belong in: the lower class,
                     the working class, the middle class, or the upper class?
                      1. Lower class
                      2. Working class
                      3. Middle class
                      4. Upper class
                      8. DK
                      9. NA

UNEMP   18. At any time during the last ten years, have you been un-
(23)   employed and looking for work for as long as a month?
                      1. Yes

2. No
8. DK
9. NA

We are faced with many problems in this country, none of which can be solved easily or inexpensively. I'm going to name some of these problems, and for each one I'd like you to tell me whether you think we're spending too much money on it, too little money, or about the right amount. Are we spending too much, too little, or about the right amount on [19, 20, 21]?

NATEDUC
(24)

19. Improving the nation's educational system?
    1. Too little
    2. About right
    3. Too much
    8. DK
    9. NA

NATFARE
(25)

20. Welfare?
    (Same answers as NATEDUC, #19)

TAX
(26)

21. Do you consider the amount of federal income tax that you have to pay to be too high, about right, or too low?
    1. Too high
    2. About right
    3. Too low
    8. DK
    9. NA

SPKATH
(27)

22. If somebody who is against all churches and religion wanted to make a speech in your city/town/community against churches and religion, should he be allowed to speak or not?
    1. Yes, allowed to speak
    2. Not allowed
    8. DK
    9. NA

SPKCOM
(28)

23. Suppose a man who admits he is a Communist wanted to make a speech in your community. Should he be allowed to speak or not?
    (Same answers as SPKATH, #22)

SPKHOMO
(29)

24. Suppose a man who admits he is a homosexual wanted to make a speech in your community. Should he be allowed to speak or not?
(Same answers as SPKATH, #22)

CAPPUN
(30)

25. Do you favor or oppose the death penalty for persons convicted of murder?
1. Favor
2. Oppose
8. DK
9. NA

GUNLAW
(31)

26. Would you favor or oppose a law that would require a person to obtain a police permit before he or she could buy a gun?
(Same answers as CAPPUN, #25)

GRASS
(32)

27. Do you think the use of marijuana should be made legal or not?
1. Should
2. Should not
8. DK
9. NA

COMMUN
(33)

28. Thinking about all the different kinds of government in the world today, which of these statements comes closest to how you feel about Communism as a form of government?
1. It's the worst kind of all
2. It's bad, but no worse than some others
3. It's all right for some countries
4. It's a good form of government
8. DK
9. NA

HAPPY
(34)

29. Taken all together, how would you say things are these days—would you say that you are very happy, pretty happy, or not too happy?
1. Very happy
2. Pretty happy
3. Not too happy
8. DK
9. NA

HEALTH
(35)

30. Would you say your own health, in general, is excellent, good, fair, or poor?
    1. Excellent
    2. Good
    3. Fair
    4. Poor
    8. DK
    9. NA

PARTYID
(36)

31. Generally speaking, do you usually think of yourself as a Republican, Democrat, Independent, or what?
    0. Strong Democrat
    1. Not very strong Democrat
    2. Independent, close to Democrat
    3. Independent (neither, no response)
    4. Independent, close to Republican
    5. Not very strong Republican
    6. Strong Republican
    7. Other party, refused to say
    8. DK
    9. NA

POLVIEWS
(37)

32. I'm going to show you a seven-point scale on which the *political* views that people might hold are arranged from extremely liberal—point 1—to extremely conservative—point 7. Where would you place yourself on this scale?
    1. Extremely liberal
    2. Liberal
    3. Slightly liberal
    4. Moderate, middle of the road
    5. Slightly conservative
    6. Conservative
    7. Extremely conservative
    8. DK
    9. NA

HELPFUL
(38)

33. Would you say that most of the time people try to be helpful or that they are mostly just looking out for themselves?
    1. Try to be helpful
    2. Just look out for themselves
    3. Depends (volunteered)
    8. DK
    9. NA

FAIR
(39)

34. Do you think most people would try to take advantage of you if they got a chance, or would they try to be fair?
   1. Would take advantage of you
   2. Would try to be fair
   3. Depends (volunteered)
   8. DK
   9. NA

SATCITY
(40)

35. Tell me the number that shows how much satisfaction you get from the city or place you live in.
   1. A very great deal
   2. A great deal
   3. Quite a bit
   4. A fair amount
   5. Some
   6. A little
   7. None
   8. DK
   9. NA

SATFAM
(41)

36. Tell me the number that shows how much satisfaction you get from your family life.
   (Same answers as SATCITY, #35)

SATFRND
(42)

37. Tell me the number that shows how much satisfaction you get from your friendships.
   (Same answers as SATCITY, 35)

SATJOB
(43)

38. On the whole, how satisfied are you with the work you do—would you say you are very satisfied, moderately satisfied, a little dissatisfied, or very dissatisfied?
   0. Not applicable due to no job
   1. Very satisfied
   2. Moderately satisfied
   3. A little dissatisfied
   4. Very dissatisfied
   8. DK
   9. NA

SATHEALT
(44)

39. Tell me the number that shows how much satisfaction you get from your health and physical condition.
   (Same answers as SATCITY, #35)

I am going to name some institutions in this country. As far as the *people running* these institutions are concerned, would you say that you have a great deal of confidence, only some confidence, or hardly any confidence at all in them [40–52]?

CONFINAN
(45)

40. Banks and financial institutions
    1. A great deal
    2. Only some
    3. Hardly any
    8. DK
    9. NA

CONBUS
(46)

41. Major companies
    (Same answers as CONFINAN, #40)

CONCLER
(47)

42. Organized religion
    (Same answers as CONFINAN, #40)

CONEDUC
(48)

43. Education
    (Same answers as CONFINAN, #40)

CONFED
(49)

44. Executive branch of the federal government
    (Same answers as CONFINAN, #40)

CONLABOR
(50)

45. Organized labor
    (Same answers as CONFINAN, #40)

CONPRESS
(51)

46. Press
    (Same answers as CONFINAN, #40)

CONMEDI
(52)

47. Medicine
    (Same answers as CONFINAN, #40)

CONTV
(53)

48. TV
    (Same answers as CONFINAN, #40)

CONJUDG
(54)

49. U.S. Supreme Court
    (Same answers as CONFINAN, #40)

CONSCI
(55)

50. Scientific community
    (Same answers as CONFINAN, #40)

CONLEGI
(56)

51. Congress
    (Same answers as CONFINAN, #40)

CONARMY
(57)

52. Military
    (Same answers as CONFINAN, #40)

DRUNK
(58)

53. Do you sometimes drink more than you think you should?
    0. Total abstainer
    1. Yes
    2. No

8. DK
9. NA

SMOKE
(59)

54. Do you smoke?
1. Yes
2. No
9. NA

ANOMIA1
(60)

55. In spite of what some people say, the lot/situation/con-
dition of the average man is getting worse, not better. Do
you more or less agree with that, or more or less disagree?
1. Agree
2. Disagree
8. DK
9. NA

ANOMIA2
(61)

56. It's hardly fair to bring a child into the world with the way
things look for the future.
(Same answers as ANOMIA1, #55)

ANOMIA3
(62)

57. Most public officials (people in public office) are not really
interested in the problems of the average man.
(Same answers as ANOMIA1, #55)

FINALTER
(63)

58. During the last few years, has your financial situation been
getting better or getting worse, or has it stayed the same?
1. Getting better
2. Getting worse
3. Stayed the same
8. DK
9. NA

GETAHEAD
(64)

59. Some people say that people get ahead by their own hard
work; others say that lucky breaks or help from other
people are more important. Which do you think is most
important?
1. Hard work most important
2. Hard work, luck equally important
3. Luck most important
8. DK
9. NA

Please tell me whether or not *you* think it should be possible
for a pregnant woman to obtain a *legal* abortion [60–65].

ABDEFECT   60. If there is a strong chance of serious defect in the baby.
(65)   1. Yes
                     2. No
                     8. DK
                     9. NA

ABNOMORE   61. If she is married and does not want any more children.
(66)   (Same answers as ABDEFECT, #60)

ABHLTH   62. If the woman's health is seriously endangered by the
(67)   pregnancy.
                     (Same answers as ABDEFECT, #60)

ABPOOR   63. If the family has a very low income and cannot afford any
(68)   more children.
                     (Same answers as ABDEFECT, #60)

ABRAPE   64. If she became pregnant as a result of rape.
(69)   (Same answers as ABDEFECT, #60)

ABSINGLE   65. If she is not married and does not want to marry the man.
(70)   (Same answers as ABDEFECT, #60)

APPENDIX C
A COURSE RESEARCH
PROJECT

Completing a research project on your own is much more challenging than using the data we provide in Chapter 2 or in the SPSS system file NORC84. In this appendix we outline a class research project. The subject of this research is happiness, and the questions on this survey come from the SPSS system file NORC84. This similarity will allow you to compare your results with those of a representative national sample.

This appendix includes a questionnaire you can photocopy and use in an interview. The questionnaire is designed for the interviewer to record (in the boxes on the right), the numbers that correspond to the respondent's answers. The numbers under the boxes designate the columns in which these data are to be stored when the information is placed in a computer file.

Sampling Methods

Let us suppose that you are going to administer this questionnaire to 20 people. The obvious question is which 20?

- One choice would be to go to a store and hand out questionnaires to people leaving the store.
- Another choice would be to go to a random selection of households and interview the individuals in these households.
- Or you could randomly dial telephone numbers and interview individuals over the phone.

Each of these sampling methods is reasonably good, although there are always problems with biases that might make your sample different from the general population. The store may attract people from one social class or ethnic group more than others. You may be biased in which shoppers you approach to question and which ones you let pass by. Households with many members are more likely to have someone home when you knock on the door or call on the phone; hence you may undersample single people. Households with ferocious guard dogs are judiciously skipped by prudent interviewers. People without phones will not be netted in a telephone survey.

The fact that it is nearly impossible to obtain a perfect random sample does not mean that research is impossible. Our burden as researchers is to do work that is as free from bias as we can make it, and yet humbly admit that some small distortion still creeps in. An analogy is radio reception from a distant station: Occasionally there may be static distortion, but normally you can distinguish the music and lyrics. Accepted survey practices are accepted because experience has shown that they provide reasonably accurate data about the population being sampled.

You need to consider the purpose of your research. Are there special reasons why, given that purpose, a particular sampling method is desirable or undesirable? For example, if you wanted to study homeless people, a phone survey or a household survey of a middle-class neighborhood would not be efficient or appropriate. If you wanted to survey wealthy people, passing out questionnaires at a fast-food outlet would not be the best approach. There is no substitute for careful thinking. Consider first who is in the population you want to sample, and second what would be the most efficient means of obtaining a sample of these people that is approximately random.

Once you have gathered your data, the next step is to code it. All but one of the questions in the Happiness Questionnaire are precoded; that is, all possible responses for each question have already been given a number, and columns have been designated for the responses for each variable. Precoding saves time; however, it does require painstaking forethought and pretesting of the questionnaire. Precoding usually restricts you to multiple-choice questions. The choices may help the respondents answer as they consider the alternatives, but the set of answers may not allow some respondents to express their positions precisely.

The last question on the questionnaire was deliberately left open-ended to provide the option of dealing with less structured data. If you want to have a quick and easy coding experience, stop at Question 12.

Question 12—"What do you think you could do to be happier five years from now than you are today?"—will result in a plethora of answers. Come coding time you will have to decide whether you are going to categorize these responses into numbered groups for quantitative analysis or simply keep the verbal responses as material to quote when illustrating your findings in the coded questions. Open-ended questions can be eye openers for the researcher in illustrating factors that he or she may have overlooked or in pointing out that assumptions are unfounded.

Follow your instructor's guidelines for administering the Happiness Questionnaire to a sample of people.

The DATA LIST command for Questions 1 through 11 of the questionnaire will be

```
data list fixed / id 1-4   happy 5   health 6   satfam 7
                   satfrnd 8   satjob 9
                   educ 10-11   marital 12   childs 13
                   income 14-15   sex 16   age 17-18.
```

Happiness Questionnaire

(Interviewer: Record the answer to each question in the boxes at right.)

ID

Columns 1–4

As a class exercise, we are doing a study of what affects happiness. Will you please answer twelve questions for us?

1. Taken all together, would you say that you are very happy, pretty happy, or not too happy?

1. Very happy	8. Don't know (DK)
2. Pretty happy	9. No answer (NA)
3. Not too happy	

   HAPPY

   Column 5

2. Would you say your own health, in general, is excellent, good, fair, or poor?

1. Excellent	4. Poor
2. Good	8. DK
3. Fair	9. NA

   HEALTH

   Column 6

3. Tell me the number that shows how much satisfaction you get from your family life.

1. A very great deal	6. A little
2. A great deal	7. None
3. Quite a bit	8. DK
4. A fair amount	9. NA
5. Some	

   SATFAM

   Column 7

4. Tell me the number that shows how much satisfaction you get from your friendships. (Use the same choices as for Question 3.)

   SATFRND

   Column 8

5. On the whole, how satisfied are you with the work you do? Would you say you are very satisfied, moderately satisfied, a little dissatisfied, or very dissatisfied?

0. Not applicable due to no job	4. Very dissatisfied
1. Very satisfied	8. DK
2. Moderately satisfied	9. NA
3. A little dissatisfied	

   SATJOB

   Column 9

6. How many years of formal education have you
    completed? (Enter number of years.)   EDUC
    98. DK
    99. NA   Columns 10–11

7. Are you currently married, widowed, divorced,
    or separated, or have you never been married?   MARITAL
    1. Married   4. Separated
    2. Widowed   5. Never married
    3. Divorced   Column 12

8. How many children have you ever had? Please
    count all that were born alive at any time (in-
    cluding any you had from a previous marriage).   CHILDS
    0–7. Actual number
    8.   Eight or more
    9.   NA   Column 13

9. Into which of the following groups did your
    total family income, from all sources, fall last
    year before taxes?   INCOME
    1. Under $5,000   7. $35,000 to $49,000
    2. $5,000 to $9,999   8. $50,000 to $74,999
    3. $10,000 to $14,999   9. $75,000+   Column
    4. $15,000 to $19,999   10. DK   14–15
    5. $20,000 to $24,999   11. NA
    6. $25,000 to $34,999

10. Sex.   SEX
    1. Male
    2. Female   Column 16

11. What is your age?   AGE
    0–97. Actual age
    98.   DK
    99.   NA   Column 17–18

12. This is the last question. What do you think
    you could do to be happier five years from
    now than you are today?

Thank you for your cooperation.

GLOSSARY OF SPSS/PC+ COMMANDS

COMPUTE Examples

Mathematical operators used with COMPUTE

+	plus
–	minus
*	multiplication
/	division
**	exponentiation
SQRT	square root

```
compute  answer1=450+200.

compute  answer2=450-200.

compute  answer3=450*2.

compute  answer4=450/50.

compute  answer5=5**3.

compute  answer6=sqrt(81).

compute  tinc=winc+hinc.

compute  retire=65-age.

compute  tpay=dsalary*days.

compute  avesal=payroll/nemploys.

compute  deviat=(inc-minc)**2.

compute  sd=sqrt(sumdev).
```

CROSSTABS Examples

```
data list /
     id 1-2
     educ 3-4
     sex 5
     happy 6.
begin data.
     .
     .
     .
end data.
missing values educ (-9) happy sex (0).
recode educ (0 thru 11=1) (12 thru 15=2) (16 thru 30=3).
crosstabs educ by sex.
options 4.

get file 'norc84'.
crosstabs satfam satfrnd satjob by income.
options 4.
```

DATA LIST Examples

Single record file

```
data list /
     id 1-2
     educ 3-4
     sex 5
     happy 6.
```

Free format file

```
data list free /
     id 1-2
     educ 3-4
     sex 5
     happy 6.
```

Multiple record file

```
data list records=2 /1 id 1-4 sex 6
                     /2 marital 5.
```

FREQUENCIES Examples

```
get file 'norc84'.
frequencies all/
          statistics.
get file 'norc84'.
frequencies abdefect
          abnomore
          abhlth
          abpoor
          abrape
          absingle/
          statistics.
```

(The subcommand could also be written as abdefect to absingle)

IF Examples

Comparisons used with IF

    EQ   equal

    NE   not equal

    LT   less than

    GT   greater than

    LE   less than or equal to

    GE   greater than or equal to

```
if (age le 9) agegroup=1.

if (age gt 9 and age le 19) agegroup=2.

if (age gt 19 and age le 29) agegroup=3.

if (age gt 29 and age le 39) agegroup=4.

if (age gt 39 and age le 49) agegroup=5.

if (age gt 49 and age le 59) agegroup=6.
```

```
if (age gt 59 and age le 69) agegroup=7.

if (age gt 69 and age le 79) agegroup=8.

if (age gt 79) agegroup=9.

if (tenure lt 12) newexec=1.

if (famincom gt aveincom) income=1.
```

LIST Examples

```
list.

list/cases=15.

list variables=income/
    cases=all.

data list /
    id 1-2
    educ 3-4
    sex 5
    happy 6.
begin data.
    .
    .
    .
end data.
select if (sex ne 1 or sex ne 2)
list.
```

MEANS Examples

```
data list /
    id 1-2
    educ 3-4
    sex 5
    happy 6.
```

```
begin data.
    .
    .
    .
end data.
missing values educ (-9) happy sex (0).
means happy by sex.

get file 'norc84'.
means happy by health.
```

MISSING VALUES Examples

```
missing values educ (-9).

missing values income (-9).

missing values sex religion party (0).

missing values educ (-9) happy sex (0).

data list/
    id 1-2
    educ 3-4
    sex 5
    happy 6.
begin data.
    .
    .
    .
end data.
missing values educ (-9) happy sex (0).
frequencies all.
```

PROCESS IF Examples

```
data list /
    id 1-2
    educ 3-4
    sex 5
    happy 6.
```

```
begin data.
    .

    .

    .

end data.
process if (sex eq 1).
frequencies all/
            statistics.


get file 'norc84'.
process if (age gt 49).
frequencies educ/
            statistics.
process if (age gt 24 and age lt 50).
frequencies educ/
            statistics.
```

RECODE Examples

```
recode marital (2 thru 4=1).

recode height (low thru 59=1) (60 thru 70=2) (71 thru hi=3).

recode cars (3 thru hi=2).

recode age (lo thru 15=1) (16 thru 65=2) (66 thru hi=3).
```

SELECT IF Examples

Comparisons used with SELECT IF

EQ   equal

NE   not equal

LT   less than

GT   greater than

LE   less than or equal to

GE   greater than or equal to

```
select if (educ gt 15).

select if (sex eq 1).

select if (age gt 15 or age lt 66).

select if (educ gt 16 or income gt 30000).

select if (educ gt 12 and sex eq 2).

select if (sex eq 2 and age gt 14 and age lt 45).
```

(The same cases could be selected by using two SELECT IF commands—one for SEX and one for AGE.)

```
select if (sex eq 2).

select if (age gt 14 and age lt 45).

data list /
     id 1-2
     educ 3-4
     sex 5
     happy 6.
begin data.
   .
   .
   .
end data.
select if (sex eq 1).
frequencies educ
            sex
            happy/
            statistics.
```

VALUE LABEL Examples

```
value label polviews  1 'liberal'
                      2 'middle of the road'
                      3 'conservative'.
```

```
value label overdue   1 'less than 60 days'
                       2 'more than 60 days'/
             military  1 'military personnel'
                       2 'civilian personnel'.
```

VARIABLE LABEL Examples

```
variable label  childs  'number of Children'.

variable label  income  'Gross Income'
                net      'Net Income'.
```

ANSWERS TO REVIEW QUESTIONS

Chapter 1

1.1 SPSS/PC+ stands for Statistical Package for the Social Sciences/Personal Computers enhanced edition, Version 3.0.

1.2 Input devices, central processing unit, storage devices, and output devices are parts of a computer.

1.3 A keyboard and disk drive are examples of input devices.

1.4 The central processing unit executes program commands.

1.5 A floppy disk, hard disk, and tape are examples of storage devices.

1.6 A video display screen, printer, floppy disk, and disk drive are examples of output devices.

1.7 A computer program consists of commands that instruct the computer about how to obtain, process, store, and output information.

1.8 A command keyword is followed by specification fields which provide details about the command.

1.9 No. A word or variable name cannot be split between lines of an SPSS/PC+ command.

1.10 A period indicates the end of an SPSS/PC+ command.

1.11 A set of instructions submitted to a computer for execution is a run or a job.

Chapter 2

2.1   The Hedderson case would be coded 25 in the first two columns, which indicate his identification number. The third and fourth columns would be coded 21 to indicate the 21 years of formal education; the fifth column would be coded 1 to indicate his sex; and the sixth column would be coded 1 to indicate that he stated that he felt very happy. Thus the record line for Hedderson would read

   252111

2.2   To code age, researchers usually simply employ the age of the respondent in years and record this figure in two columns. Someone who was 19 years old would be given a value of 19. Someone who was 45 years old would be given a value of 45. Grouped intervals could also be used. For example:

Age	Code
Under 10	1
10–19	2
20–29	3
30–39	4
40–49	5
50–59	6
60–70	7
Over 70	8

2.3   In the United States, political party affiliation might be coded as follows:

Party	Code
Democrat	1
Republican	2
Independent (no affiliation)	3
Other affiliation	4

The code numbers used to indicate the categories of a variable are an arbitrary choice of the researcher. In this example, Republican could just as well be coded 1 and Democrat 2. The code numbers are merely short labels used to save space.

2.4 The simplest way to code annual salary would be to use two columns and code the case's income in thousands of dollars. Thus, someone with an income of $20,000 would be given a score of 20. The last category 99 could be used for people whose annual salary is $99,000 or more. Grouped intervals (as in Review Question 2.2) could also be used.

2.5 `data list / educ 3-4.`

2.6 DATA LIST commands are not used with SPSS system files; the variable location information is already saved with the file.

2.7 `data list / income   13`
         `              sex      16.`

2.8 `missing values educ   (-9).`

2.9 `missing values income (-8) education (-9).`

2.10 `missing values   sex`
         `                 religion`
         `                 party    (0).`

2.11 Nothing need be done. A blank entry is assumed to be missing.

Chapter 3

3.1 `data list /   id      1-2`
         `              educ    3-4`
         `              sex     5`
         `              happy   6.`
         `begin data.`
         `010912`
         `021223`
         `031521`
         `041222`
         `050611`
         `061612`
         `071522`
         `081612`
         `091821`

```
        101412
        111321
        121611
        130922
        141212
        151221
        161821
        170821
        181222
        191613
        201421
        end data.
        list.
```

3.2   ```
get file 'norc84'.
list all/
    cases=20.
```

**3.3**    ```
get file 'norc84'.
list income/
    cases=all.
```

3.4   ```
frequencies all.
```

**3.5**    ```
frequencies age
            sex
            marital.
```

3.6   You would need to recode INCOME into a manageable number of categories. Otherwise there would be almost as many income categories in
the frequencies table as there are cases because most people would
have a unique income.

3.7   This output indicates that there is a variable named NEIGHBOR that
has three categories: 1, 2, and 3. In category 1 there are three cases
and that is 30.0 percent of the total number of cases for which there
are data. In category 2 there are five cases and that is 50.0 percent of
the total number of cases for which there are data. In category 3 there
are two cases and that is 20.0 percent of the total number of cases for
which there are data. There is one missing case, which means there is
one case for which we do not have the NEIGHBOR information.

3.8   ```
get file 'norc84'.
frequencies all/
            statistics.
```
```

3.9   get file 'norc84'.
         frequencies abdefect
                      abnomore
                      abhlth
                      abpoor
                      abrape
                      absingle/
                   statistics.

(The subcommand could also be written as abdefect to absingle)

3.10   get file 'norc84'.
         frequencies educ
                      health
                      happy/
                   statistics.

3.11   select if (sex eq 1).

3.12   select if (age gt 65).

3.13   select if (educ gt 16 or income gt 30000).

3.14   select if (age gt 15 or age lt 66).

3.15   select if (sex eq 2) and (age gt 14 and age lt 45).

The same cases could also be selected by using two SELECT IF commands: one for SEX and one for AGE.

         select if (sex eq 2).
         select if (age gt 14 and age lt 45).

3.16   select if (educ gt 15 and sex eq 2).
         list all/
               cases=25.

Chapter 4

4.1   Use the command MD YOURID. This is not an SPSS/PC+ command and would not be followed by a period.

4.2   Use the command CD YOURID. Again, this is not an SPSS/PC+ command and would not be followed by a period.

4.3   Enter the command SPSSPC. It is not followed by a period and does not have a slash between the SPSS and the PC.

4.4   Hold down the Alt key while pressing the M key.

4.5   The Delete key erases. The Backspace key deletes errors and moves to the left.

4.6   Press the F1 key and then the Enter key.

4.7   When the Help Display is on the screen, press the F1 key.

4.8   Hold down the Ctrl key and press the Home key.

4.9   Hold down the Ctrl key and press the End key.

4.10   The Insert key moves Review between modes.

4.11   Press the F10 key.

4.12   Press the Enter key to see the rest of the output.

4.13   The program will be in Menu mode after it has executed.

4.14   Hold down the Ctrl key and press the M key.

4.15   Output is stored in SPSS.LIS.

4.16   No. Your output file will be written over the next time you execute an SPSS/PC+ program.

4.17   Rename the file.

4.18   Press the F9 key and follow the prompts.

4.19   Commands are stored in SPSS.LOG.

4.20   Press the F9 key and follow the prompts.

4.21   Press the F3 key and follow the prompts.

4.22   Follow prompts while in the Menu mode of the Review editor program.

Chapter 5

5.1   `recode marital (2 thru 4=2).`

5.2   `recode height (low thru 59=1) (60 thru 70=2) (71 thru hi=3).`

5.3   `recode cars (2 thru hi=2).`
      or
      `recode cars (2 thru hi=2).`

5.4   recode age (0 thru 15=1) (16 thru 65=2) (66 thru hi=3).

5.5   compute family$=wife$ + husband$.

5.6   compute hourly$=salary/160.

5.7   if (tenure lt 12) newexec=1.
            if (tenure gt 11) newexec=0.

5.8   if (famincom gt aveincom) income=1.
            if (famincom lt aveincom) income=0.

5.9   get file 'norc84'.
            process if (sex eq 1).
            frequencies income/
                        statistics.
            process if (sex eq 2).
            frequencies income/
                        statistics.

5.10   get file 'norc84'.
            process if (age gt 49).
            frequencies educ/
                        statistics.
            process if (age gt 24 and age lt 50).
            frequencies educ/
                        statistics.

5.11   variable label childs 'number of children'.

5.12   variable label income 'gross income'
                          net   'net income'.

5.13   value labels polviews 1 'liberal'
                                  2 'middle of the road'
                                  3 'conservative'.

5.14   value labels overdue 1 'less than 60 days'
                                 2 'more than 60 days'/
                        military 1 'military personnel'
                                 2 'civilian personnel'.

Chapter 6

6.1   crosstabs   income by sex
                         options 4.

Although a run would occur without the OPTIONS command, the output would be more difficult to understand. It would contain the *number* of cases in each cell rather than the percent of cases.

6.2   crosstabs   sales by day/
                          options 4.

6.3   data list /   id   1-2
                            educ   3-4
                            sex   5
                            happy   6.
begin data.
010912
021223
031521
041222
050611
061612
071522
081612
091821
101412
111321
121611
130922
141212
151221
161821
170821
181222
191613
20142
end data.
missing values   educ   (-9)
                   happy
                   sex   (0).
recode   educ (0 thru 11=1)
                 (12 thru 15=2)
                 (16 thru 30=3).
crosstabs   educ by sex/
**   options 4.**

6.4   get file 'norc84'.
       crosstabs politics by religion
                    options 4.

6.5   get file 'norc84'.
       crosstabs happy health income
               by educ
                    options 4.

6.6   get file 'norc84'.
       crosstabs happy by marital by sex/
                    options 4.

6.7   statistics 1 2.

6.8   Cramer's *V* is a transformation of chi-square that ranges from 0.0 for no
       association to 1.0 for a perfect association. Unlike chi-square, Cramer's
       V size is not affected by the number of cases or cells. It is, however,
       affected by the marginal percentages of the number of cases in each
       category of the variables being used.

Chapter 7

7.1   means   income by sex.

7.2   means   health by educ income.

7.3   data list /
               id   1-2
               educ   3-4
               sex   5
               happy   6.
       begin data.
       010912
       021223
       031521
       041222
       050611
       061612
       071522
       081612
       091821
       101412
       111321

```
        121611
        130922
        141212
        151221
        161821
        170821
        181222
        191613
        20142
        end data.
        missing values
              educ        (-9)
              happy
              sex         (0).
        means happy by educ.
```

7.4   ```
get file 'norc84'.
means happy by health.
```

**7.5**    The criterion variable in a MEANS output is the variable whose mean score is given for each category of another variable.

**7.6**    In a MEANS command, the dependent variable is placed before the BY.

**7.7**    ```means income by sex by educ.```

**7.8**    ```
means income by educ /
        statistics all.
```

7.9   ```
select if educ eq 12 or educ eq 15
means income by educ /
        statistics all.
```

## Chapter 8

**8.1**    ```plot income with educ.```

**8.2**    ```plot income educ with age.```

**8.3**    ```correlation happy health.```

**8.4**    ```
correlation income age famsize carsize /
        option 2 5.
```

8.5   Such a scatterplot would not be revealing because there would not be enough variance in the number of cars per family. There would be too many cases clustered in the 1 to 3 range.

8.6   There would be too many cases per point in the scatterplot. The problem could be solved by using the SAMPLE command to select out a suitable proportion of the cases. See the discussion of SAMPLE in Appendix A.

8.7   Technically, the correlation coefficient is meant for interval variables that are linearly associated. The technique is robust, and will usually produce reasonably accurate estimates for ordinal variables. Nominal variables with only two categories may also be used with the correlation coefficient. Nominal variables with more than two categories are absolutely inappropriate and produce nonsensical coefficients.

8.8   The correlation coefficient presumes a linear relationship. Therefore, an exponential negative relationship would not be measured accurately. Using a COMPUTE statement to create a new variable (which is the log of the infant death rate) and then doing the correlation analysis with the new variable would be appropriate. See the discussion of the COMPUTE statement in Section 5.2.

8.9   The negative coefficient indicates that as one variable increases in value, the other variable tends to be lower in value. The positive coefficient indicates that as one variable increases in value, the other variable tends to be higher in value.

8.10   Remembering that the correlation coefficient squared is the true measure of the strength of the association, the relative strengths would be $.20^2$ to $.30^2$ or .04 to .09. The association between HEALTH and EDUC is only four-ninths as strong as the association between HEALTH and INCOME. (The associations in this question are purely hypothetical.)

Chapter 9

9.1   Theoretically, the dependent and independent variables in a multiple regression analysis should be interval variables. In practice, ordinal variables are often used. Two-category nominal variables, also called dichotomous variables, can be used as well if neither category has fewer than 20 percent of the cases.

9.2   `regression variables=health`
                        `income`

```
                                    educ                                    ⋆
                                    happy
                                    age
                                    sex/
                    dependent=health/
                    method=enter.
```

9.3   ```
        if (relig eq 1) d1=1.
        if (relig ne 1) d1=0.
        if (relig eq 2) d2=1.
        if (relig ne 2) d2=0.
        if (relig eq 3) d3=1.
        if (relig ne 3) d3=0.
        if (relig eq 4) d4=1.
        if (relig ne 4) d4=0.
        regression
            variables=happy
                         income
                         health
                         d1
                         d2
                         d3
                         d4 /
            dependent=happy /
            method=enter.
```

**9.4**   The multiple R is the correlation between the dependent variable and the entire set of independent variables. The multiple R squared is the proportion of variance in the dependent variable associated with variance in the independent variables.

**9.5**   Multicollinearity problems exist when there are high intercorrelations among the independent variables. Multicollinearity causes unreliable estimates of beta: that is, estimates that fluctuate greatly from one sample to another. The problem can be resolved by dropping one of two highly correlated variables from the set of independent variables or combining them into a composite variable. There is no problem when more than one independent variable is highly correlated with the dependent variable. Only when two or more independent variables are highly correlated with each other do we have multicollinearity problems.

**9.6**   When the plot of the standardized residuals by the standardized pre-
```

dicted values is not random, the association between the dependent variable and the set of independent variables is not linear. Either the dependent variable or one or more of the independent variables needs to be transformed.

9.7   ```
regression variables=health
                   income
                   educ
                   happy
                   age
                   sex/
                   dependent=health/
                   method=enter/
                   scatterplot (*res *pre).
```

## Chapter 10

**10.1**    MANOVA will enable the reader to use a covariate, to obtain significance tests for multiple predictor variables, and to analyze group differences on a set of dependent variables. Other techniques would perform a separate analysis for each dependent variable.

**10.2**    When there is only one dependent variable, MANOVA assumes its variance within each of the groups is normal and the same. For more than one dependent variable, MANOVA requires the additional assumption that the joint distribution of the dependent variables is multivariate normal. The variances of the dependent variables need not equal one another, but the distribution of scores on one dependent variable for all the cases with a particular score on another dependent variable should be normal.

**10.3**    `manova educ by marital (1,5) by sex (1,2).`

**10.4**    Yes. MANOVA assumes that there are some cases for each value in the range indicated.

**10.5**    `manova educ by marital (1,5) sex (1,2) with income.`

**10.6**    `manova confinan to conarmy by relig(1,5) sex(1,2).`

**10.7**    It would mean that the differences between MARITAL groups, controlling for SEX, would occur from sampling error only 2 times out of 1,000.

**10.8**    It would mean that the differences between the sexes in the effects of
```

marital status would occur from sampling error less than 1 time out of 1,000.

10.9   Marital status would be a significant variable in the analysis because of the way it influenced the differences in scores by sex. It would not matter that the effects of marital status alone were not significant.

10.10 Pillai's trace.

Chapter 11

11.1
```
discriminant groups=class(1,4) /
variables=sex
           race
           age
           income
           educ
           defense
           spend.
```

11.2
```
get file 'norc84'.
    select if (sex eq 2).
    if (childs eq 0 and wrkstat ge 4) famwork=1.
    if (childs ne 0 and wrkstat ge 4) famwork=2.
    if (childs eq 0 and wrkstat lt 4) famwork=3.
    if (childs ne 0 and wrkstat lt 4) famwork=4.
    dscriminant groups=famwork/
    variables=race
              educ
              income
              age
              memploy
              class.
```

11.3   The primary purpose of a discriminant analysis is to improve our ability to classify cases. Compare the percent of cases that were misclassified by the discriminant analysis to the percent that would be misclassified by chance. The proportion improvement is equal to

$$\frac{\text{Random error proportion} - \text{Discriminant model-error proportion}}{\text{Random error proportion}}$$

11.4   The expected percent of correct classifications is equal to the sum of the squared proportion in each group.

11.5   The statistical significance of a discriminant analysis is produced for the Wilks' lambda statistic in the Canonical Discriminant Functions table of the output.

11.6   Compare the percent of cases classified correctly with that function in the analysis to the percent classified correctly when that function is not in the analysis. This procedure can be done with the FUNCTIONS sub-command. FUNCTIONS 1 will include only the first and most powerful function; FUNCTIONS 2 will include the two most powerful functions; and so forth. The difference between the percent of cases classified correctly with function 2 and with function 1 is the improvement made by the second function. The difference between the percent of cases classified correctly with function 3 and with function 2 is the improvement made by the third function.

11.7   The statistical significance of individual functions can be assessed from the output in the Canonical Discriminant Functions table. The statistical significance is approximated by the drop in the statistical significance after the function's effects are removed. The statistical significance for Wilks' lambda (the ratio of the within-groups sum of squares to the total sum of squares) is used.

11.8   To determine the contribution of a particular variable to the discriminant analysis classification accuracy, redo the analysis, dropping the variable in question from the VARIABLES subcommand. The change in the percent of cases classified correctly when the variable is dropped represents the variable's contribution.

Contribution = percent correct with variable − percent correct without
variable

11.9   To approximate the contribution of a particular variable to the statistical significance of a discriminant analysis, drop the variable in question from the analysis and compare the statistical significance of the analysis using the variable to the statistical significance without the variable. Letting P^2 equal the statistical significance without the variable and P^1 equal the statistical significance with the variable, the formula would be

$$\text{Contribution} = \frac{P^2 - P^1}{P^2}$$

This contribution is the proportionate reduction in the likelihood that the group differences are the result of sampling probability error.

11.10 To classify new cases, use the SELECT subcommand to choose the cases used for calculating the discriminant function, and use the command STATISTICS 13, 14 to produce for each of the new cases its predicted group membership.

Chapter 12

12.1 Regression analysis assumes that the dependent variable and the predictor variables are interval and that the dependent variable is normally distributed for each value of the predictor variables.

12.2 When a table has three or more variables and many cells, log-linear analysis with the HILOGLINEAR command will allow the user to see more easily what the significant relationships are.

12.3 A log-linear analysis of health (four categories) by marital (five categories) by religion (five categories) would normally require (4 × 5 × 5) × 5 = 500 cases.

12.4 `hiloglinear health (1,4) marital (1,5) religion (1,5)/`
            `print all.`

12.5 The first-order effects would indicate whether each cell in the table has the same number of cases. This statistic is uninteresting because we do not expect to have an equal number of cases in each category of these variables.

12.6 The second-order effects would indicate whether any of the bivariate associations controlling for the effects of the third variable were significant—for example, whether the association between HEALTH and MARITAL is significant controlling for the effects of RELIG.

12.7 The third-order effects would indicate interaction effects—for example, whether the association between HEALTH and MARITAL is the same for each value of RELIG.

12.8 The chi-square and probability of the highest-order effects are given in the output in the table entitled TESTS THAT K-WAY AND HIGHER ORDER EFFECTS ARE ZERO.

12.9 The partial chi-square is a measure of the association between HEALTH and MARITAL controlling for the effects of RELIG. A partial chi-square probability of .023 would indicate that an association at least this strong would occur 23 times out of 1,000 through sampling error.

12.10   The strength of the association is most easily measured by comparing the observed frequencies in the categories of the dependent variable for the different categories of the predictor variables.

Chapter 13

13.1   A factor is a composite variable underlying the variance in a set of variables.

13.2   A factor loading is a measure of the association between a variable and a factor of which it is one component. Factor loadings range from -1.0 to 1.0. A 0.0 indicates no association; a 1.0 indicates a perfect association. The sign of the loading indicates whether the association is positive or negative.

13.3   The eigenvalue is a measure of variance in the set of variables in the factor analysis. The total eigenvalue is equal to the number of variables in the analysis.

13.4   The communality of a variable is the proportion of its variance accounted for by the variables in the analysis. The communality is 0.0 for no association and 1.0 for a perfect association. The communality of all the variables will be 1.0 when the number of factors equals the number of variables.

13.5   A factor score is the value of the factor for a particular case.

13.6   In an orthogonal rotation, the correlation between the factors in the analysis is kept at 0.0. In an oblique rotation, some correlation is permitted among the factors in the analysis. The default level of correlation in an oblique rotation will usually be below an absolute value of 0.30.

13.7   The factor extraction technique used by default for FACTOR is principal components.

13.8   The default rotation technique is a varimax orthogonal rotation.

13.9   The default rotation technique for the ROTATION = OBLIQUE/ is oblimin.

13.10   `factor variables=confinan to conarmy/`

Chapter 14

14.1   A PUMS file is a sample of households and individuals. An STF data file has as units geographic areas for which aggregate statistics are available.

14.2   Yes. You could use a PUMS file for this task.

14.3   You could not use an STF data file for this task because the necessary individual data would be lacking.

14.4   When you want the information on a household record applied to the individuals who reside in the household, you must use a FILE TYPE command.

14.5   Use a SELECT IF command with the variable SUMRYLV, which indicates geographic level.

14.6   Use a SELECT IF command with the variable RECOIND, which indicates ethnic and racial group.

14.7   There is not a household-value variable for which you can produce a frequencies table. Rather, each cell in the household value distribution is a variable that must be named and included in a LIST command.

14.8   In the STF data files, a 0 value can indicate that the information was suppressed or it can indicate that the coded value was 0. You need to use an IF statement with the variable that indicates suppression to change zero to a missing value when suppression is indicated.

INDEX